1995

W9-CLF-732

THE DISTAFF SIDE

THE DISTAFF SIDE

Representing the Female
in Homer's *Odyssey*

Edited by
BETH COHEN

New York   Oxford
OXFORD UNIVERSITY PRESS
1995

Oxford University Press

Oxford   New York
Athens   Auckland   Bangkok   Bombay
Calcutta   Cape Town   Dar es Salaam   Delhi
Florence   Hong Kong   Istanbul   Karachi
Kuala Lumpur   Madras   Madrid   Melbourne
Mexico City   Nairobi   Paris   Singapore
Taipei   Tokyo   Toronto

and associated companies in
Berlin   Ibadan

Published by Oxford University Press, Inc.,
200 Madison Avenue, New York, New York 10016

Library of Congress Cataloging-in-Publication Data
The Distaff side : representing the female in Homer's Odyssey /
edited by Beth Cohen.
p. cm.
Includes bibliographical references and index.
ISBN 0-19-508682-1; ISBN 0-19-508683-X (pbk.)
1. Homer. Odyssey. 2. Epic poetry, Greek—History and criticism.
3. Women and literature—Greece—History. 4. Goddesses, Greek, in literature.
5. Art and literature—Greece. 6. Homer—Characters—
Women. 7. Women in literature. 8. Women in art.
9. Art, Greek.
I. Cohen, Beth.
PA4167.D57   1995
883'.01—dc20   94–6749

1 3 5 7 9 8 6 4 2

Printed in the United States of America
on acid-free paper

To the memory of my mother

Preface

This is the first book to examine the representation of female characters of the *Odyssey* from the diverse disciplinary perspectives of art history, classics, and history. It contains eleven new essays by twelve contributors. Eight of these essays are revised and expanded versions of talks presented at a symposium entitled "The Female Figures of Homer's *Odyssey*: Goddesses, Monsters, and Women," which was held at Bard College on February 1, 1992, in conjunction with the exhibition *The Odyssey and Ancient Art: An Epic in Word and Image*.

The introduction to this book consists of three overviews: A. J. Graham, a specialist on Greek colonization, presents the evidence supporting a probable eighth-century date for the *Odyssey*'s composition in order to employ the epic poem as historical evidence for certain roles of Greek women during the Age of Exploration. Seth L. Schein surveys the nature of Homer's female representations, contrasting the threatening characters in Odysseus' first-person narrative with honorable "heroic" women elsewhere in the poem. Diana Buitron-Oliver and I examine the earliest representations of the *Odyssey*'s female characters in Greek art of the sixth and fifth centuries B.C., revealing how Classical artists' visualizations reflected the roles of women in contemporary Greek society.

In the second part of this book, classicists noted for their work on the *Odyssey* reconsider the diverse roles of important individual female characters in the poem: Sheila Murnaghan focuses on Athena, Lillian Eileen Doherty on Homer's Sirens, and Helene P. Foley on Penelope. Froma I. Zeitlin discusses the bed wrought by Odysseus as an emblem figuring Penelope's fidelity. The essays in the final section interpret the visualization of the *Odyssey*'s female characters by ancient artists. Here art historians, specializing in iconography, vase painting, sculpture, and theory, point out dangerous aspects of Odysseus' female encounters as they are revealed in Greek, Etruscan, and Roman art. H. A. Shapiro surveys the erotic aspects of the imagery of the virgin princess Nausikaa, and Richard Brilliant discusses the visualization of Kirke's transforming and seductive powers. Jenifer Neils considers the depiction of Odysseus' nautical encounter with the Sirens versus those with Skylla and perhaps Charybdis. Finally, Christine Mitchell Havelock provides a formal analysis of the rare representations of the aged maidservant Eurykleia's recognition of Odysseus.

My preparatory work as a cocurator of the exhibition at Bard College, which began in 1989, provided an excellent opportunity both to read the *Odyssey* time and again and to read widely about it. This made me especially aware of the recent work by classicists exploring female aspects of the poem, particularly through the characterization of Odysseus' wife, Penelope. I was eager to share this new direction with my colleagues in art history—where much of the work on the iconography of Homeric legend had centered on the exploits of male heroes—to make the visualizations of Homer's females in ancient art more accessible to classicists and to broaden the scholarly discussion to include more of the key female characters. The important symposium at Bard College opened an interdisciplinary dialogue on the *Odyssey*, feminine in orientation, but not solely feminist in approach. The present expanded and more comprehensive volume is a fuller realization of those goals.

I am grateful to Diana Buitron-Oliver, for inviting me to join her as a cocurator of the *Odyssey* exhibition, thus inspiring my interest in the poem. Bard College made the symposium possible. I owe thanks to President Leon Botstein and Executive Vice President Dimitri Papadimitriou, as well as to Linda Weintraub, then director of the Edith C. Blum Art Institute of Bard College. Marci Acita, formerly of the Blum Art Institute, has provided invaluable aid during the planning of the symposium and in her support of the present project. I would particularly like to thank the eight symposium speakers: Richard Brilliant, Lillian Eileen Doherty, Helene P. Foley, A. J. Graham, Christine Mitchell Havelock, Jenifer Neils, H. A. Shapiro, and Froma I. Zeitlin. I am indebted to Seth L. Schein for providing translations of the *Odyssey* for several art history chapters (3, 10, 11).

Among the many institutions and individuals who have provided photographs and the permission to publish them, I would particularly like to thank the following: Jerry Mallick, National Gallery Photographic Archive, Washington, D.C., for making available photographs originally acquired for the *Odyssey* exhibition; Carmen Arnold-Biucchi, American Numismatic Society; Art Resource; Gregory Callimanopulos, New York; Melody Ennis, Museum of Art, Rhode Island School of Design; Fred S. Kleiner, *American Journal of Archaeology*; John A. Larson, The Oriental Institute, University of Chicago; Joan R. Mertens, Metropolitan Museum of Art; Mark D. Stansbury O'Donnell, St. Paul; Marion True and Jacklyn Burns, J. Paul Getty Museum; Cornelius C. Vermeule III and Karen L. Otis, Museum of Fine Arts, Boston; P. Flourentzos, Department of Antiquities, Nicosia, Cyprus; Flemming Johansen, Ny Carlsberg Glyptothek; Dyfri Williams and I. D. Jenkins, British Museum; Alain Pasquier, Musée du Louvre; the National Archaeological Museum, Athens; F. W. Hamdorf, Staatliche Antikensammlungen und Glyptothek, Munich; Gertrud Platz and Ursula Kästner, Antikensammlung, Staatliche Museen zu Berlin-Preussischer Kulturbesitz; Katrin Bemmann, Deutsches Archäologisches Institut, Rome; Francesco Nicosia and Mario Iozzo, Soprintendenza Archeologica della Toscana-Firenze; Fratelli Alinari; Margot Schmidt, Antikenmuseum Basel und Sammlung Ludwig; and Prefect Leonard E. Boyle, Biblioteca Apostolica Vaticana.

I would like to take this opportunity to thank Angela Blackburn of Oxford University Press for her belief in and support of this book. Several individuals have provided special help during its preparation. I thank Andrew Oliver, Jr., for reading the manuscript by me and Diana Buitron-Oliver, and for tolerating the many hours Diana and I spent working together. H. A. Shapiro contributed both practical and scholarly assistance, and I owe him many thanks. Finally, I would like to express my gratitude to my husband, John F. Burleigh, for his help and patience throughout all stages of this project.

New York   B. C.
January 1994

Contents

Plates follow page 58

Contributors

Richard Brilliant is Professor of Art History and Archaeology and the Anna S. Garbedian Professor in the Humanities at Columbia University. He has published many books and articles on aspects of ancient art, most notably *Gesture and Rank in Roman Art* (1963), *The Arch of Septimius Severus in the Roman Forum* (1967), *Visual Narratives* (1984), and *Commentaries on Roman Art* (1993). He is also engaged in the study of problems in the history of art resulting in *Portraiture* (1991) and the forthcoming studies *My Laocoon* and *The Concept of Style*.

Diana Buitron-Oliver is a Classical archaeologist and art historian with specialties in Attic pottery and Cypriot archaeology. She is author of *Douris* (1995), a monograph on the Attic vase painter, and *The Sanctuary of Apollo at Kourion: Excavations in the Archaic Precinct* (1995), as well as several exhibition catalogues. She was cocurator of the exhibition *The Odyssey and Ancient Art* held at Bard College in 1991–92 and is currently Professorial Lecturer at Georgetown University.

Beth Cohen is an art historian who has published on Greek sculpture, vase painting, and iconography, as well as the relationship between the Renaissance and Classical antiquity. She is the author of *Attic Bilingual Vases and Their Painters* (1978) and coauthor of the exhibition catalogue *The Odyssey and Ancient Art: An Epic in Word and Image* (1992). Recently she was Associate Director and Adjunct Associate Professor of Art History for the University of Rochester in Italy at Arezzo.

Lillian Eileen Doherty is Associate Professor of Classics at the University of Maryland, College Park. Her articles on Homer have appeared in *Arethusa*, *Helios*, and the *American Journal of Philology*. She is the English-language translator of Jacqueline de Romilly's *Short History of Greek Literature* (1985) and the author of *Siren Songs: Gender, Audiences, and Narrators in the Odyssey*, forthcoming from the University of Michigan Press.

Helene P. Foley is Olin Professor of Classics, Barnard College, Columbia University. Her publications include *Ritual Irony: Poetry and Sacrifice in Euripides* (1985) and *The Homeric Hymn to Demeter* (1993). She is also editor of *Reflections of Women in Antiquity* (1981) and coauthor of *Women in the Classical World: Image and Text* (1994), published by Oxford University Press.

A. J. Graham is Professor of Classical Studies and Allen Memorial Professor in Greek at the University of Pennsylvania. His longest-standing interest has been in Greek colonization, and he has contributed the chapters on that subject to the *Cambridge Ancient History* (1982). He is the author of *Colony and Mother City in Ancient Greece* (1983).

Christine Mitchell Havelock is Professor Emerita of Art History at Vassar College. Her main interest has been Greek sculpture, especially the archaistic style. She has published *Hellenistic Art: The Art of the Classical World from the Death of Alexander the Great to the Battle of Actium* (1981), and she is the author of a book on the Aphrodite of Knidos and the female nude in Hellenistic sculpture forthcoming from University of Michigan Press.

Sheila Murnaghan is Associate Professor of Classical Studies at the University of Pennsylvania. Her areas of interest include Greek epic and tragedy and women in antiquity. She is the author of *Disguise and Recognition in the Odyssey* (1987).

Jenifer Neils is Professor of Art History and Chair of the Department of Art History and Art at Case Western Reserve University. Her research specialty is Greek vase painting and iconography. Her publications include *The Youthful Deeds of Theseus* (1987) and several contributions to the *Lexikon Iconographicum Mythologiae Classicae*. Recently she was the curator of *Goddess and Polis: The Panathenaic Festival in Ancient Athens*, as well as the editor of the exhibition catalogue.

Seth L. Schein teaches Comparative Literature and Classics at the University of California, Davis. He has published mainly on Homeric epic and Attic tragedy. His writings include *The Iambic Trimeter in Aeschylus and Sophocles: A Study in Metrical Form* (1979) and *The Mortal Hero: An Introduction to Homer's Iliad* (1984), and he has edited *Reading the Odyssey: Selected Interpretive Essays*, forthcoming from Princeton University Press.

H. A. Shapiro is Professor of Classics in the University of Canterbury, Christchurch, New Zealand. His books include *Art and Cult under the*

Tyrants in Athens (1989) and, most recently, *Myth into Art* (1994). He is coauthor of *Women in the Classical World,* published by Oxford University Press.

Froma I. Zeitlin is Charles Ewing Professor of Greek Language and Literature and Professor of Comparative Literature at Princeton University. She is author of *Under the Sign of the Shield: Semiotics and Aeschylus' Seven against Thebes* (1982) and numerous articles on Greek myth and literature. She coedited *Before Sexuality: The Construction of Erotic Experience in the Ancient Greek World* (1990) and *Nothing to Do with Dionysos? Athenian Drama in Its Social Context* (1990) and edited *Mortals and Immortals* (1991), a collection of essays by Jean-Pierre Vernant.

Abbreviations

ClAnt	*Classical Antiquity*
CP	*Classical Philology*
CQ	*Classical Quarterly*
CVA	*Corpus Vasorum Antiquorum*
CW	*Classical World*
EtCl	*Les études classiques*
JAC	*Jahrbuch für Antike und Christentum*
JdI	*Jahrbuch des Deutschen Archäologischen Instituts*
JHS	*Journal of Hellenic Studies*
JRGZM	*Jahrbuch des Römisch-Germanischen Zentralmuseums, Mainz*
JWalt	*Journal of the Walters Art Gallery*
LIMC	*Lexikon Iconographicum Mythologiae Classicae* (Zurich and Stuttgart 1981–)
MusHelv	*Museum Helveticum*
OJA	*Oxford Journal of Archaeology*
ÖJh	*Jahreshefte des Österreichischen archäologischen Instituts in Wien*
Para	J. D. Beazley, *Paralipomena: Additions to Attic Black-figure Vase-painters and to Attic Red-figure Vase-painters* (2d ed.) (Oxford 1971)
RA	*Revue archéologique*
RhM	*Rheinisches Museum für Philologie*
RM	*Mitteilungen des Deutschen Archäologischen Instituts, Römische Abteilung*
Roscher	*Ausführliches Lexikon der griechischen und römischen Mythologie*, ed. W. H. Roscher, I–IV (Leipzig 1884–1921)
TAPA	*Transactions of the American Philological Association*
WS	*Wiener Studien*

I

Introduction

1

The *Odyssey,* History, and Women

A. J. Graham

If we include the goddesses and semidivine women, the *Odyssey* presents a great panorama of womanhood. This is a fascinating prospect for Greek historians, starved as they are for information about women in Greek history generally, and especially in the early period. Before they can use that material for historical reconstructions and conclusions, however, it is necessary to consider the question of the *Odyssey* as historical evidence. Because that question is not only complicated and multifaceted but also very important, it cannot be balked at or skimped, and it must be dealt with before the women of the *Odyssey* can be used for history.[1]

Very many and diverse theories have been put forward about the nature and composition of the *Odyssey*—theories that I, as an ancient historian, am not very well qualified to judge. However, I am glad to see that there is now a reasonable consensus in favor of the opinion, in which I have always believed, that the poem is a unified work of art, composed by a single poet at a single time.[2]

This enables the historian to treat the poem, even though it is primarily a literary work of fiction, as a piece of historical evidence. Modern historians, blessed—or even embarrassed—as they are by a superabundance of sources, would never think of using an epic poem as historical evidence, but it is a different matter for the ancient historian who is desperately short of source material, particularly in the early period, whenever exactly that may be, when the *Odyssey* was composed. This brings us to the all-important question, for a historian, of date. Can we establish when the *Odyssey* was composed?

It must be confessed straightaway that what we would most like to have—a precise and reliable external date—does not exist. The dates for Homer given by later Greeks were manifestly not based on definite knowledge. When Herodotos says (2.53.2) that he thinks that Hesiod and Homer lived four hundred years before his own time and not more, he reveals clearly that their date was a matter of uncertainty and dispute. His estimate puts the two early epic poets in the ninth century B.C.

In default of reliable external dating, scholars have used a variety of inevitably less satisfactory methods to try to establish the date of composition of the Homeric epics: internal evidence of various kinds, linguistic development, literary comparisons and development, and evidence from archaeology and art.

The internal evidence consists of things mentioned in the poem, places, peoples, or material objects that it seems possible to date by other means. For example, the references to Sicily in the *Odyssey* are thought to provide us with a *terminus post quem* for its composition, namely, the reopening of the western Mediterranean to the Greeks about the middle of the eighth century B.C. On this argument the *Odyssey* would have been composed after ca. 750 B.C. A *terminus ante quem* has been seen in the introduction of the type of warfare based on heavily armed infantrymen, the so-called hoplites, and the associated armor and weapons, the earliest evidence for which is dated to the period ca. 700–675 B.C. The "orthodox" view has been that the fighting in Homer is very different from, and therefore earlier than, hoplite warfare.[3] Recently there has been a strong movement in Homeric scholarship in favor of the "unorthodox" idea that Homer's fighting, too, was based on massed infantry.[4] If correct, that interpretation would weaken the chronological significance of the introduction of hoplite tactics. However, the arguments supporting the unorthodox interpretation can be shown to be unconvincing.[5] So it is still justifiable to argue that the introduction of hoplite tactics represents a *terminus ante quem* for the composition of the Homeric poems. The references to Sicily and the introduction of hoplite warfare were two of the main arguments used by H. L. Lorimer in her impressive *Homer and the Monuments*, a very detailed and lengthy comparison of the objects in the Homeric poems and those in the archaeological record, based largely on the scholarship up to the Second World War.[6] From these and other indications she came to a time bracket for the poem's composition between ca. 750 and 675 B.C.[7]

A more recent use of an internal dating argument has been based on the Homeric references to Egypt, especially to the great city of Egyptian Thebes (mentioned at *Iliad* 9.381 ff.). W. Burkert has argued that this passage could not be a reminiscence of the great Bronze Age city, preserved in an old poetic formula by the bards who preceded the poet or poets of the *Iliad* and the *Odyssey*, because the language of those lines shows recent elements.[8] So he proposed to see the passage as a reference to the rebuilt Thebes, supposedly the capital of the Twenty-fifth Dynasty, which lasted from ca. 715–663 B.C. He therefore argued that these dates were a *terminus post quem* for the composition of the *Iliad*, which he dated ca. 650 B.C. The *Odyssey*, which is universally agreed to be, if not contemporary with, then later than the *Iliad*, would on this argument not have been composed earlier than about the middle of the seventh century. But Burkert's argument is quite unconvincing. The magnificence and wealth of Egypt and its greatest city in the Bronze Age were obviously proverbial, and these references in the Homeric poems offer no chronological precision. Nor is it at all probable that the activities of the short-lived Ethiopian Dynasty, which never established control over all of Egypt and whose capital was probably not at Thebes, would have produced references to the greatness of Egypt and Egyptian Thebes in the Homeric poems.[9] Finally, the whole basis for Burkert's argument is removed by the observation that old elements in the poems can be described in recent language.[10] This rather obviously failed attempt to use internal evidence for a chronological conclusion would not have deserved a mention, had the thesis not been adopted in S. West's part of the Introduction to the new *Commentary on the Odyssey*, with the result that a mid-seventh-century date for the composition of the *Odyssey* is likely to have wide dissemination.[11]

A chronological argument from literary development can be made on the basis of the reasonable assumption that Homer (and Hesiod) are earlier than the lyric poets.[12] Among the early lyric poets, Archilochos can be confidently dated about the middle of the seventh century,[13] so the Homeric poems would be earlier than that. The chronological conclusions are very imprecise, however, and not all experts in Greek literature would even accept the premise that the Homeric poems are necessarily earlier than the early lyric poets.[14]

A different argument from literary development was put forward by Morris, who believes on the basis of analogies from other cultures and times that the *Iliad* and *Odyssey*, being oral compositions, could not have been preserved until and unless they were written down. Otherwise, each new oral performance would have altered the poems.

This gives him a *terminus post quem* for their composition in the introduction of alphabetic writing to Greece, dated "close to *c.* 750 B.C."[15] (He cannot find a *terminus ante quem* on any such arguments, so for that he accepts dates reached by other methods.) However, an argument based on comparative analogies does not constitute proof, and this one is by no means universally accepted.[16]

It is a relief to turn to the more objective combination of linguistic and literary criteria used by R. Janko in his important book, *Homer, Hesiod and the Hymns.*[17] His method was to study the variations between older and newer linguistic usages in the *Iliad,* the *Odyssey,* Hesiod's *Theogony* and *Works and Days,* and the Homeric *Hymns.* By this means he was able to put these works in a relative chronological order, namely, to confine ourselves to the works of interest to us, *Iliad, Odyssey, Theogony,* and *Works and Days.* For establishing absolute chronological intervals and dates, Hesiod was very important to Janko. Because we know that the *Theogony* and the *Works and Days* were composed by one man, the differences that Janko found between the two works indicate an interval no longer than the term of a man's active life. The differences between the *Iliad* and the *Odyssey* are no greater than those between the *Theogony* and the *Works and Days.* So Janko argued that the *Odyssey* and the *Iliad* could also have been composed within the timespan of an active human life.

Finally, Janko used Hesiod to give absolute dates to the works he studied. There are historical reasons for dating Hesiod's *floruit* to about 700 B.C.[18] With this precise date to work from, Janko's preferred range of dates for the composition of the *Iliad* was ca. 750 to 725 and for the *Odyssey* ca. 743 to 713.[19] This is a very bold and ambitious chronological argument, and it undeniably contains many uncertainties. But it also has many interlocking chronological indications and many additional arguments, to which a brief summary cannot do justice.

In the category of archaeology and art the most sensational contribution to the chronology of the Homeric poems comes undoubtedly from the so-called Nestor's Cup, discovered in a grave on Pithekoussai, the island in the Bay of Naples called Ischia today.[20] This Late Geometric cup bears an incised inscription that may be translated as follows: "Nestor's cup was fine to drink from. But whoever drinks from this cup will immediately be seized by the desire of fair-crowned Aphrodite." The cup itself and other objects in the same grave may be dated ca. 720 to 710. It has been generally recognized that the humorous graffito shows a familiarity with epic poetry, and the reference to the cup of Nestor is inevitably reminiscent of

Iliad 11.632–37. It is possible to argue—and it has been argued—that this evidence does not necessarily prove that our *Iliad* was known in Pithekoussai and therefore also in Euboia, whence the colonists originated, before ca. 720, because it could merely attest the diffusion of the general epic tradition about the heroes, which we know from the Homeric poems.[21] But this possible argument has a look of special pleading. We are not just dealing with a reference to Nestor; it is specifically to his cup. Surely the easiest and simplest conclusion is that our *Iliad* was well known in the Greek world generally before ca. 720.

Although not so striking and not so early, we also have important artistic evidence bearing on the date of the *Odyssey*. There are no fewer than three representations of the blinding of Polyphemos on Greek painted pottery of the second quarter of the seventh century.[22] Once again it is possible to argue that the artists knew the story but need not necessarily have known Homer's version of it in *Odyssey* Book 9.[23] The easiest conclusion, however, is surely that it was precisely this very striking part of our *Odyssey* that led to the popularity of the scene with Greek vase painters.

We have now briefly looked at four different ways of trying to determine the date of composition of the *Odyssey*. Internal indications suggested the period ca. 750–675; an argument from the character of oral poetry gave a suggested *terminus post quem* of ca. 750; a bold and ambitious use of linguistic and literary developments gave a date of ca. 743–713; and art and archaeology rather strikingly supported that dating because Nestor's Cup seems to show that the *Iliad* was composed no later than the third quarter of the eighth century, and the representations of the blinding of Polyphemos seem to show that the *Odyssey* was current before ca. 675, and at least that the low date for the *Odyssey*'s composition, ca. 650, cannot be right. Because these chronological arguments are independent of each other and yet they all point in general terms to the period ca. 750–700, there seems to be good reason for confidence that the composition of the *Odyssey* fell within this period. Naturally we cannot claim certainty—our evidence and arguments are not of that quality—but we have a probable hypothesis, which is the most we are likely to achieve in this early period of Greek history.

So the historian has in the *Odyssey* a piece of historical evidence with a fairly precise and secure date. There is still one issue to consider before we can proceed to use this evidence for historical purposes. It is widely and correctly believed that the bardic poetry of which the *Odyssey* is a part represented a very ancient tradition, going back into the Bronze Age. Not only are there embedded in the Homeric epics descriptions of objects that did not exist after the Bronze Age but also the political geography can be shown to be that of the Bronze Age; the poet knows that he is describing heroic events earlier than his own time and employs some conscious anachronisms in order to do so. So the question inevitably arises, Is the *Odyssey* evidence for the world in which it was composed or for that earlier world—say, of the late Bronze Age—which the poet tried to depict? This was a matter of scholarly controversy in the past, but it is now generally recognized that the material that goes back into the Bronze Age is very restricted, and the general historical environment of the poem is that of the poet's own day.[24]

We have seen that that time is the second half of the eighth century B.C. This period is characterized by historians of Ancient Greece as the beginning of the Greek Renaissance from the so-called Dark Ages, which followed the collapse of the great civilizations of the late Bronze Age. There are many aspects of this renaissance, such as economic and demographic growth and new achievements in art and architecture, but two of great importance were the growth in overseas trade and the beginning of the great movement of colonization of the Archaic period, which established new Greek communities over large parts of the coasts of the Mediterranean and Black Seas. The world of the *Odyssey* is preeminently one of seafaring, of new and strange lands reached by ship, and of the strange peoples who inhabited them. There is important evidence in the poem for the historian concerning both overseas trade and colonization, and some of that evidence relates to the role of women in both these activities. We may begin with trade.

One of the oddities in some modern works about early Greece has been the belief that normal, regular trade came relatively late. There seems to be a strange desire to interpret the undeniable exchange of goods well attested in the archaeological record as evidence, not of trade, but of gift exchange. It is certainly true that the *Odyssey* is full of examples of heroic gift exchange, but that should not blind us to the clear fact that it is also a storehouse of evidence about regular sea trade undertaken for profit.[25]

The regularity of the activity is revealed in the standard question asked of strangers who arrive by sea: "who are you, sirs? From what port have you sailed over the highways of the sea? Is yours a trading venture; or are you cruising the main on chance, like roving pirates, who risk their lives to ruin other people?"[26] (3.71–74). In many of the made-up narratives throughout the work, trading voyages occur, as those Odysseus himself is said to have undertaken in Book 19 (282–86). Such trading could be performed by the leaders of society. The fictional king Mentes, whom the goddess Athena pretends to be in Book 1, claims to be sailing to Temesa with a cargo of iron, which they intend to trade for copper (182–84); and Menelaos collects much livelihood and gold when sailing to Egypt (3.299–302, 311–12), Cyprus, Phoenicia, and Libya, among other destinations (4.81–91).

Special trading ships are mentioned, with the characteristic that they are broad (5.250; 9.323), and there are specialist traders, whose captain is mindful of his cargo and of the profits he has made (8.161–64). One particularly interesting feature is that we already meet the individual merchant who travels on another's ship (2.318–19; 14.295–96), a specialist in trading. We also have some indications of trade goods, though the *Iliad* offers a larger list, such as metals (1.182–84), papyrus (21.390–91), trinkets (15.415–16), and, notably, slaves.

Although this regular trading activity can perfectly well be carried on by Greeks, the *Odyssey* frequently mentions the foreign traders par excellence, the Phoenicians. They are providers of a fine bowl of silver and gold (4.615–19); in one of Odysseus' fictional tales a Phoenician trading ship sails from Crete to the western Peloponnese and returns to Sidon (13.272–78); in another, Odysseus relates that a deceiving Phoenician takes him from Egypt to Phoenicia and later tries to take him on a trading voyage to Libya, with the secret intention of selling him as a slave (14.287–97). These stories suit well the other evidence we have for Phoenician activities in the eighth century and earlier.[27] We know of their settlements in North Africa, Spain, Sardinia, and Sicily, and their trading efforts can be seen in archaeological finds in these and many other areas of the Mediterranean. These finds include fine metal bowls of silver and bronze.[28] Their connection with Crete in the *Odyssey* is especially interesting because there are striking Phoenician objects in the Cretan archaeological record[29] and a Phoenician shrine, attesting actual Phoenician presence, has recently been recognized at Kommos on the south coast of the island.[30]

The most memorable tale involving the Phoenicians is in the Eumaios story. When he was a boy, a Phoenician trading ship arrived in harbor with a cargo of trinkets. One of the slave women in Eumaios' father's house, Eumaios' nurse, was herself Phoenician, and she established close relations with the Phoenician sailors. So when they finally sailed after a whole year of trading and taking on cargo, the woman slipped away to sail with them, taking Eumaios with her to be sold as a slave (15.415–84).

This story finally brings us to women. The Phoenician slave

woman claimed that she had been captured by pirates and sold into slavery. There are several women slaves in the *Odyssey* who had been objects of trade. The most notable is Eurykleia, the old nurse, whose purchase by Laertes, Odysseus' father, for the price of twenty oxen is described in Book 1 (429–31). It is certainly true that the slave trade is prominent in the references to trade in the *Odyssey* because these transactions are a necessary device to explain the movements of individuals, but we need not doubt that the buying and selling of people as slaves was a regular feature of life at the time when the poem was composed, and that many of those slaves were women.[31]

Turning now to overseas colonization, two passages in the poem have been seen to reflect that experience.[32] The first is the description of the Utopian city of the Phaeacians, which is expressly stated to have been recently founded by an act of emigration and colonization:

> These Phaeacians had once lived in the broad lands of Hypereia, and had been neighbours to the Cyclopes, a quarrelsome people, who took advantage of their greater strength to plague them, till the day when their king, Nausithous, made them migrate and settled them in Scheria, far from the busy haunts of men. There he laid out the walls of a new city, built them houses, put up temples to the gods, and allotted the land for cultivation.   (6.4–10)

The city's layout is carefully described at 6.262–72:

> Our city is surrounded by high battlements; it has an excellent harbour on each side and is approached by a narrow causeway, where the curved ships are drawn up to the road and each owner has his separate slip. Here is the people's meeting-place, built up on either side of the fine temple of Poseidon with blocks of quarried stone bedded deeply in the ground. It is here too that the sailors attend to the rigging of the black ships, to their cables and their sails, and the smoothing of their oars.

This might be a description of many Greek colonies where an isthmus site was chosen, such as Sinope in the Black Sea, which made the city easily defensible from the land, and provided the two harbors that were so useful. Later Odysseus is said to have "marvelled at the harbours with their well-found ships, at the meeting-place of these sea-lords and at their long and lofty walls, which were surmounted by palisades and presented a wonderful sight" (7.43–45).

Very different is the colonial passage from the story of the Kyklopes, where we are shown, not a well-established Greek colony, but a promising colonial site:

Not very far from the harbour on their coast, and not so near either, there lies a luxuriant island, covered with woods, which is the home of innumerable goats. The goats are wild, for man has made no pathways that might frighten them off, nor do hunters visit the island with their hounds to rough it in the forests and to range the mountain-tops. Used neither for grazing nor for ploughing, it lies for ever unsown and untilled; and this land where no man goes makes a happy pasture for the bleating goats. I must explain that the Cyclopes have nothing like our ships with their crimson prows; nor have they any shipwrights to build merchantmen that could serve their needs by plying to foreign ports in the course of that foreign trade which ships have established between the nations. Such craftsmen would have turned the island into a fine colony for the Cyclopes. For it is by no means a poor country, but capable of yielding any crop in due season. Along the shore of the grey sea there are soft watermeadows where the vine would never wither; and there is plenty of land level enough for the plough, where they could count on cutting a deep crop at every harvest-time, for the soil below the surface is exceedingly rich. Also it has a safe harbour, in which there is no occasion to tie up at all. You need neither cast anchor nor make fast with hawsers: all your crew have to do is to beach their boat and wait till the spirit moves them and the right wind blows. Finally, at the head of the harbour there is a stream of fresh water, running out of a cave in a grove of poplar-trees.   (9.116–41)

This may be seen as an idealized description of one of the favorite sites for Greek colonies, the offshore island.[33]

In the episode of the Kyklopes we are also vividly reminded of the fears of barbarous non-Greek peoples, whom colonists might meet. Often in the poem Odysseus is eager to learn of the inhabitants of some strange land "whether they are cruel, and wild, and unjust, or whether they love strangers and fear the gods in their thoughts" (9.171–76). In the case of the Kyklopes, they meet the worst examples of the first sort, murderers and cannibals.

It is in the relations of Greek colonists and native peoples that the women engage our attention. There is a theory, widely held today, that Greek women did not participate in the foundations of Greek colonies in the Archaic period and that only men went, who ensured the continuance of their settlements by taking wives from the local native population.[34] I have argued against this theory in print,[35] but it is hard to overturn a widely held belief.[36] So I make no apology for returning to the subject now, especially as I think that the *Odyssey* can supply an additional argument to those I marshaled earlier.

One reason for the adoption of the theory against which I am arguing is that there is quite a lot of evidence for intermarriage between Greeks and non-Greeks, both within the colonial world and in general. But those instances of intermarriage are quite different from the belief that all the women in a new Greek colony were non-Greeks.[37]

A second support for the theory is a famous passage of Herodotos about the foundation of Miletos (1.146.2–3), which I quote:

> Those who set out from the prytaneum of the Athenians, and who consider themselves the most noble of the Ionians, did not take women to the colony, but married Carian women, whose fathers they killed. Because of this killing the women themselves made a law and imposed an oath on themselves (which they handed down to their daughters), never to eat with their husbands, nor to call their own husband by his name, for the reason that the men had killed their fathers, husbands and sons, and then, after doing that, married them.

This passage forms part of a patently tendentious chapter in which Herodotos is claiming that the Ionians are thoroughly mixed racially. The story also belongs to a well-known category, called *aetiological;* that is, it explains the reason for some custom or institution. The story's aetiological character is clearly shown by the information that the law, which the women had imposed on themselves, was passed on to their daughters, for this provided the necessary link between the existing customs and the events of long ago that were thought to explain them. An aetiological story cannot be taken as historical evidence for the facts it contains, but it could still be argued that it provides a general testimony to ancient Greek practices. This raises the question whether Herodotos thought the supposed actions of the Ionian settlers normal or abnormal. It seems to me that his words "did not take women to the colony" imply clearly enough that in Herodotos' opinion it was normal for colonists to include women. Even if this interpretation is not accepted, the Herodotean story about Miletos cannot be called sufficient evidence for the belief that in Greek colonization of the Archaic period it was the rule for the colonists to find their wives among the native population.

The remaining arguments in favor of the thesis are more or less uncertain instances of intermarriage in Greek colonization and the absence of mention of Greek women going as colonists. The latter, as an argument from silence, is inevitably suspect, and the more so in this case, because our Greek historical sources make a practice of ignoring women. We have several reports of colonization in the fifth century by the best of historians, Thucydides. He invariably uses the masculine gender in his description of the colonists.[38] Yet we definitely know that the colonists who went to the Athenian colony of Thourioi in this very period brought their wives with them.[39] It is also striking that one Greek historian, writing, admittedly, about the Hellenistic period, regarded the presence of women and children as characteristic of a colonial expedition and their absence as indicative of a military campaign.[40]

Curiously enough, among the very few individual colonists whose names we know from the Archaic period, two are women.[41] Both these women were priestesses. This is the clue, I maintain, that leads to a very strong indirect argument against the theory that Greek women did not go to Archaic Greek colonies. That argument, in brief, is the importance of Greek women in Greek religion.

It is easy to show, as has been stated, that "religion in Greece was suffused with women from top to bottom."[42] At the top were the great priestesses, very distinguished and powerful women, of the greatest importance to the community. There were frequently strict rules about eligibility for these high offices. But there were also many cults in which the worshipers were women, and any Greek woman had an important role to play in the religious life of the community.[43]

It is also an easy task to show that religion was of the highest importance in Greek colonies, just as in the cities of Old Greece.[44] I therefore argued that all Greek colonies would need Greek women in order to ensure a proper relation between the community and its gods, and it is absurd to imagine that native women, who did not even speak Greek, could be entrusted with these important tasks.

When I published this argument, I naturally drew attention to the passage in the *Iliad* where Theano, wife of Antenor, who has been chosen priestess of Athena by the people, is alone empowered to open the doors of the temple so that the goddess can be supplicated (6.296–300).[45] There is also archaeological evidence for great priestesses as early as ca. 800, if the occupants of the two very rich female graves discovered at Eleusis of that date were, as has been suggested, priestesses.[46] One of the graves contained a figurine of the Egyptian goddess Isis, whom the Greeks identified with Demeter.

It now seems to me that the *Odyssey* also can contribute to this question. In the great panorama of womanhood presented by the *Odyssey,* the non-Greek female element consists either of slave women or of divine or semidivine creatures, such as Kirke, Kalypso, the Sirens, Skylla, and Charybdis. While some of these characters had definite attractions, they were all, if in different degrees, sinister and destructive.

Contrast these with the Greek women, either wives or maidens before marriage. Penelope obviously stands alone, but at the ideal Greek colony of the Phaeacians we find the distinguished queen Arete, whom the castaway Odysseus is advised to supplicate, and the ideal of an unmarried maiden, Nausikaa. These are the women that Greeks of the eighth century thought of as appropriate wives and partners in a Greek community. I would be the first to admit that this argument is impressionistic, but I would still maintain that the *Odyssey* here faithfully reflects a view of women that makes it impossible to imagine that Greek colonists would expect to establish a new Greek community in which the women were not Greek.

Notes

1. The very extensive bibliography on this subject can be reached by consulting recent works with very full lists, e.g. Morris, 1986, 130–38; Raaflaub, 1991, 252–56. I therefore confine my bibliographical references to either those strictly pertinent or representative selections.

2. See, e.g., Heubeck, West, and Hainsworth, 1988, 6–7.

3. Cf., e.g., Murray, 1980, 54 and 120.

4. See, e.g., Raaflaub, 1991, 225–30; Wees, 1988 (from whom I borrow the terms "orthodox" and "unorthodox") 1–2.

5. In establishing the unorthodox interpretation Latacz, 1977, has been very influential, but his arguments from Homer's words for military formations were already shown to be uncertain by Leimbach, 1980, in his review. The authority of Pritchett, 1985, 1–33, also added weight to the unorthodox interpretation, but his reliance on analogies often very distant in place and time (e.g., the Battle of Agincourt!) and on an inaccurate classification of Homer's many fights between individuals as formal *monomachiai* indicates the weakness of his case. The very full, detailed, and convincing analysis by Wees, 1988, may be seen, positively, as an excellent description of Homeric battle tactics and, negatively, as a complete rebuttal of the unorthodox interpretation.

6. More recently, *Archaeologia Homerica*, founded by F. Matz and H.-G. Buchholz, 1967– , has been covering more comprehensively similar (but more extensive) ground to Lorimer's.

7. Lorimer, 1950, 462–64.

8. Burkert, 1976.

9. For a full account of Egypt under the Twenty-fifth Dynasty, see James, 1991, esp. 677–708. I am grateful to David O'Connor for advice on this subject. On Homer and Egypt, see Braun, 1982, 32–35.

10. Kirk, 1968, 95; Janko, 1992, 8–9.

11. West, 1988, 33–34.

12. See, e.g., the chronology in Easterling and Knox, 1985.

13. Barron and Easterling, 1985a, 117; Graham, 1978, esp. 72–86.

14. E.g., those mentioned previously who would date the *Iliad* and *Odyssey* to ca. 650 or later.

15. Morris, 1986, 83–94.

16. See, e.g., Nagy, 1992, 33–36.

17. Janko, 1982.

18. See, e.g., Janko, 1982, 94–98, 228–31; Barron and Easterling, 1985b, 93.

19. Janko, 1982, 230–31. In Janko, 1992, 18–19, he now dates the *Iliad* to before 750.

20. Meiggs and Lewis, 1988, no. 1; Hansen, 1983, no. 454, unfortunately marred by multiple misprints of the date. (These are corrected in the *Addenda et Corrigenda ad CEG 1*, Hansen, 1989, 304). I do not follow the restoration in the first line that Hansen supports because I find his formal arguments lead to a less satisfactory sense. See, however, Meiggs and Lewis, 1988, no. 1, apparatus. Cf. also Graham, 1982, 99.

21. See, e.g., Hansen, 1976, 42–43; Hiller, 1976, 30.

22. See, e.g., Friis Johansen, 1967, 34–36; Fittschen, 1969, 192–94; Brillante, 1983, 103.

23. Cf., e.g., Lowenstam, 1992, 166–68; Morris, 1986, 91–92; Kirk, 1968, 284–85. It is admittedly very possible to see representations of the Homeric epics in scenes that are too vague to bear the weight of the interpretation. This seems to me to be done, e.g., by Schefold, 1991, who dates Homer on these arguments to ca. 800; see 519.

24. Morris, 1986, 86–91.

25. For a well-balanced and well-documented account, with full treatment of modern interpretations, see Wees, 1992, 219–48. Kopcke, 1990, 121–28, is also useful and well informed.

26. The translations of this and all subsequent quotations from the *Odyssey* are by Rieu, 1946, and are published by kind permission.

27. Culican, 1991; Niemeyer, 1984.

28. Culican, 1991, 478; Frankfort, 1954, 195–201; Markoe, 1985; note, however, the review by Winter, 1990.

29. E.g., the inscribed bronze bowl from a tomb at Knossos; Coldstream, 1982, 271–72.

30. Shaw, 1989.

31. Wickert-Micknat has maintained that there are few slave women in the Homeric epics and that the situation about slavery and freedom was very different from what we know in other periods of the ancient world; see, briefly, Wickert-Micknat, 1982, 83, and, fully, Wickert-Micknat, 1983. But her attempt to deny the obvious rests on unconvincing a priori assumptions, improbable meanings attributed to Greek words, and weak arguments from silence.

32. See, e.g., Beloch, 1924, 231–32; Schaefer, 1960, 77–78.

33. Cf. Beloch, 1924, 231–32; Bremmer, 1986.

34. See, e.g., Rougé, 1970; Compernolle, 1983; Coldstream, 1993.

35. Graham, 1984.

36. Cf., e.g., Dalby, 1992, 19–20 n. 29, who shows no proper understanding of the poverty of our source material and rejects my thesis without specific criticisms, except the phrase "a paper of patchy logic," for which an author would welcome precise justification.

37. Graham, 1984, 293–94.

38. E.g. 1.27.1 (Epidamnos); l.100.3, 4.102.2–3 (Amphipolis); 3.92.5 (Herakleia in Trakhis).

39. Diodorus Siculus 12.10–11, esp. 11.1. Cf. Graham, 1984, 302.

40. Diodorus Siculus 20.41.1. Cf. Meister, 1984, 396–97.

41. Pausanias 10.28.3; Strabo 4.1.4 (C 179). Cf. Graham, 1984, 302–4.

42. Schaps, 1979, 73.

43. Cf. Graham, 1984, 304–10.

44. Ibid., 311–12.

45. Ibid., 304–6.

46. Coldstream, 1977, 78–80.

2

Female Representations and Interpreting the *Odyssey*

Seth L. Schein

The representation and description of a variety of females—human women, goddesses, and monsters—are among the most striking features of the *Odyssey*. For the most part, women and the goddess Athena are described or represented by the voice of the poem's (implied) narrator; other goddesses and nonhuman females occur mainly in the stories told in the first person by Odysseus, sometimes in secondary narrative by characters whom Odysseus quotes and whose accounts, as in the case of Kirke's description of the Sirens, he seems to accept. Only Kalypso figures in both authorial and embedded narrative.

The *Odyssey* gives relatively few descriptions of its female characters' physical appearances and characteristics, such as Athena's gray eyes (*passim*), Penelope's "thick hand" (21.6), and the white arms of Arete (7.233,335; 11.335), Nausikaa (6.101, 186, 251; 7.12), Helen (22.227), and servants in both Scheria and Ithaka (7.239; 18.198; 19.60). Nevertheless, it offers quite a lot of what might be called the phenomenology of appearance: accounts of specific characters' appearances that are grounded in the effects they have on other characters or on themselves. Odysseus, for example, refers to several of his companions meeting the wife of the Laistrygonian Antiphates, "as large as a mountain top, and they loathed her" (10.113); quoting Kirke, he gives an extended description of the monstrous Skylla

17

(12.85–100). Perhaps it is no accident that these two females are man-eaters, like the Kyklops Polyphemos, whom Odysseus calls a "monstrous marvel, and he didn't resemble / a man who eats bread but a wooded pinnacle / in the high mountains" (9.190–93). Presumably the appearance of these dangerous figures was correlative in Odysseus' mind with their hideous actions, which motivated his descriptions of them.

Penelope is a poetically more important example of the phenomenology of appearance. We do not learn what she actually looks like, but we hear that Odysseus prefers her to Kalypso, even though she is "slighter in form and stature to look at face-to-face" than the goddess (5.217); that Athena enhanced Penelope's "beautiful face" with ambrosial beauty of the kind Aphrodite uses, and "made her taller and fuller to see and whiter than sawn ivory" (18.192–96), so that the Suitors desired her all the more and "prayed to lie beside her" (18.212–13); that she herself did not even want to wash the tears off her face when she was leaving her bedroom for the main hall of the palace, and felt the immortals "destroyed [her] excellence in both form and build," when Odysseus went with the Greeks to Troy (18.178–81, 251–53 = 19.124–26). This emphasis on the effects of Penelope's physical appearance makes sense, given the importance in the poem of the themes of appearance and disguise, mutability and subjectivity.[1]

Each depiction or description of a female in the *Odyssey* is aimed either at the external audience of the poem or at some internal audience of one or more characters as well as the external audience. Each appeals to, or plays against, audiences' conceptions of females generally as well as the expectations shaped by representations of particular females in the mythology and oral poetic tradition behind the poem. None of these descriptions or representations within the *Odyssey* is totally authoritative; taken together, they contribute greatly to the poem's narratological, dramatic, and moral complexity. In particular, the multiplicity and complexity of females represented as making decisions, taking actions, and telling stories challenge listeners and readers to shape views of Odysseus' distinctive heroic identity, evaluate his authority as a narrator, and consider how his interactions with females help constitute both his identity and his authority, even while these representations make problematic any particular interpretation of the hero, the females, and the poem.[2]

For many readers, the most memorable section of the *Odyssey* is Odysseus' narrative to the Phaeacians in Books 9–12 of his adventures since leaving Troy. The traditional story patterns and folktales on which this narrative draws are carefully adapted to the distinctive themes, ethical concerns, and symbolic patterns of the *Odyssey* as a whole, but this is not what makes them so memorable. Rather, they constitute a series of diverse, wide-ranging stories about the pleasures and dangers of human existence, stories that tend to represent what is "human" as male and most of the "pleasures" and "dangers"—or what a male imagination fantasizes as such—as female.

I say "male imagination" precisely because these stories are narrated in the first person by Odysseus and constitute *his*, not the poem's, versions of heroic experience. Many of them involve nonhuman female figures who threaten the hero or his return homeward. These females, to hear Odysseus tell of them, are often monstrous, and their menace is literally or symbolically sexual—specific instances of the general danger of being swallowed, engulfed, concealed, or obliterated, against which he constantly struggles. In this respect they are vividly imagined versions of the sea itself in which Odysseus is lost, through which he struggles to return home, and with which, according to Teiresias' prophecy (11.121–37), he must make his ultimate peace by bringing knowledge of ships and the worship of the sea god Poseidon to inland agriculturists among whom they are yet unknown. Odysseus represents his experiences with sea dangers as encounters with the feminine and repeatedly tells of escaping these dangers when the threatening females eventually befriend him, after he survives or overcomes them.[3]

The power of these dangerous, nonhuman females is sometimes signaled by the prototypically female activities of weaving (Kirke, Kalypso) and singing (Kirke, Kalypso, the Sirens).[4] In other instances the threat to Odysseus is that of being swallowed, literally eaten alive (Skylla, Charybdis). Polyphemos, the Kyklops, though apparently a male figure, might well be included in this list of dangerous females in that he seems to be symbolically feminized by the cave-womb in which he dwells, within which the hero is Nobody and from which the hero is, so to speak, (re)born, conspicuously insisting on his identity as Odysseus.[5]

Kalypso and her island offer a suggestive example of how the encounters with females that Odysseus narrates work and how each constitutes a coherent episode, thematically and ethically relevant to the entire poem. As I have said, this is the only one of the adventures that is told both by the poem's narrator and, more briefly, by Odysseus in his first person narratives to the Phaeacians (7.244–66; 12.447–50) and to Penelope (23.333–37). Kalypso is referred to emphatically in the opening of the poem (1.13, 15, 49–57), and Odysseus' departure from Ogygia is the first adventure narrated after the Telemachy. These features make the episode especially prominent and give it a paradigmatic status in relation to the other adventures.

Kalypso, whose name means "concealer," is a good instance of the poem's characteristic punning and etymological wordplay on the names and attributes of its characters—punning and wordplay that reflect these characters' essential natures and functions. Kalypso "conceals" Odysseus on her island at the "navel of the sea" (1.50), which means, in effect, that as long as he is with her he is lost at sea and not himself—not able to function as Odysseus. All he "does," until the intervention of Hermes in Book 5, is sit passively weeping, gazing out over the sea that should be the medium of his heroic achievement but now is merely a barrier to it, "longing to see even the smoke / rising from his native land" (1.58–59). He does, however, resist Kalypso's invitation to become her immortal consort, which would mean permanently "concealing" his mortality and his return homeward, as well as abandoning his distinctive heroic pattern of suffering, endurance, and ultimate triumph for the life of ease that characterizes the gods' existence. Despite temptation, Odysseus keeps his mind on "thoughtful Penelope," though "she is slighter than you [Kalypso] in form and stature to look at; / for she is mortal, but you are immortal and unaging" (5.216–18); he keeps longing "to go homeward and see the day of returning home" (5.220). In effect he chooses to be remembered as the hero of the *Odyssey* over the oblivion among mortals that would accompany an existence as Kalypso's husband.[6] This choice is every bit as significant as Achilles' decision to die at Troy and achieve "imperishable glory" rather than to return home to a long life with no glory (*Iliad* 9.412–16). In each epic the hero chooses, in a different way, to be a hero, and so chooses life (in heroic song) over death (through being forgotten).[7]

The Sirens apparently constitute a danger for Odysseus different in kind from that of Kalypso and the other threatening, nonhuman females he tells of in his first-person narrative of his adventures. They neither invite him into a sexual relationship nor threaten to engulf or swallow him. Rather, they sing a song in a "honey-sweet voice" (12.187) and claim,

> when anyone has delighted in it, he will go on his way knowing more;
> for we know all things, as many as, in broad Troy,
> the Trojans and Argives toiled at by the will of the gods,
> and we know as many things as happen on the earth that feeds many. (12.188–91)

The song with which the Sirens tempt Odysseus suggests by its content and diction the kind of heroism associated with the *Iliad* and the Iliadic poetic tradition.[8] If Odysseus were to give way to their temptation and relapse, as it were, into that poetic genre, he would be destroyed and his bones would join those of other men rotting, as Kirke tells him, on the Sirens' meadow, for no warrior heroism can resist the power of the Sirens' song. Only the heroism of *nostos* poetry—poetry celebrating a hero's "return home"—grounded in Odysseus' characteristic cunning intelligence and mental toughness, is sufficient to withstand the Sirens' temptation. It is noteworthy that whereas the diction and content of the Sirens' song are Iliadic, the dangerous pleasure it offers is distinctively Odyssean because it is fundamentally sexual. This is shown by *terpsamenos* ("has delighted in," 12.189), a participial form of the verb *terpō*, which is frequently used of sexual delight, and by the sexually connotative *thelgousin*, Kirke's word in 12.44 for the "enchanting" effect of the Sirens' singing (and a word also used by Odysseus at 10.318 and by Kirke at 10.326 for the "enchanting" effect of her own metamorphosing drugs). In addition, the "flowery meadow" (*leimōn' anthemoenta*, 12.159), in which, Kirke says, the Sirens sit and sing and the bones of their victims rot (12.44–46), also suggests a scene of sexual activity, given the erotic associations of meadows (and grass and gardens) in early Greek poetry.[9] Thus, through their singing and their landscape, the Sirens menace Odysseus sexually, even though they do not explicitly invite him into a sexual relationship like Kirke and Kalypso and seem to tempt him with knowledge rather than with sexuality.

By contrast, the human females whom the poem describes Odysseus as meeting—Nausikaa, Arete, and especially Penelope—are invariably helpful. Penelope might well be considered a beneficent version of the seductive and dangerous nonhuman females Odysseus encounters. When she weaves a plan or a garment, she helps preserve Odysseus' home and kingdom. When he goes to bed with her in Book 23, he is neither threatened with destruction nor deflected from his journey homeward. Rather, their sexual union marks the end of his wanderings, at least in this poem,[10] and his restoration to his full identity as husband and king.

But how should a listener or reader of the *Odyssey*, as opposed to its hero, understand Penelope's loyalty and resourcefulness? The poem not only represents these qualities as existing for the sake of Odysseus and as an adjunct to his heroic identity, but it also characterizes them and her in such a way as to call into question this representation and even to raise doubts about the possibility of any single, straightforward interpretation of the epic.

Looked at in one way, Penelope, throughout the *Odyssey*, protects the *oikos* ("house" and "household") of Odysseus and Telemachos. Like Arete, she spends her time supervising servants and working wool, but *her* weaving of a shroud for Laertes is absolutely unique in kind and so important that it is described at length three times (2.94–110, 19.138–56, 24.129–46). Undoing by night what she accomplishes during the day, she uses this typically female activity to deceive the Suitors, delay her remarriage, and preserve the *oikos*.

In this salutary deception, Penelope shows the same cunning intelligence that is characteristic of Odysseus. The poem even shows hers to be superior to his when, at 23.176–80, she tests the stranger who claims to be Odysseus by ordering Eurykleia to prepare his bed—the one, we hear, Odysseus himself had made—outside their bedroom. Odysseus rises to the bait: By suspecting that another man has entered their bedroom and cut the rooted olive trunk that formed one leg of the bed, he in effect acknowledges the power of Penelope over him—the possibility that she has been or could be unfaithful. By describing the construction of the bed, he provides her with the certain sign that he really is Odysseus and gives her the opportunity to assert clearly her actual faithfulness and her resourcefulness in preserving their marriage and household.[11]

The mental similarity between Odysseus and Penelope is obvious both at 18.281–83, where he enjoys the way she trickily charms gifts from the Suitors while "her own mind is eager for other things," and in the continuation of the recognition scene in Book 23, when Penelope wishes to learn about the future trial imposed on Odysseus by Teiresias before going to bed with her husband, controlling her desire as so often in the poem he controls his (23.257–62). This mental likeness, or mutuality, is the poem's main example of the kind of harmony in marriage that Odysseus wishes for Nausikaa at 6.181–85:

> may the gods provide a husband and a house and unity of mind
> that is good; for nothing is better and stronger than *this*,
> than when the two of them, man and wife, keep house,
> being of one mind in their thoughts; with many pains for their enemies
> and joy for their well-wishers, and they themselves are especially glorious.

The verb translated as "are . . . glorious"—*ekluon*, a form of *kluō* ("hear")—is linguistically cognate with *kleos*, the Iliadic word for "heroic glory." It is characteristic of the *Odyssey* and its genre that having a harmonious marriage and an *oikos* can generate the kind of glory that in the *Iliad* and the Iliadic poetic tradition comes only from heroic warfare. It is equally characteristic that a woman, Penelope, can win such *kleos* for her "excellence" (*aretē,* 24.197) in "remembering" (*memnet',* 24.195) her husband—*kleos* that Odysseus himself, in a striking "reverse simile," compares to that of a good king who righteously upholds justice and under whose rule the land is fruitful, the herds are safe and strong, the fish in the sea plentiful, and the people well off (19.108–114).[12] As Agamemnon's shade says to that of Achilles at 24.194–98,

> How good was the mind of blameless Penelope,
> daughter of Ikarios; how well she remembered Odysseus,
> her wedded husband; therefore, for her the glory of her excellence
> will never perish, and for those living on the earth the immortals will
>   make
> a song of grace for sensible Penelope.

In the *Iliad* "imperishable glory" is attained by warriors through celebration in poetry when they have performed heroic deeds. Here in the *Odyssey,* the "excellence" (*aretē*) that leads to such glory is redefined to refer not to supremacy in battle but to the mental toughness and faithfulness illustrated by Penelope "remembering" Odysseus. This makes sense because, elsewhere in the poem, remembering is the activity of mind that most distinguishes Odysseus from his Companions; enables him to return home to Ithaka, his *oikos,* and his wife; and makes him the hero of the epic. For her "remembering," the shade of Agamemnon says, Penelope earns a "song of grace" in the future—a kind of reward that in the *Iliad* is limited to warriors and to Helen (6.358) considered as the "cause" of warfare. In the *Odyssey* Helen, with her drug Nepenthe that "banishes grief and allays wrath, causing forgetfulness of all evils" (4.221), seems morally trivial in large part because she is more concerned with forgetting than with remembering; Penelope, by contrast, becomes a virtually equal, second hero of the poem, along with Odysseus.[13]

Penelope's "song of grace" is contrasted by Agamemnon's shade to the "song of hate" (24.200) he prophesies for Klytaimestra and to the "harsh reputation" Klytaimestra "will cause to attend / on female women, even on one who does well" (24.201–2). In the world of the *Odyssey,* it seems, a woman who preserves or betrays her husband and *oikos* is as much the object of praise or blame as a man in the *Iliad* who acts heroically or like a coward, just as a return homeward, which in the *Iliad* is incompatible with heroic glory, is in the *Odyssey* itself the source of such glory.

In the kind of traditional poetry exemplified by the *Odyssey*, the *oikos* is a suitable object of song; the poetic world is divided into those loyal to the *oikos* and those who would destroy it; the hero is permitted to kill in defense of his *oikos* and to escape the reprisals that usually would follow such killing. Furthermore, because women's place is in the *oikos,* their role and importance in the *Odyssey* is far greater than in the *Iliad.* This has even led some readers, notably S. Butler, to suppose that the poem was composed by a woman.[14] However unlikely this may seem, such a view reflects not only the prominence of women in the *Odyssey* but also the sympathy with which they are portrayed. For example, Eurykleia, who for several generations has been part of Ithaka's royal *oikos* and nursed its rulers, is conspicuous for her fierce loyalty to it and to Laertes, Odysseus, and Telemachos. Throughout the poem, the role of the wife—in the persons of Helen, Arete, and Penelope and in contrast to the poem's threatening, nonhuman females—is given special honor, and women's intelligence—especially Penelope's—is equated with men's.

All this seems clear and convincing. Nevertheless, I think it would be naive to equate the interpretations by Agamemnon and other male characters in the poem, even Odysseus, of the proper relations between husbands and wives with that of the *Odyssey* itself. For Penelope's plans and behavior can be seen to have their own motivation, quite apart from her loyalty to Odysseus and his *oikos.*[15] For example, although the contest of the bow and the axes *results* in the death of the Suitors and the restoration of Odysseus to the kingship, when Penelope declares her intention to hold the contest (19.570–81), she must be understood to do so fully prepared for imminent marriage to one of her wooers. Similarly, when she solicits gifts from the Suitors at 18.274–80, we have only Odysseus' reported understanding that she is merely leading them on, "enchanting their feeling / with pleasing words, though her mind was eager for other things" (18.282–83). Why, however, should we accept Odysseus' reading of the situation, which obviously is self-serving? By the same token, should we accept the statement by the shade of the Suitor Amphimedon to the shades of Achilles and Agamemnon that Penelope set up the contest at the bidding of Odysseus (24.167)? This directly contradicts what happens in Book 19, where, as the poem makes explicitly clear, Penelope and Odysseus do *not* recognize one another, and she sets up the contest for her own reasons.[16] If we cannot trust Amphimedon's statement, why should we accept, and how are we to evaluate, the praise of Penelope by Agamemnon, to which that statement gives rise?

Finally, what are we to make of Penelope's implicit comparison of herself to Helen (23.218–24), immediately after she recognizes Odysseus by his knowledge of their bed and tells him of her continual fear during his absence that "someone of mortal men might come and deceive me / with words. For many men plan evil profits" (23.216–17)? Is it that she distrusts herself and therefore tests Odysseus, who clearly fits the description of the kind of man against whom she says she was on guard? Penelope asserts:

> Argive Helen, born from Zeus,
> would not have mingled in the bed of love with a foreigner
> if she knew that the warlike sons of the Achaeans
> were going to bring her back again homeward to her dear fatherland.
> Surely a god drove her to do an unseemly deed;
> earlier she had not put in her own heart the disastrous
> moral blindness, from which, to begin with, sorrow came to us
> also. (23.218–24)

This is the most sympathetic thing anyone in the *Odyssey* says about Helen. Penelope refuses to join in the otherwise universal condemnation of her by the poem's male characters, a condemnation that usually is considered by readers to be that of the poem itself. Yet Penelope's independence of judgment should caution readers not to assume too readily that the poem, as opposed to certain of its characters, even makes such a straightforward, uncomplicated condemnation. In light of Penelope's comment, it might be more accurate to say that in the end the poem leaves the question of Helen's moral responsibility and even the moral status of adultery open and in doubt, however it may tempt a listener or reader to share in the majority judgment against her and her behavior.

The poem similarly tempts its audience to accept as its own the judgments of various male characters, including Odysseus, about Penelope. According to these judgments, her glory lies in loyalty to her husband and *oikos* and in the resourcefulness with which she expresses this loyalty. But the poem also shows a Penelope with a mind of her own, not merely one in harmony with her husband's. It would be simplistic to adopt the standard, patriarchal reading of Penelope and of the roles of women and other females in the *Odyssey* generally without recognizing how the poem partly undoes this reading.

In the case of Penelope, as elsewhere, the *Odyssey* implies that its

own main values and most frequently expressed viewpoints are neither unproblematic nor the only ones possible. Rather, they are to
some extent open to criticism and negative evaluation, and the poem
itself is correspondingly open-ended, interpretively ambivalent or
indeterminate, and irreducible to a single, straightforward, one-
dimensional reading.[17]

Notes

I would like to thank Beth Cohen for inviting me to contribute to the
present volume and for her constructive criticism and editorial advice. I also
wish to thank Laura Slatkin for criticism and suggestions that improved this
essay.

1. As might be expected, there are far more, and more varied, accounts
of Odysseus' appearance than of any female character's. Cf. Griffith, 1985,
310. For perceptive interpretations of the poem's descriptions of Odysseus'
physical appearances, see Bell, 1991 and Bassi, 1994.

2. On the "threat posed by female narrators," especially the Sirens and
Helen, to Odysseus' "privileges as narrator and focalizer of his own story"
and the ways in which "the epic narrator contains this threat," see Doherty,
Chapter 5, this volume.

3. Cf. Nagler, 1977.

4. Male bards (*aoidoi*) such as Phemios and Demodokos sing epic poetry
about heroes and gods; the subject matter of the songs sung by nonhuman
female singers, apart from the Sirens, is not specified. This is the kind of
singing I call "prototypically female."

5. Cf. Dimock, 1956, 56–57.

6. Cf. Vernant, 1982.

7. Güntert, 1919, argues that Ogygia is symbolically a Land of the Dead,
Kalypso a goddess of the dead, and "concealment" the equivalent of death.
Cf. Anderson, 1958; Vernant, 1982; Powell, 1977, 5, n. 13, who refers to the
interpretation of Kalypso and "concealment" by Hölscher, 1939, 67; Porter,
1962, 3–5, who terms Ogygia "an Eden-like Hell, or a hellish Eden." For a
recent discussion of Kalypso with a summary of relevant scholarship, see
Crane, 1988, 15–29.

8. See Pucci, 1979; Segal, 1983.

9. The "soft meadows" (*leimōnes malakoi*) of Kalypso's Ogygia (5.72)
have a similar connotation. Cf. Motte, 1973, 50–56, cited by Vernant, 1982,
15, n. 10.

10. In the later epic sequel to the *Odyssey* entitled the *Telegony*, Odysseus' further adventures included journeys, wars, a second marriage to
Kallidike, Queen of the Thesprotians, and death at the hands of Telegonos,
his son by Kirke. In the *Odyssey* itself, Odysseus tells Penelope of the
"immeasurable toil there will still be in the future, / [toil] abundant and

difficult that it is necessary for me to finish completely" (23.249–50), according to Teiresias' prophecy (23.251, 267–84), and he says he will go raiding to replenish the herds destroyed by the Suitors (23.357).

11. On the specific poetic significance of "the sign of the bed," see Zeitlin, Chapter 7, this volume.

12. Cf. Foley, 1978.

13. For recent discussions of Penelope, see Murnaghan, 1986, reworked and expanded in Murnaghan, 1987, 118–47; Felson-Rubin, 1987 and 1993; Winkler, 1990; Doherty, 1990; and Katz, 1991, who is especially instructive on Penelope and *kleos*.

14. Butler, 1967.

15. Cf. Felson-Rubin, 1987 and 1993. On Penelope as an independent "moral agent," see Foley, Chapter 6, this volume.

16. Nevertheless, several scholars have argued that Penelope unconsciously or intuitively recognizes Odysseus in Book 19. See, for example, Harsh, 1950; Amory, 1963; Russo, 1982. Cf. Winkler, 1990, 150–61, who describes Penelope as "only 99% certain" that the stranger "was really Odysseus" (160).

17. On the poem's open-endedness and "indeterminacy," especially in regard to Penelope, see Katz, 1991, esp. 3–19, 155–95.

3

Between Skylla and Penelope: Female Characters of the *Odyssey* in Archaic and Classical Greek Art

Diana Buitron-Oliver
Beth Cohen

The *Odyssey* is the only surviving epic poem that describes the Return of a Greek hero after the Trojan war. Thus it portrays neither the heroism and tragedy of war nor the normal order of daily life in peace, and in Classical antiquity it must have presented a particular challenge for visual artists. It is memorably rich in unusual physical adventure and suspenseful psychological drama, and ancient artists tapped both of these aspects as they struggled with the compositional difficulties of representing fantastic creatures from Odysseus' exploits as well as with representing the poem's subtler nuances of human characterization, particularly from its account of the hero's homecoming.

When faced with films based on literary sources, movie critics often ask, "Is the picture faithful to the book?" As art historians, we are dealing with specific works of visual art adapted from famous stories in a work of ancient literature. The representations preserved in Greek art from the Archaic and Classical periods were not text illustrations,[1] and thus the way in which a story or a character was shown originally must have reflected a variety of influences, which now may no longer be fully reconstructed. In pre-Classical Greece, soon after the poem's composition, probably in the late eighth century

B.C., one important factor may have been artists' limited knowledge of the poem, for they seem to have depicted only certain *Odyssey* stories.[2] In Athens the entire epic poem would have become more widely known during the sixth century B.C. with the formal recitation of Homer by competing rhapsodes at the Panathenaic festival,[3] and in fifth-century Athens playwrights created and oversaw many theatrical productions interpreting *Odyssey* subjects.[4] Several of the key preserved Archaic and Classical *Odyssey* representations are Athenian, and Athenian developments had far-ranging influence in the contemporary Greek world as well as later in Classical antiquity. Yet the particular circumstances that led to the occurrence of a particular Homeric image in a particular context at a particular time in antiquity are today often obscure.

Our subject is the visualization of the *Odyssey*'s female characters by ancient artists. Focusing specifically on when and how some of the poem's important females were first introduced in Greek art during the centuries following the composition of the poem, we will contrast the depiction of *Odyssey*-related imagery and stories from the Archaic period with the pointed refinements and changes that occurred in the Classical period of the fifth century B.C. Today our conception of these characters is to a degree refracted through these powerful visual representations that are not necessarily direct reflections of Homer's verbal configurations in the epic poem.

Nonhuman Females

It was the *Odyssey*'s dangerous nonhuman females—whether monster or divine temptress—who first and most often captured the imagination of ancient artists and their patrons. The earliest identifiable examples seem to be the Sirens.

The Sirens

Although Sirens are bird women in Greek art, this is not the way Homer depicts them. As Homer's two Sirens sing, the poet's hero mentions no particular aspect of their physiognomy, perhaps implying that, although they are magical, their appearance is in no way exceptional (nonhuman). The goddess Kirke, who instructs Odysseus about resisting the Sirens' song, also remains silent about their appearance:

> First you will reach the Sirens, who enchant
> all human beings, whoever comes to them.
> He who approaches in ignorance and hears the voice

of the Sirens—his wife and little children do not
stand beside him when he has returned home and have joy of him,
but the Sirens work enchantment with their clear-sounding song,
sitting in a meadow. Around them is a great heap of bones
of men rotting away, with the skins shriveling around them.
$$(12.39–46)^5$$

In Greek art human-headed birds initially appeared during the late eighth century B.C. as creatures employed in decorative, nonnarrative contexts, and they continued to have ornamental functions for hundreds of years.[6] The first indication that these popular composite avian monsters were equated with Homer's Sirens comes from depictions on Corinthian pottery of the first half of the sixth century B.C. (plates 39, 44, 45) in which Odysseus' ship is shown passing the Sirens in the specific manner advised by Kirke (12.47–52)—with sails stowed and Odysseus bound to the mast so that he can listen to the Sirens' seductive song, while his crew takes the ship safely past the peril, their ears deafened by beeswax. On a Corinthian black-figure aryballos in the Museum of Fine Arts, Boston (plate 39), two of the woman-headed birds familiar from decorative art now stand on a promontory above a boar-prowed ship with a man tied upright against the mast. The danger inherent in this adventure is suggested by two enormous birds hovering ominously above Odysseus' ship.[7]

Although Sirens in Greek *Odyssey* representations usually have wings, they generally do not fly. Ordinarily, neither their flowery meadow nor the lethal nature of their threat is explicitly depicted. To find the bleached skeletons of the Sirens' shipwrecked victims one must turn to a fantastic *Odyssey* seascape (plate 1) in a Roman wall painting from Pompeii of the first century A.D.[8] Here the bird-bodied Sirens have human arms and accompany their song on musical instruments.

Music-making Sirens belong to an old visual tradition, the best early example of which occurs on a black-figure Athenian wine pitcher (oinochoe) in the Callimanopulos collection (plates 2, 3) of ca. 515–505 B.C.[9] Here, in the first inscribed depiction of the *Odyssey* episode, the three Sirens' increased anthropomorphism and femininity are enhanced by the white color conventional for female flesh as well as by their finely coifed hair tied with red ribbons, and their jewelry.[10] By accompanying themselves on the lyre and pipes, their singing is shown in a contemporary Greek way, and thus the seductive power of the Homeric Sirens' song has been translated into readily understandable visual terms.

Pipes (*auloi*) and stringed instruments such as the lyre or kithara are commonly played by Sirens down through the Roman period (cf. plate 1). Usually in a trio of Sirens (more common in art than Homer's duo), two instrumentalists flank a singer, but a pentimento on the Callimanopulos oinochoe (plates 2, 3) must have been intended as a third musical instrument—the incised (but not colored) disc-shaped object in the left hand of the centralmost Siren. Its flat, round form brings to mind the tympanon, a tambourine-like percussion instrument.[11] This instrument is played by an alluringly curvaceous Siren of a developed Late Classical / Hellenistic type (bird below the hips and fully human female nude above) in the only preserved fourth-century depiction of the *Odyssey* episode (plate 4)—the comic burlesque on a South Italian (Paestan) red-figure bell-krater attributed to Python,[12] in which a not-so-mighty Greek hero hangs from the ship's mast by his wrists, with his feet dangling above his crew.

The Late Archaic and Early Classical music-making Sirens with human arms are woman-headed bird monsters civilized, and multiple associations for them existed in Greek art and culture. Music itself was considered by the ancients as one of the main characteristics of civilization.[13] Although professional musicians in public performances were male, playing musical instruments was a skill commonly mastered by women. The tympanon, for example, regularly played by maenads and satyrs in later Attic and South Italian red-figure Dionysiac scenes, was an instrument actually played by Greek women during the celebration of mystery cults.[14] In the female quarters of the Greek home, respectable women entertained each other with music and also played the pipes to set the pace for working on the loom. Female prostitutes (*hetairai*) playing the pipes or a stringed instrument, such as the barbitos, to entertain men at drinking parties (symposia) are well attested in Late Archaic Attic vase painting.[15] And on the name vase of the Sappho Painter the famous poetess herself is envisioned as a bejeweled and elaborately coifed young woman playing the barbitos.[16]

In the early fifth century Pindar put music high on the list of requirements for a good life (*Pythian Ode* 10, 37–44; fr. 129, 6–7). Later in a Pythagorean saying and in Plato (*Republic* 617b), each Siren sings a musical note, a tradition that may be traced back to Alkman, who linked the Siren with the Muse.[17] For the ancient Greeks, music was also a requirement for a good death. E. Buschor entitled his seminal study of Sirens *Die Musen des Jenseits*, and a South Italian bronze vessel (*askos*) in the form of a Siren in the J. Paul Getty Museum (plates 5, 6) provides important early evidence of the creature's dual association with Muses and the underworld.[18]

The Getty Siren's straight-lipped yet compellingly human face with heavy-lidded eyes and a strong nose, which exemplifies the Early Classical ideal of the second quarter of the fifth century B.C., is juxtaposed with a sturdy, finely feathered bird's body set on powerful feet.[19] Significantly, this Siren is demurely dressed, wearing a chiton or tunic just over her chest, which covers her human female breasts. The latter surprising anatomical feature foreshadows the increased anthropomorphism of Late Classical Sirens (cf. plate 4).[20] Her musical instrument is unusual for a Greek Siren—a syrinx, often called Pan pipes.[21] The Muse of epic poetry, Kalliope herself, plays this rustic wind instrument on the famous François vase, an Attic black-figure volute-krater of ca. 570 B.C.[22] The Getty Siren has interrupted her music and, with one of her human hands, offers a fruit. It is the many-seeded pomegranate, associated in Classical antiquity not only with fertility and sex but also with blood, death, and the underworld.[23] This Siren askos must have been made for a funerary context.

Women played an important role at Greek funerals; not only serving as professional mourners but also preparing the body of the deceased at home and accompanying it to the grave counted among the crucial duties of the wife and other female members of the household.[24] Apparently, in Late Archaic to Early Classical Greek art, the newly refashioned *Odyssey* Sirens were not merely lethally seductive but also were harnessed in popular belief to serve as sympathetic, beautiful female mourners whose sad music eased the journey of the soul of the deceased to the next world.[25] Greek artists, in further anthropomorphizing the conventional Siren birds inherited from seventh-century Orientalizing art, also humanized and civilized them, creating complex magical creatures who subsumed diverse roles suitable for divine and mortal women in Greek society.[26]

The handle of the Getty askos is in the form of a male human figure standing on the Siren's back.[27] This juxtaposition of small man with large bird woman brings to mind the name vase of the Siren Painter (plate 47), a stamnos in the British Museum of ca. 475–70 B.C., which bears the only known depiction of the *Odyssey* episode in Attic red-figure.[28] Significantly, this famous image intentionally retains three old-fashioned, armless, woman-headed Sirens so big that they dwarf the bound Odysseus and his deafened crew. Homer is as silent about the Sirens' size as he is about their appearance in general, but Greek artists may have inferred from the descriptions of Polyphemos (9.187–92) and Skylla (12.89–97, 248–49), for example, that other dangerous beings encountered by Odysseus were also giants. Vase-painters enjoy contrasting the Kyklops' larger-than-life size with the

human scale of Odysseus and his Companions even in the earliest
certain *Odyssey* depictions of the seventh century B.C., showing the
blinding of Polyphemos (plate 7).[29]

The big Siren, on the British Museum's stamnos, who plunges
head down from her rocky perch, is unique (plate 47). Although her
wings are outstretched, her eyes are closed, and her bird legs and
feet, rather than being drawn up as in flight, extend most pitifully;
thus she has long been seen as the best early evidence for a tradition
known from later literature (e.g., Lykophron, *Alexandra* 5.712–16)
that the Sirens commit suicide when their song is resisted.[30] If so, this
Early Classical Athenian vase painting depicts the *Odyssey* episode
with a typically fifth-century twist—the male hero does not merely
outwit these seductive bird monsters but vanquishes them.

The rare representations of the *Odyssey's* Sirens episode dating
from the Late Archaic to the Late Classical Period (plates 2, 3, 7)
breathe life independently from the poem. Beginning with these representations (cf. plates 47, 49, 50, 4), the Sirens tend to be portrayed
in art as standing on two separate rocky cliffs that tower over the sea,
whereas in Homer it is Skylla who inhabits a cave in such a setting.

Skylla

Whereas the Sirens are not described in the *Odyssey*, the poet describes the monster Skylla in detail: She is a creature with twelve feet
and six necks, each terminating in a head with two triple rows of teeth.
As with the Sirens, the noise Skylla makes seems to be the clue that
helped artists interpret the image. The Sirens sing and are shown with
bird parts; Skylla yelps like a newborn puppy (12.86). Thus in the
earliest known probable representation of Skylla (plate 8), in the uppermost figural frieze on an Etruscan ivory pyxis in Florence of the
Early Archaic Period (variously dated from ca. 620–570 B.C.), an
octopus-like sea monster with several long tentacle-like necks terminating in dog heads is shown beside a ship that may be understood as
that of Odysseus.[31]

Following this Etruscan example, which faithfully adheres to certain aspects of the poetic description of Skylla, no depictions of this
Odyssey monster are known in Archaic Greek art, yet this may simply
be an accident of preservation. When Skylla reappears in the mid-fifth
century, she has undergone a process of idealization involving anthropomorphism and taming. On a terra-cotta Melian relief of ca. 460 B.C.
in the British Museum (plate 9), a Skylla with a human female upper
body assumes a typically placid and nonthreatening Classical Greek

guise.[32] Her neatly waved hair is bound with a headband (*sphendonē*), and she wears a short chiton with a pleated skirt that cleverly masks the transition to the finned, fishy tail of a sea monster that forms her lower body. She is poised with one hand on her hip and the other thoughtfully raised to her chin. Skylla's disposition of human and nonhuman anatomical features recalls Greek artists' typology for the Sirens.

Although her general appearance has been established, fifth-century artists remain uncertain about how to depict the canine aspect that forms an important part of her poetic image (12.86). On the Melian relief (plate 9) dog heads are shown emanating from her waist, but on a contemporaneous gem in a finger ring from Cyprus (plates 10, 11) they issue from her shoulders.[33] On both of these works Skylla is well dressed and impeccably coifed. Her fashionable attire and quiet demeanor serve to civilize this anthropomorphized Skylla,[34] and her visualization in fifth-century Greek art brings to mind the later literary tradition that she was originally a beautiful woman transformed into a monster by a goddess's jealousy.[35] Although we recognize in the Classical hybrid creature the model for Skylla employed throughout subsequent ancient art, her specific identification as Homer's unconquerable female monster rests on the later depictions.[36]

In the second half of the fifth century, Skylla appears with some frequency on the silver coinage of South Italy and Sicily. On a stater of Cumae she shares the field with a mussel shell,[37] and on a tetradrachm of Acragas (Agrigento) with a crab.[38] In both cases Skylla dominates the die at the expense of the mussel shell or crab that would be the normal reverse type. In the Cumaean series one of Skylla's dogs is attached at her waist and two at her shoulders; on Sicilian coins the dogs, usually two, project only from her waist. On Cumaean coins Skylla may wear a short tunic or a covering of seaweed, but on Agragantine coins as well as on the coinage of Magna Graecia generally she is nude down to the waist. Like later Classical Sirens, Skylla provided a rare context for representing the exposed female torso outside the cult of Aphrodite in Greek art.[39]

On the Cumaean and Agragantine coins, Skylla might be seen as a marine creature common to the seas around Sicily and South Italy, for ancient tradition had placed her dwelling directly in the Strait of Messina.[40] But her use on these local coinages may also be related to the character of this *Odyssey* monster, particularly the inevitability of her swift attack, which was eminently appropriate for a fighting emblem. Even Odysseus could do nothing to avert her onslaught.

On coins of Herakleia and Thourioi, from the late-fifth to the fourth century, Skylla, posed with one arm raised in a threatening gesture, actually appears as an emblem decorating the helmet of the warrior goddess Athena (plate 12). Sometimes the Skylla on the coinage of Thourioi does not merely hold a trident, a rudder, or a staff, but hurls a spear or a stone (plate 12)—a particularly menacing fighting symbol.[41]

On tetradrachms of Syracuse and Acragas of ca. 415–405 B.C. Skylla appears in the exergue, while in the main scene Nike crowns a victorious winged charioteer (plate 13). C. M. Kraay associated the Skylla in this context with a marine victory of Syracuse, in which case this sea monster may again be seen as a formidable fighting symbol.[42]

Kirke

Although not a hybrid monster like Skylla or the Sirens, Kirke is nevertheless not human; she is a "dread goddess endowed with speech" (10.136). When the Companions arrived at Kirke's house in the *Odyssey*, "They heard Kirke inside singing in a lovely voice, / working at a great, immortal web on a loom" (10.221–22). This charming singing combined with the deceptively homely appeal of a domestic task, which was also a mortal woman's daily occupation, lured Odysseus' men into the goddess's trap. Homer describes Kirke as a beautiful woman with lovely hair and a sweet voice (10.136, 221), who, along with her charming aspects, had the frightening magical power of transforming men into swine.

Kirke is the only female character of the *Odyssey* other than the Sirens who achieves widespread popularity in Archaic art. In fact, Odysseus' encounter with her is second in frequency only to the Polyphemos adventure. The earliest representations focus on Kirke's transformation of Odysseus' Companions into a variety of beasts (rather than just swine, cf. 10.239–40) and seem almost folkloric in nature (plates 31, 32).[43] The tools of her trade, always at hand, become her attributes: the wand, handy for stirring, and a deep cup to hold the magic potion.[44] The recipe for Kirke's magic brew is actually given in the *Odyssey*,

> for them she stirred cheese and barley and yellow honey
> in Pramnian wine, but she mixed in with the food
> harmful drugs so they would forget their native land completely.
> (10.234–36)

Most of these ingredients belong to the usual Homeric pharmaceutical stock, but barley can have a hallucinogenic effect under certain circumstances.[45]

The most famous Archaic depiction of Kirke appears on the Attic black-figure cup of the mid-sixth century B.C. by the Painter of the Boston Polyphemos (plate 32). Here, although Odysseus appears on the left, sword drawn, denoting the subjugation of the goddess to come, the emphasis is on the hieratic arrangement of partially metamorphosed Companions—male figures with animal heads—around a nude Kirke mixing her brew.[46] The unusual exposure of her body in Archaic art, emphasized by the white color conventional for female flesh (cf. plate 31), has no precedent in the poem; it expresses the strength of Kirke's powers in visual terms that may allude to actual witchcraft practices.[47]

On a group of black-figure lekythoi of the late sixth century B.C., the Kirke composition has been adjusted to fit this tall cylindrical vase shape. The sorceress is generally shown seated or as just having risen from her stool, and Odysseus may not always be present.[48] But Kirke continues to stir her magic potion and is flanked as before by transformed Companions with heads of various animals. Although now clothed, the powerful Kirke is still given center stage.

Just as the female monsters in *Odyssey* representations are beautified and civilized by the fifth century, so does the goddess Kirke undergo a process of demystification. Representations still allude to her special powers through the cup and the wand, and usually through the presence of a few animal-headed Companions as well, but the focus has shifted from Kirke's transforming magic with its frightening folkloric overtones to a later moment in the story—the goddess retreating in fear before a threatening, sword-wielding Odysseus. Excerpts involving only the two main characters occur in the Early Classical period. First, on a column-krater in Sydney, Australia, of ca. 480 B.C., Kirke, wand in hand, offers her cup to an Odysseus who is just drawing his sword.[49] In two slightly later representations, Kirke flees, and Odysseus chases her, flashing his sword.[50]

By the third quarter of the fifth century, the comical aspects of this male-female chase are emphasized. A double-register calyx-krater in New York attributed to the Persephone Painter exemplifies the now-common scheme (plate 34).[51] Odysseus, sword drawn, pursues Kirke, who drops her cup and wand as she flees with her arms outstretched. Kirke's vacant chair occupies the center of the composition, and animal-headed transformed Companions with outstretched arms follow along behind the charging hero. H. Froning has suggested the influence of a satyr play,[52] but this type of representation may simply be moving closer to the *Odyssey* itself and away from the folkloric versions popular in the Archaic period.[53] In either event, the Kirke episode is now interpreted as a male-female pursuit (the prelude to a sexual encounter)—a popular generic compositional type in the fifth century. In the poem, Kirke, once subdued, becomes Odysseus' lover and advisor, and her palace is his home for a year. In Classical representations the dominant male figure, as well as comic elements, such as the dropped cup, signify the artists' taming of this dangerously powerful goddess.[54]

These nonhuman creatures—Kirke, Skylla, and the Sirens—appear to have been not only the first female characters of the *Odyssey* represented in Greek art but also the ones who had the greatest and most enduring popularity in Classical antiquity. Initially visualized as fearsome creatures (plates 39, 8, 32), they were humanized, beautified, dressed fashionably, civilized, tamed, or domesticated by Greek artists before the end of the fifth century B.C.

Human Females

During the Classical Period of the fifth century, human female characters of the *Odyssey* finally play a significant role in Greek art. The earliest surviving examples, in a variety of media—terra-cotta relief, vase painting, and marble sculpture—all date ca. 470 / 460–440 B.C. As befits the subtle and idealized imagery of this time, these women often appear in relatively quiet scenes inspired by the epic poem, which represent women's work and elements of domestic setting and emphasize psychological characterization and human interaction.

Several of the surviving images, which came to light in the nineteenth century, have long been associated with lost monumental painting, as well as with the style of the greatest Classical painter, Polygnotos of Thasos.[55] This popular and important concern of early modern scholarship was supported by the invaluable evidence given by the ancient author Pausanias, who recorded in his second-century A.D. guidebook to Greece several now-lost Classical paintings that appear to have included women of the *Odyssey*, ranging from maiden princess to wife and servant.[56]

Shades of Women in the Underworld

Polygnotos' lost *Nekyia*, which appeared alongside his *Iliupersis* in the Clubhouse of the Cnidians at the Sanctuary of Apollo, Delphi, is described in great detail by Pausanias (10.28.1–31.12). Apparently, the artist employed later literary sources in addition to Book 11 of the *Odyssey*, yet his painted vista of the underworld recalled Homer's description. It contained some seventy figures, including Odysseus, who had come to consult the shade of the seer Teiresias, as well as the shades of many legendary figures of different generations, all dwelling together in a vast and timeless landscape. Pausanias' description, along with the recent reconstruction by M. D. Stansbury-O'Donnell (plates 14, 15),[57] indicates that the organization of Polygnotos' painting included several iconographically appropriate groupings of shades, such as those of Greek enemies of Odysseus, of Trojan heroes, and of Greek women. Many of Polygnotos' monumental figures simply stood quietly or sat on rocks and must have been identified solely by inscriptions giving their names. Pausanias mentions distinctive yet quiet poses for Polygnotos' Phaidra, seated on a swing, and Eriphyle, standing and fingering her necklace through the folds of her garment.

In the *Odyssey* (11.84–89, 150–224) Odysseus has touching encounters with the shade of his mother Antikleia just before and after he consults the shade of Teiresias. In Pausanias' description of Polygnotos' *Nekyia*, Antikleia sits on a rock behind Teiresias, who approaches the hero crouching over the pit of blood (10.29.8). In the poem, Odysseus asks Teiresias,

> But come and tell me this and relate to me accurately:
> I see here the ghost of my dead mother,
> but she sits in silence near the blood, and doesn't bring herself
> to look at her own son face-to-face or to speak to me;
> tell me, lord, how might she recognize me as the man I am?
> (11.140–44)

Only after Odysseus has allowed Antikleia to drink the blood of the slaughtered sheep is she able to tell him about her own death as well as about the state of affairs in Ithaka. After this poignant encounter, Odysseus recognizes the souls of many women, "the wives and daughters of princes," sent by Persephone (11.225–33).

Odysseus' roster of famous women in the underworld is probably related in some way to the Hesiodic *Catalogue of Women*, composed during the sixth century B.C., which ostensibly was a listing of women who bore offspring fathered by gods, and thus it was also a genealogy of heroes.[58] In Book 11 of the *Odyssey* as well, Odysseus sees not simply ordinary women chosen at random, but women drawn partly from the descendents of Aiolos (eponym of the Aeolians), who was one of the sons of Helen (eponym of the Hellenes), as well as from Theban and Attic saga.

However, Homer's poem and Polygnotos' lost painting apparently did not include the same figures. In all, Odysseus observes the shades of fourteen legendary women in the *Odyssey*'s underworld, whereas Pausanias describes nineteen in Polygnotos' painting.[59] According to Pausanias, Polygnotos depicted most of the women from the Aiolid stemma mentioned by Odysseus: Tyro, Chloris, Iphimedeia, Klymene, and Eriphyle.[60] Besides these five women of the Aiolid group, the nine other women who appear in both the *Odyssey* and the wall painting include well-known heroines such as Ariadne and Phaidra, as well as less famous mythological women, such as Prokris, daughter of Erechtheus and wife of Kephalos, and Maira, perhaps the daughter of Proitos, king of Tiryns, and his Lycian wife, Anteia.[61]

Although several famous women in the *Odyssey*'s underworld (Antiope, Alkmene, Epikaste) appear to have been absent from the painting, Polygnotos included other well-known women mentioned in the Hesiodic *Catalogue* but not in Homer, such as Auge, the mother of the hero Perseus, and Kallisto, the mother of Arkas (king and eponym of Arcadia). Certain female figures in Polynotos' underworld such as the Amazon queen Penthesilea and Megara, the bride of Herakles, do not appear in either literary work.

Of course, the original fifth-century B.C. inscriptions in Polygnotos' *Nekyia* could well have been restored and even changed during the intervening six hundred years down to Pausanias' day. Moreover, Pausanias himself sometimes made mistakes in his descriptions. Thus perhaps too much emphasis should not be placed on discrepancies. Still, the differences between the names of the figures in Pausanias' description of Polygnotos' lost painting and those in Homer's underworld may attest to the variety of sources drawn upon by Polygnotos in forming his own painted assemblage of shades. If at least part of the original painting can be regarded as a visual genealogy, that genealogy might well have reflected the time in which it was constructed, particularly those relationships between cities and families believed engendered by legendary marriage or divine union that would have conveyed a message comprehensible to the fifth-century Greek viewer.[62] Above all, the inclusion of legendary women in the painting, as in the poem, emphasizes their important generative role in the perpetuation of the noble lines that constituted the civilized Greek world.

Polygnotos' *Nekyia*, of the mid-fifth century B.C., is the earliest known monumental painted *Odyssey* landscape. A later painted representation of the underworld has survived as part of the famous *Odyssey* Landscapes in the Vatican Library, which once belonged to the Second Style decorative scheme of a Roman room of the first century B.C. In this wall painting, generally thought to depend on a lost Hellenistic original, consecutive moments from Odysseus' journey homeward are depicted in continuous narrative as they unfold over time and space throughout an illusionistic land and seascape.[63] Here the classic dominance of human figures over their environment has been inverted.

The dreamlike rocky terrain of the underworld appears in two sections. In one Odysseus consults the shade of Teiresias; the shades of women standing nearby include Phaidra, Ariadne, and Leda, whose names are inscribed. The second section (plate 16) contains three identifiable male figures who also appear in the *Odyssey*'s underworld: Sisyphos with his rock (11.593–600), the hunter Orion with his club (11.572–75), and the giant Tytios (11.576–81).[64] In the foreground a graceful group of diminutive female figures pour water from clay pots into a vat. They appear to be engaged in a traditional occupation of women, but their work will never be done: A Greek inscription identifies these female shades as the Danaids, doomed forever to attempt to fill a leaky vat. Although prominent in the *Odyssey* Landscapes, the Danaids do not appear in the epic poem.[65] These female figures, however, recall the nameless women attempting to fetch water with broken jars who appeared in Polygnotos' *Nekyia* at Delphi (Pausanias 10.31.9, 11) (plate 15). Thus both ancient paintings evidence the interpretive freedom exercised by visual artists in representing Homer's underworld.

Nausikaa

The underworld and all of the nonhuman females previously discussed appear during a flashback in the epic poem: Odysseus' own account of his adventures given at the court of the Phaeacian king Alkinoos and his queen Arete. In Book 6, the goddess Athena, as part of her plan to aid Odysseus, who had washed up naked on the shore of Scheria, the land of the Phaeacians, inspired the daughter of this royal couple, the young princess Nausikaa, to wash clothes at the river in preparation for her upcoming marriage.[66] This ruse resulted not only in clean clothing for Odysseus but also in his direction to the Phaeacian palace. However enchanting the encounter of the fair maiden with the naked hero at the riverbank may be in the *Odyssey*, it is among the episodes most rarely represented in ancient art.

In fact, as with the *Odyssey's* other human females, no certain
images of Nausikaa are preserved before the fifth century B.C.[67]
Pausanias (5.19.9) interpreted a now-lost Archaic representation, on
the Chest of the Corinthian tyrant Kypselos at Olympia, as Nausikaa
and a servant girl going down to the river in a mule cart. In the story
the princess and her maidservants first washed the clothes and then
played ball along the riverbank. The naked hero awakened and approached Nausikaa for help, covering his exposed genitals with a
branch, and the as-yet-unmarried maiden, heartened by the goddess
Athena, bravely stood her ground before the naked stranger.

Pausanias (1.22.6) saw a panel painting by Polygnotos in the picture gallery of the Propylaea on the Athenian Akropolis representing
Odysseus coming upon the Phaeacian princess Nausikaa and her servant women washing clothes at the river, "just as Homer described
it."[68] But Polygnotos' now-lost painting, at least in Pausanias' description, evidently differed from the narrative of the *Odyssey* (6.126–44),
where the encounter takes place during the girls' ballgame after the
clotheswashing. Significantly, by altering the story, Polygnotos created a monumental context for representing women's work. Two of
the rare depictions of the encounter of Nausikaa and Odysseus in Attic
red-figure vase painting (plates 24, 25, 27) include young women
doing laundry rather than playing ball, and thus aspects of both images may ultimately depend upon the lost Polygnotan composition.[69]

On the pyxis lid by Aison of ca. 420 B.C. in the Museum of Fine
Arts, Boston (plate 27), one laundress is as yet unaware of the encounter of her mistress with the naked hero.[70] She wrings out one end of a
wet garment, while clasping its opposite end between her thighs. In
order to keep her own garment dry and to provide greater mobility for
the work, this laundress wears her chiton rolled up at the waist and
secured by a belt; its shortened skirt swirls around her thighs, expos-
ing her lower legs. The vase painter has captured the allure of a young
maidservant's physical beauty as innocently revealed in a domestic
chore—a theme with enduring resonance in the history of art.

On the amphora in Munich (plates 24, 25)—the name vase of
Beazley's Nausicaa Painter—all of the Phaeacian maidens, who still
hold pieces of laundry, have hiked up their chitons to a mid-calf
length; shortened skirts, of course, would also be convenient for playing ball.[71] The rightmost of the three young laundresses on the amphora's reverse wrings out a garment in a manner recalling the charming motive on the Boston lid (plate 27), and this shared detail has been
believed to derive from Polygnotos' famous lost painting.[72]

On the obverse of the Munich amphora, the goddess Athena,

making a rare appearance in an *Odyssey* depiction, stands between the naked Odysseus and a Phaeacian maiden probably meant to be Nausikaa.[73] Although Pausanias does not mention an Athena in Polygnotos' panel painting, the Munich amphora's goddess functions with particular subtlety amidst the laundry theme. Here the helmeted goddess of war wears her aegis over a wool peplos, which hangs down to her ankles. Protruding from beneath her peplos are the linen sleeves of a fine chiton worn as an undergarment.[74] This stately virgin goddess in full formal dress contrasts with the Phaeacian maidens caught down at the river's edge with their chitons shortened. Although Athena may have inspired the women's work, her dress indicates that she has not engaged in it. The naked hero on the Nausicaa Painter's amphora stands before a tree draped with drying laundry (plates 24, 25). This detail, which departs from the poem's narrative,[75] makes little visual sense, for here Odysseus could literally have clothed himself rather than grabbing some foliage. The Nausikaa episode in Classical Greek art not only plays upon the mores of proper dress versus undress inherent in the lines of the poem but also underscores the role of garments made from woven cloth as an emblem of civilization. In this *Odyssey* context motives from the everyday life of women came to be shown in a famous now-lost painting by a great artist in the city goddess's major sanctuary.

Another focus of Polygnotos' lost painting, of course, must have been the Phaeacian princess herself. A richly dressed maiden whose name is inscribed as Nausikaa is located 180 degrees around the Boston pyxis lid (plate 24) from Odysseus, between the working laundress and the perhaps too elegantly dressed maidservants,[76] who run in fright at the sight of the disheveled, naked hero. This Nausikaa, standing her ground as in the poem, is a study of arrested movement. Her right arm is folded across her waist; her left arm and hand reach upward toward her chin to suggest an appropriate inquisitive perplexity.[77] These arm gestures add to the subtly characterized picture of human hesitation.

Penelope

Similar quiet and yet distinctive poses and gestures, designed to betray the movements of the soul, unite the delineation of human female characters from the *Odyssey* in the repertory of fifth-century Greek art,[78] overshadowing the role of identifying attributes in the Archaic Period. Foremost among Early Classical inventions of Homeric females is Odysseus' wife, Penelope, whose visual imagery also conveys something of her complex characterization in the poem. The compelling Classical Penelope types have been preserved both in works of art from the fifth-century B.C. (plates 17, 18, 20, 54) and in later Greek and Roman variations and copies (plates 19, 60). This wide-ranging corpus in a variety of media has invited scholarly speculation about the nature of the originals and about the sources for Penelope's typology as well as its significance.[79] But here we shall examine the familiar images of Penelope and emphasize their place in *Odyssey* representation.

A Penelope preserved in a broad narrative context appears on the name vase of Beazley's Penelope Painter, an Attic red-figure skyphos in Chiusi of ca. 440 B.C., which has *Odyssey* characters on both obverse and reverse (plates 17, 56).[80] Here the handsome young Telemachos stands before his seated mother,[81] and the vase painting has a rare architectonic backdrop—a carefully depicted loom, which must bear the unfinished shroud for Odysseus' father, Laertes, that Penelope herself wove by day and unraveled by night, attempting to forestall commitment to a Suitor in her husband's absence. The remarkable shadow cast on the cloth by Telemachos' profile probably reflects the influence of an unknown lost monumental painting.[82] His heroic paired spears, by crossing the horizontals of the loom at the central vertical axis of the composition, set off Penelope in her own compositional box.

Penelope is seated on a stool with her legs crossed, her left hand resting at the edge of the seat, and her downcast head propped up on the back of her right hand. Her face is drawn in a three-quarter view—noteworthy in a vase painting—and her hair is parted in the middle. Over her delicate linen chiton, she wears a himation of heavier cloth, which is drawn around the front of her body and over the back of her head. Enveloped as well by her own sad predicament, occasioned by her husband's interminable absence, she pays her son no heed. In Book 19 of the Odyssey, Penelope describes her state of mind.

> Therefore I pay attention neither to strangers nor to suppliants
> nor in any way to heralds who work for the public;
> but longing for Odysseus I waste away in my own dear heart.
> These men are eager for a wedding, but I spin out deceptions.
> (19.134–37)

The Penelope scene on the Chiusi skyphos does not represent a specific episode in the *Odyssey;* Telemachos never confronts his mother before her loom in the women's quarters of Odysseus' house.

Furthermore, the footwashing of Odysseus on the reverse of the same skyphos (plate 56) deviates widely from the actual *Odyssey* episode in Book 19.[83] Yet the Penelope Painter's two images work well together as decoration for a single vase. Here the aristocratic Penelope, enthroned before the elaborately patterned cloth she has woven,[84] is rendered unheeding by her abject despair. She contrasts sharply with the crouching maidservant on the reverse, who in the process of carrying out a lowly domestic task—washing the feet of a supposed stranger—will discover her master in disguise.[85] And on the Chiusi skyphos this woebegone, faithful Penelope recalls the suspenseful irony of the poem itself for, unbeknownst to her, her husband is close at hand.[86]

The seated Penelope in red-figure vase painting (plate 17), facing toward the viewer's left, with her himation drawn over the back of her head, is similar to the Penelope type employed in monumental Classical Greek sculpture, documented by Roman copies as well as by a headless fragmentary Greek marble statue found at Persepolis (plates 18, 19). In the sculptural type, Penelope wears a veil over the back of her head, but her upper body is not wrapped in her himation, and her fine chiton clings to her breasts. Good evidence for the Classical conception of Penelope's face, which is not well preserved on the Chiusi skyphos, is provided by the Roman marble copy in Copenhagen (plate 19).[87] Homer's Penelope may deny that she retained her physical beauty after Odysseus' departure (19.123–28), but the despairing mature Penelope in Classical art, of course, is ideally young and fair. Her regular features recall other Early Classical males and females, who often suffer faint melancholy.[88] But her downturned head—with slightly narrowed eyes and an emphatically bowed, thin upper lip—belies her distraught state. In the *Odyssey* Penelope cries time and again, as when she learns of Telemachos' departure on a quest for Odysseus.

> A cloud of grief came over her, breaking her heart, and she no longer had the heart
> to keep sitting on a chair, although there were many in the house,
> but she sat on the threshold of her elaborately adorned bedroom,
> weeping pitifully, . . .   (4.716–19)

One wonders whether Penelope's tears could also have appeared in Classical art.

During the Classical Period variant images of Penelope also are found on terra-cotta Melian reliefs of ca. 460 B.C. In one compositional type (plate 20) the unheeding Penelope, seated with one foot on a footstool (cf. 19.57–59), is approached by a gaunt Odysseus, disguised as a beggar, who takes her by the wrist while male figures, who must be Telemachos, Eumaios, and Laertes, look on.[89] A wool basket placed beneath Penelope's seat alludes to the weaving so strongly associated with her Homeric characterization. However, this composition depicts neither the first encounter of Odysseus and Penelope in the great hall of their palace as described in Book 19 nor their reunion in Book 23; fifth-century art often prefers assemblages of characters that evoke the *Odyssey* to strict delineations of particular episodes.[90] In another compositional type also found on Melian reliefs representing Eurykleia washing Odysseus' feet (plates 54, 55), Penelope stands in the background with one arm folded across her body and her other hand raised to her chin, a second reflective pose, which remained popular in Etruscan and Roman art.[91]

In the sixth century, gestures involving a person's hand touching or supporting the chin or head had generally been used to convey sadness, particularly in scenes of mourning.[92] These traditional gestures of mourning recur in funerary contexts into the fourth century and beyond. During the fifth century B.C., however, such hand-to-head gestures were enthusiastically pressed into service by artists to convey a variety of psychological states in both male and female figures, from puzzle solving, as in the case of Oedipus and the Sphinx, to exhaustion, as in the case of Herakles with the freshly killed Nemean lion.[93] Individual artists, moreover, may even have favored certain gestures and thus introduced them in a variety of contexts.[94] But a hand-to-head gesture by a seated mythological character wrapped in a himation may have first been employed in Greek art for the angry and despairing hero Achilles.[95]

Two of the many contexts in fifth-century art for seated poses with telling hand gestures are particularly relevant for Penelope. The first is a Classical motive employed for her husband, which is preserved on the cheekpiece of a bronze helmet in Berlin and elsewhere in the decorative arts; it reflects a "mourning" Odysseus—the hero seated in despair with hand to head. This seated pose may have been conceived as a pendent to Penelope. Although the narrative context of the lost, undoubtedly famous prototype is not known, modern scholars normally associate this image with Odysseus on Kalypso's isle of Ogygia, longing to return home.[96]

The preparation of the bride before the wedding, often shown in a mythic guise, is an important context for representing seated, elegantly dressed female figures in an interior setting during the latter part of the fifth century B.C., and many examples are preserved in

Attic vase painting.[97] The seated Penelope, a faithful wife faced with uncertain marital status, is a poignant counterpart to these joyous, anticipatory bridal scenes. However, the depiction of another Homeric female character wryly partakes of the actual wedding-preparation formula—namely, Helen, the wife of Menelaos, being pursuaded by Aphrodite and Eros to go off with Paris. A red-figure cup in Berlin from the third quarter of the fifth century B.C. shows Helen, seated in a chair with a jewelry box on her lap, turning away from both deities of love and from the handsome young Trojan prince.[98] Her inclined head resting in her hand and her frowning lips express the throes of weightier decision making than determining which bauble to pull from her jewelry box.

The persuasion of Helen is depicted with even more intensity on a red-figure pointed amphoriskos in Berlin of ca. 430 B.C., the name vase of the Heimarmene Painter (plate 21).[99] Here Aphrodite has taken the decision-making Helen directly into her lap. Details of this seated Helen's dress and gesture strongly recall images of Penelope: The back of her inclined head is veiled, and her left arm is raised to her face while her right arm crosses her body (cf. plate 54).

Viewed in light of the depiction of Helen, Penelope's seated pose and hand-to-head gestures in Classical art may denote neither simply mourning nor faithfulness, but anguished thought and, more specifically, sexual decision making. With Telemachos grown, Penelope should decide to marry one of the Suitors and thus leave the home and property of her long-lost husband to their son. She should do what Helen did do, but should not have done.[100] In the *Odyssey* at the reunion of Odysseus and Penelope (23.218–24), the faithful wife actually mentions the contrasting example of Helen, defending the latter's infidelity because it was caused by a god.[101] In Classical art, there also appears to have been a subtle mirror-imaging of Helen and Penelope as *brides*, specifically contrasting the married Helen's adulterous decision, which began the Trojan War, with the married Penelope's faithful indecision, which helped bring the final Return of a Greek hero to a successful conclusion.

The memorable Classical typologies for Penelope endure into Roman art, as, for example, on an Early Imperial Roman relief in the British Museum (plate 60), which represents the spectrum of female characters in Odysseus' household. Here the classic unheeding Penelope, seated above her wool basket, is approached by the faithful old nursemaid Eurykleia, while two young women stand on the left gossiping. The latter can only be traitorous maidservants who sleep with Suitors.[102] A tradition for their representation also goes back to the art of the fifth century B.C.—in works depicting the slaughter of the Suitors itself.

Maidservants at the Slaughter of the Suitors

One of the rare preserved depictions of the slaughter of the Suitors is found on a second Attic red-figure skyphos with *Odyssey* imagery on both sides, also attributed to the Penelope Painter (plates 22, 23). Here Odysseus aims an arrow at the Suitors (on the reverse) as two young maidservants, standing directly behind the hero, look on.[103] Their gestures reveal their anxiety over the Suitors' fate: the first wrings her hands while the second folds one arm across her waist and raises her other hand to her cheek—an ignoble variation on the Classical arm gestures of Penelope (plate 54) and Nausikaa (plate 27). After Odysseus' victory, a grim death also awaits these traitorous maidservants; however, heightening the shock of the archery massacre by showing the immediate reaction of women in Odysseus' household has no precedent in the poem. Given the addition of these female onlookers, perhaps it is appropriate that Odysseus has not flung off his beggarly attire revealing himself in heroic nudity (cf. *Odyssey* 22.1 and plates 24, 25).

The Penelope Painter's image of Suitors being slain beside their banqueting couches in the great hall of Odysseus' house has long been associated with a lost Classical mural painting, but it is not likely to have been derived from Polygnotos' lost depiction of Odysseus *after* the slaughter seen by Pausanias (9.4.2) in the Temple of Athena Areia at Plataea.[104] Nevertheless, the inclusion of female figures to enhance the universality of monumental representational art so characteristic of the Classical Period has often been associated with an early impetus from Polygnotan painting.[105]

In this essay we have examined the changes that occur from the Archaic to the Classical period in the way artists represent some of the female characters of the *Odyssey*. When Classical Greek artists depict its nonhuman female characters, they civilize and tame them. Visualized as monsters in early representations, the Sirens are the first creatures to be beautified and humanized. In addition to singing, they play familiar Greek music to seduce the senses. In portraying these humanized Siren birds as easing the passage of the deceased to the underworld, Greek artists create a positive role for them outside the context of the *Odyssey*. Skylla is conceived as a beautiful woman in her upper half, and, divorced from the *Odyssey* episode, she takes on a positive role as a fighting emblem, based on her devastating, inevitably successful attack. Kirke, whose image in art is always that of a fully human female figure, loses her dread, magical aspect, indicated earlier by her nudity and her compositional prominence. Even with her cup and her wand identifying her as a female magician, the goddess is now outclassed and appears as just another woman chased and subdued by a hero.

The more idealized terms in which Classical artists conceive of the Sirens and Skylla reflect wide-ranging fifth-century developments. The change in the representation of Kirke from powerful sorceress to pursued female might also be seen as an idealization, at least from the male point of view, for in these images she has ceased to be regarded as a threat to men. This selection of a later moment in the story of Kirke introduces a vulnerable human element that has more to do with the representation of women than with all-powerful goddesses.

Fifth-century artists are the first to extract human female characters from the *Odyssey* as subject matter for art, and several overlapping themes are consistently important in the depiction of these characters. The first is the theme of marriage and generation. This was given particular emphasis in the *Nekyia* by Polygnotos, whose attentive representation of female figures in this painting as well as in others has earned him the epithet *painter of women*.[106] The second theme is the role of women's work in civilized life. This includes the importance of women as weavers and caretakers of woven garments, which is emphasized in the Classical depictions of Penelope and Nausikaa. Third, in Greek art as in Greek life, women are seen as preservers of the household. In the poem Penelope preserves Odysseus' household by staying chastely at home, unable to arrive at the decision to remarry for twenty years.[107] Fifth-century artists choose to depict Penelope in a seated pose that denotes her homebound decision making.

Such representations of the *Odyssey*'s female figures reflected a newfound interest in the human psyche. This concern with representing the psychological dimension of events permeated all the arts in the fifth century B.C.[108] As a result, Classical artists created visual images that more closely approached the power of Homer's characterizations, which were more than two hundred years earlier in date and described a somewhat different society. Insofar as visual artists' work reflects the society and time in which they and their patrons live, Classical painters, sculptors, and craftsmen, in their representation of human women from the *Odyssey*, emphasized female virtues still important in their own time, notably, the crucial role of women in assuring the continuity of civilized society through correct marriage, child-bearing, and preservation of the household. Their images reaffirmed the proper place of the female in the social structure of the Greek world.

NOTES

1. See Havelock, Chapter 11, this volume, and Lowenstam, 1992, particularly 169–70. For the phenomenon of text illustration in the Classical world, see Weitzmann, 1959 and 1970.

2. See Graham, Chapter 1, this volume; Powell, 1992, 183; and Shapiro, 1992, 73. Early representations were drawn, in particular, from the Polyphemos adventure (plate 7).

3. This may have been regulated by the Peisistratid tyrant Hipparchos in the last quarter of the sixth century; see Shapiro, 1993a and 1992, 72; cf. Shapiro, 1989, 43–46.

4. *LIMC* VI, s.v. "Odysseus," (O. Touchefeu-Meynier), 946; Touchefeu-Meynier, 1968, 306, table 2.

5. The translations of the *Odyssey* here and in Chapters 10 (Neils) and 11 (Havelock) are by Seth L. Schein.

6. For early Greek Sirens outside *Odyssey* depictions and their Ancient Near Eastern sources, see Neils, Chapter 10, this volume; Buitron and Cohen, 1992, 109–10, 125–33; Hofstetter, 1990.

7. See Vermeule, 1979, 203; *LIMC* VI, s.v. "Odysseus," 962, no. 151; cf. Brilliant, Chapter 9, this volume.

8. Ling, 1991, 118, 119, fig. 120, "provenance unknown." I. D. Jenkins has confirmed the Pompeiian provenance of the painting in the records of the British Museum in a letter of September 1, 1993.

9. The Callimanopulos oinochoe has often been incorrectly dated to the first quarter of the fifth century, e.g., *LIMC* VI, s.v. "Odysseus," 962, no. 154. On the importance of this early representation, see Buitron and Cohen, 1992, 128, with bibliography; and Hofstetter, 1990, 100, no. A 139, 116–17.

10. See also Neils, Chapter 10, this volume. For the Sirens' seductive and erotic aspect, see Touchefeu-Meynier, 1968, 186–87, and Buitron and Cohen, 1992, 132.

11. Paquette, 1984, 206. This instrument was held in the left hand and beaten with the right and may be a more likely identification than the cymbal, which would have been used in a pair; cf. Christie's, cat. 1988, no. 34.

12. Trendall, 1987, 158, no. 272; *LIMC* VI, s.v. "Odysseus," 962, no. 156.

13. See West, 1992, 13.

14. Paquette, 206, figs. 209–11, P5–P10; e.g., tympana in South Italian vase painting, Trendall, 1989, figs. 52, 83, 119, 162.

15. Maas and Snyder, 1989, 58, 85–86, 114–15, 121. For music in the lives of Greek women, see also Berard, 1989, 91–92.

16. Warsaw, National Museum (ex Goluchow 32): Haspels, 1936, 228, no. 56; *CVA* Goluchow [Poland 1] plate 16,3; Maas and Snyder, 1989, 120.

17. West, 1992, 235, 224; see also Doherty, Chapter 5, this volume.

18. Buschor, 1944. See Neils, Chapter 10, this volume, on white ground lekythoi (plates 49, 50) and on later funerary contexts for Sirens.

19. Cf. the Sirens on the reliefs from the so-called Harpy tomb in Lycia who grasp souls of the deceased in their talons; Pryce, 1928, plates 21, 22.

20. E.g., Buitron and Cohen, 1992, 123, 133, no. 45, and Woysch-Méautis, 1982, 96–97, 137–39.

21. Paquette, 1984, 63–65.

22. *ABV* 76,1; represented in the Wedding Procession of Peleus and Thetis. See Paquette, 1984, 66, S1. In Etruscan art Muselike Sirens also play the syrinx (cf. plate 52). On the relationship of and contest between Sirens and Muses, see Touchefeu-Meynier, 1968, 183–84, and Buschor, 1944.

23. The story of Persephone, preserved in the Homeric *Hymn to Demeter*, 372, best exemplifies beliefs about this fruit in early Greece. Although daughter of the goddess Demeter, Persephone was bound to dwell in the underworld as wife of Hades half of each year because of the pomegranate seed (or seeds) she had eaten there. On the date of the hymn as not later than the end of the seventh century B.C., see Athanassakis, 1976, 73, and on the pomegranate's chthonic associations, 78; see also Foley, 1994, 34–35, 56–57.

24. Alexiou, 1974, 102–3; Vermeule, 1979, 14; Garland, 1990, 233; and Berard, 1989, 103–4.

25. Usually viewed as a later phenomenon, e.g., Buschor, 1944, especially 55–77. On this later tradition in art, see also Neils, Chapter 10, this volume.

26. Sirens change again in the Late Classical Period, when their nudity reaffirms their association with nature, and their emphatic gestures suggest professional ritual mourning—aspects monumentalized in funerary sculpture. In subsequent centuries as well as in the Etruscan (cf. Neils, Chapter 10, this volume, and plate 52) and Roman civilizations, there is a shifting interplay of bird and human in visualizations of these liminal creatures in the art of Classical antiquity. For summaries of the Sirens' development, see Buitron and Cohen, 1992, 109–35, 150–51, no. 51; Brommer, 1983, 83–88.

27. A stopper for the vessel's mouth, at the top of the Siren's head, would have hung from a chain attached to the ring hanging from the man's left arm.

28. *ARV²* 289,1; 1642; *BAdd²* 210; *LIMC* VI, s.v. "Odysseus," 962, no. 155.

29. Buitron and Cohen, 1992, 33; Fellmann, 1972, 10–14. See Lowenstam, 1992, 168, for checks on the size of Polyphemos in Greek art. Cf. the muscular Polyphemos in the escape of Odysseus from the Kyklops' cave on another red-figure stamnos attributed to the Siren Painter: Greifenhagen, 1982, 211–17, figs. 1, 2; and Sotheby's, cat., 1990, no. 13.

30. See Buitron and Cohen, 1992, 131, with bibliography, and par-

ticularly Weicker, 1902, 45, 49, and fig. 18, for a proposed earlier example of the Sirens' suicide; see also Hofstetter, 1990, 130, 351, n. 587. On the Siren Painter's stamnos, see Neils, Chapter 10, this volume.

31. Also included in the scene are the rams escaping from the cave of Polyphemos from Odysseus' earlier adventure. Krauskopf, 1974, 8–9, questions the association of this sea monster with Skylla.

32. Jacobsthal, 1931, 54, no. 71.

33. Boardman, 1991a, 163, no. 286/32, plate 6.

34. At least one other type of female monster undergoes a similar beautification process during the Classical Period—the Gorgon; see examples of Perseus and Medusa in Schefold and Jung, 1988, 101–6.

35. For this literary traditon and the later representations of Skylla, see Neils, Chapter 10, this volume.

36. Her savage cannibalism as described in the *Odyssey* (12.98–100, 244–59) would have had little appeal for Classical artists, and she first seizes men, presumably Companions of Odysseus, in Hellenistic art of the third century B.C.: Buitron and Cohen, 1992, 137; Schefold and Jung, 1989, 344, fig. 307, bronze mirror cover Berlin, Pergamonmuseum 8391. See also Neils, Chapter 10, this volume.

37. Kraay, 1976, plate 42 no. 725, and Rutter, 1979, 14, nos. KR 127–29.

38. Franke and Hirmer, 1972, plate 60, no. 175.

39. On interpreting Skylla's nudity, which does not become common until the fourth century, see Neils, Chapter 10, this volume.

40. Cf. Rutter, 1979, 12; Neils, Chapter 10, this volume.

41. Herakleia: Kraay, 1976, 193, no. 737; Franke and Hirmer, 1972, plate 89, nos. 257–58; Thourioi: Kraay, 1976, 196; Franke and Hirmer, 1972, plates 87, nos. 252–53 and 88, no. 254. Skylla also appears on real helmets in Hellenistic and Roman times; see Buitron and Cohen, 1992, 137, 213; Andreae, 1983, 35 and fig. 18.

42. On the proposed link between the coins and the victory of Syracuse over the Athenian fleet in 413 B.C., see Kraay, 1976, 222; Franke and Hirmer, 1972, plate 37, no. 107. See also Robinson, 1971, 95, no. 279. The association of coins with historical events has been called into question by C. Arnold–Biucchi, 1990, 20–21, but see also Tudeer, 1913, 33–37, 142–44. For the tetradrachm of Acragas, see Franke and Hirmer, 1972, plate 61, no. 176.

43. Other important early Kirke representations include: Boston 99.519, Attic black–figure cup, *ABV* 69,1; *BAdd*[2] 18; Touchefeu–Meynier, 1968, 85–86, no. 170; *LIMC* VI, s.v. "Kirke," (F. Canciani) 52, no. 13, plate 26; British Museum 88.2–8.114e, 160e and 1952.5–5.14, Clazomenian amphora fragments from Tell Defenneh, *LIMC* VI, s.v. "Kirke," 52, no. 18; and Pseudochalcidian amphora in Vulci, *LIMC* VI, s.v. "Kirke," 53, no. 19, plate 26.

44. The wand as an attribute of a sorceress or magician originated in Middle Kingdom Egypt; see Bourriau, 1988, 110–16. Another approach to

depicting the encounter of Odysseus and Kirke, in which the goddess also has her cup and wand but appears alongside her loom (plate 38), occurs on Boeotian black–figure vases from the Sanctuary of the Cabiran gods near Thebes, which range in date from the late fifth to the third quarter of the fourth century B.C. Moret, 1991, has associated these caricaturized representations with rituals of the Cabiran cult. For the imagery of Kirke on Cabiran vases, see also n. 84 in this chapter and Brilliant, Chapter 9, this volume.

45. See Tzavella-Evjen, 1983, 185–88.

46. Boston 99.518, see *ABV* 198; *BAdd*² 53; Touchefeu-Meynier, 1968, 86–87, no. 171; *LIMC* VI, s.v. "Kirke," 52, no. 14; and on the partially metamorphosed men, Brilliant, Chapter 9, this volume.

47. For Kirke's nudity and its connection with witchcraft, see Devambez, 1973, 17–18 and nn. 1–3; and Boardman, 1991b, 83. Cf. Neils, Chapter 10, this volume. On interpreting Kirke's nudity in a narrative context, see Snodgrass, 1982, 5–8.

48. E.g., Odysseus arriving, holding sword: Berlin 1960, now lost, Brommer, 1983, 71, fig. 29; *LIMC* VI, s.v. "Kirke," 52, no. 16; Taranto 9125, Touchefeu-Meynier, 1968, 87–88, no. 173, plate 13,1–2; Odysseus seated: Athens 1133, Touchefeu-Meynier, 1968, 89–90, no. 176, plate 14,3; *LIMC* VI, s.v. "Kirke," 52, no. 17, plate 26; Odysseus absent: Taranto 20324, Touchefeu-Meynier, 1968, 88, no. 174, plate 13,3–5; *LIMC* VI, s.v. "Kirke," 51, no. 5, plate 24; for the black–figure amphora, in a private collection, Ostermundigen, see Blatter, 1975, plate 29,2; *LIMC* VI, s.v. "Kirke," 51, no. 5bis, plate 24.

49. Sydney private collection: Connor, 1988, 41–53, figs. 1–4; *LIMC* VI, s.v. "Kirke," 53, no. 21.

50. Red-figure Lekythos, Erlangen 261, *ARV*² 651,21; *BAdd*² 276; Raeck, 1984, 19, fig. 10; *LIMC* VI, s.v. "Kirke," 53, no. 22, plate 26; and red-figure oinochoe, Louvre G 439, *ARV*² 775; *BAdd*² 288; Buitron and Cohen, 1992, no. 24; *LIMC* VI, s.v. "Kirke," 53, no. 23, plate 27.

51. *ARV*² 1012,1; *BAdd*² 314; Buitron and Cohen, 1992, 90–91, no. 90; *LIMC* VI, s.v. "Kirke," 53, no. 25, plate 27.

52. Froning, 1988, 190–93.

53. Cf. the Attic red-figure calyx-krater attributed to the Phiale Painter, Bologna, Museo Civico 298; *ARV*² 1018,62; *LIMC* VI, s.v. "Kirke," 53, no. 24; Oakley, 1990, 76–77, no. 62 and plates 42, 43, a, c–d; the Attic bell-krater in Warsaw, Poland, National Museum 140352 (ex Lancut, Potocki 7653); *LIMC* VI, s.v. "Kirke," 53, 26, plate 27.

54. Cf. Wohl, 1993, 25.

55. For a discussion of the early bibliography in this scholarly tradition, regarding the lost paintings of *Odyssey* themes, see Müller, 1913, 80–118; the work of Robert, particularly 1892, was especially important.

56. On the evidence for lost Greek paintings in Pausanias, see Pollitt, 1990, 127–44; for the lost paintings of *Odyssey* themes, see Brommer, 1983, 112–13.

57. Stansbury-O'Donnell, 1990, reconstructs a composition that would have been divided between three walls of the building; for all of his drawings, 220–221, figs. 3–5. Our plate 14 reproduces his drawing of the north wall, which includes, in addition to Odysseus, the following legendary women: Antikleia, Eriphyle, Tyro, Megara, Klymene, Prokris, Thyia, Chloris, Phaidra, Ariadne, Iphimedeia, and Auge. In his reconstruction of the south wall, our plate 15, the following female figures appear: women with water jars, Pero, Nomia, Kallisto, and Penthesilea. For Polygnotan painting, see Robertson, 1975, 1:241–59.

58. The Hesiodic *Catalogue* was composed by a poet writing in Hesiodic style as a continuation of the *Theogony,* but it clearly depends on earlier traditions of genealogical verse; see West, 1985, 2, n. 7; Stanford, 1961, 389–90; cf. Heubeck and Hoekstra, 1989, 90–91. For the interpretation of the women in Homer's *Nekyia,* cf. Wohl, 1993, 36–37.

59. Odysseus also observes the shades of twelve men plus the apparition of Herakles in the *Odyssey's* underworld, whereas Pausanias describes thirty-one male heroes in Polygnotos' painting; only seven appear in both.

60. Only Leda appears in the *Odyssey* (11.298) but is not mentioned in Pausanias' description of Polygnotos' *Nekyia.*

61. *Iliad* 6.160. Cf. Apollodoros, *Library* 2.11.2, who does not name Maira among the daughters of Proitos and Anteia.

62. Kebric, 1983, esp. 2 and 28–29, proposes that the figures in Polygnotos' *Nekyia* and *Iliupersis* taken together would have referred to the genealogy of the Athenian general Kimon and recalled his victory over the Persians at Eurymedon of ca. 466 B.C. For a recent interpretation of the *Nekyia,* relating its iconography to ethical polarities between Greeks and Trojans as well as to the importance of initiation in the Eleusinian mystery cult, see Castriota, 1992, 118–27.

63. For associations of this Roman frieze, which is interrupted by painted pilasters, with a lost continuous Hellenistic prototype see Blanckenhagen, 1963, and cf. Pollitt, 1986, 185–86, 208–9, 314–15, nn. 25–31.

64. See Brommer, 1983, 82. Some of the picturesque sinners of the underworld had already appeared in art during the Archaic Period, such as Sisyphos with his rock, whom Odysseus observed among other evildoers suffering torments (11.593–600); see Buitron and Cohen, 1992, nos. 31–32.

65. Ling, 1991, 111, associates the inclusion of the Danaids, as well as several other elements, with their importance in South Italy.

66. On Athena's role in Phaiakia and on the female figures in Odysseus' earlier adventures, see Murnaghan, Chapter 4, this volume. For the representation of the Phaeacian queen Arete, which is not known before the fourth century B.C., see Buitron and Cohen, 1992, 25, 28, 30, no. 3; *LIMC* I, s.v. "Alkinoos I," (O. Touchefeu-Meynier) 545, no. 1.

67. *LIMC* VI, s.v. "Nausikaa," (O. Touchefeu-Meynier), 712–14. Cf. the interpretation of a black-figure kothon in Baltimore, The Walters Art

Gallery, 48.198, by Brommer, 1980, 109–12 and 1983, 95–96, as the meeting between Odysseus and Nausikaa, rejected by Boardman, 1981, 38; see also Buitron and Cohen, 1992, 27, 29, no. 2; and *LIMC* VI, s.v. "Nausikaa," 713, no. 5.

68. Trans., Shapiro, Chapter 8, this volume; note his detailed analysis of the Nausikaa episode in Classical art. See also *LIMC* VI, s.v. "Nausikaa," 712–14.

69. Hauser, 1905, 21–32, and Touchefeu-Meynier, 1968, 211–12. On the association of the lost play by Sophokles, *Nausikaa* or the *Plyntriai* (Laundresses), see Shapiro, Chapter 8, this volume.

70. 04.18: *ARV²* 1177,48; *BAdd²* 340; *LIMC* VI, s.v. "Nausikaa," 713, no. 3; Hauser, 1905, 21.

71. Munich 2322: *ARV²* 1107,2; *BAdd²* 329; *LIMC* VI, s.v. "Nausikaa," 713, no. 2. See Woodford, 1986, 53, fig. 70, for an illustration of the chiton and how it is belted when worn.

72. Hauser, 1905, 26.

73. For the identification of Nausikaa on Munich 2322 see Shapiro, Chapter 8, this volume. For Athena, cf. the black-figure cup attributed to the Painter of the Boston Polyphemos (plate 33) and Shapiro, Chapter 8, this volume. On Athena's role in Phaiakia, see Murnaghan, Chapter 4, this volume. Athena appeared far more often in ancient art as the protectress of other heroes, such as Perseus, Theseus, and especially Herakles; see the many examples in Schefold, 1978; and Schefold and Jung, 1988.

74. See Woodford, 1986, 56, fig. 73, for an illustration of the peplos and how it is worn. On the great painter Polygnotos' love of distinguishing special garments and of representing fine cloth, see Simon, 1963, 58, 61; Pliny, *Natural History*, 35.58.

75. See Shapiro, Chapter 8, this volume. The conveniently placed tree bearing human or heroic attributes set aside was a convention of Archaic Greek art; for clothing in trees, cf. the Attic black-figure hydria, Leyden xv e 28 (PC 63), attributed to the Antimenes Painter, *ABV* 266,1; *BAdd²* 69; Berard, 1989, 94, fig. 128; and Hurwit, 1991, 40.

76. Cf. Shapiro, Chapter 8, this volume. For the tunics worn by handmaidens on Aison's lid, which need not have been inspired by theatrical costumes, see also Miller, 1989, especially 314 and 329.

77. Hauser, 1905, 20–21; cf. Neumann, 108–9.

78. Hauser, 1905, 21.

79. For the Classical sculptural type, see Ridgway, 1970, 101–3; for a political interpretation related to the discovery of a torso of the Penelope type in Persepolis (plate 18), see Gauer, 1990, particularly 44–65. Gauer's discussion, in general, is inspired by Robertson, 1975, 209–10: "I have wondered if this mourning woman might have stood for Hellas Unredeemed (perhaps in parable: Penelope or Electra waiting for Odysseus or Orestes to rescue her from her oppressors), and replicas have been set up in the cities of the Delian League, devoted to freeing all Greeks from the Persian yoke."

80. *ARV*² 1300,2; *BAdd*² 360.

81. Müller, 1913, 81, compares the Classical contrapposto pose of Telemachos to the Oinomaos, from the east pediment of the Temple of Zeus, Olympia; see Ashmole and Yalouris, 1967, plate 18. Cf. the pose of Paris in the persuasion of Helen on Berlin, Antikensammlung (Charlottenburg) 30036; see n. 99, this chapter.

82. Recently, Gauer, 1990, 49–50, has convincingly argued for the invention of the Penelope type in Polygnotan painting and its subsequent adaptation in Classical sculpture.

83. On the interpretation of the Chiusi skyphos, see Lowenstam, 1992, 179; cf. Havelock, Chapter 11, this volume.

84. See Atchity and Barber, 1987, 28–29, on the ability to weave elaborately patterned cloth as a sign of an upper-class woman. We have suggested elsewhere (Buitron and Cohen, 1992, 92) that Kirke at her loom on Cabiran vases (e.g., plate 38) recalls the depiction of Penelope in Ithaka, and thus the imagery of the seductive enchantress playfully parodies that of the faithful aristocratic wife.

85. Murnaghan, 1987, 39, on the significance of the recognition of Odysseus by servants. The kneeling servant on the Chiusi skyphos is marked as a slave by her short hair and sleeveless chiton; see Schefold and Jung, 1989, 321.

86. On the human limitations of Penelope's knowledge, cf. Murnaghan, Chapter 4, this volume.

87. The head type has been identified on the basis of the copy in Berlin that preserves traces of Penelope's hand; see Ridgway, 1970, 101; Gauer, 1990, 33, no. 5. The hair of the sculptural type which has no central part differs from that of Penelope on the red-figure skyphos (cf. plates 19, 17). On Penelope's appearance in the poem, see Schein, Chapter 2, this volume.

88. Cf. the head from a marble statue known as the Blond Boy, Athens, Acropolis Museum, 689; Ridgway, 1970, plate 72.

89. See Foley, Chapter 6, this volume, on Odysseus' gesture.

90. See Buitron and Cohen, 1992, no. 55, on the evidence for a seam in the mold for the terra-cotta relief, indicating the onlookers were added to the Odysseus and Penelope group. The reversed direction of the Penelope motive on the Melian relief is also related to its manufacture in a mold; cf. the similar reversal of the Penelope image in impressions made from gold rings, e.g., Touchefeu-Meynier, 1968, 211, no. 385, plate 40, 8.

91. See Havelock, Chapter 11, this volume, on discrepancies between this composition and the *Odyssey* episode. Cf. the pose of Penelope with that in the painting from the Macellum of Pompeii in Naples; Schefold and Jung, 1989, 328, fig. 289.

92. E.g., the black-figure plaque by Exekias, Berlin, F 1813; *ABV* 146,22; *BAdd*² 41; see Neumann, 1965, 139, fig. 69.

93. Oedipus and the Sphinx: red-figure cup in the Vatican attributed to the Oedipus Painter, *ARV*² 451,1; *BAdd*² 242; Neumann, 1965, 129, fig. 62;

Herakles and Nemean lion: metope from the Temple of Zeus at Olympia, Ashmole and Yalouris, 1967, plate 143 and fig. 18. Cf. Herakles on the calyx-krater in Palermo, Museo Nazionale 13840, attributed to the Painter of the Wooly satyrs, ARV^2 613,4; $BAdd^2$ 269; Boardman, 1989, fig. 14. For a recent discussion of this community of gesture and pose between Penelope and other figures in fifth-century B.C. art, see Gauer, 1990, 39–44.

94. E.g., the different contexts for the chin-resting-on-hand gesture in the Phiale Painter, Oakley, 1990, 75, no. 53, plate 37, A: Agrigento, Museo Archeologico Regionale, AG 7, Perseus contemplating the bound Andromeda (ARV^2 1017,53); 75, no. 54, plate 38, A: Vatican, Museo Gregoriano Etrusco 16586, a nymph onlooker (ARV^2 1017,54; 1678); 89, no. 139, plate 110: Munich, Staatliche Antikensammlungen 6254 (2798) a mourning woman at a tomb (ARV^2 1022,138).

95. Friis Johansen, 1967, 123–27, mourning Achilles receiving arms; 155–60, Briseis led away; 166–78, mission to Achilles; see also Buitron-Oliver, 1991a, 65, 72–73, with nn. 34–36. On distinguishing the different armings of Achilles, Lowenstam, 1992, 168 and nn. 12, 13.

96. On the comparison of "weeping Odysseus" with a mourning wife, *Odyssey* 8.523–31, see Foley, 1978, 7; for Odysseus on Ogygia, see Schein, Chapter 2, this volume. On the helmet cheekpiece, Berlin, Antikensammlung (Charlottenburg) Misc. 7863, and its interpretation, see Schefold and Jung, 1989, 316 and 317, fig. 275; see also *LIMC* VI, s.v. "Odysseus," 947–48 and no. 22; Stanford and Luce, 1974, 157, illustrations 125, 126, 112 (or Odysseus mourning for Ajax?); Touchefeu-Meynier, 1968, 192–96. Cf. Odysseus' pose at the entrance to the underworld, Attic red-figure pelike, ca. 440 B.C., attributed to the Lykaon Painter, Museum of Fine Arts, Boston 34.79; ARV^2 1045,2; $BAdd^2$ 320; often associated with Polygnotan painting: Touchefeu-Meynier, 1968, 135, no. 227, plate 21, 1; *LIMC* VI, s.v. "Odysseus," 961, no. 149; see also Cohen, 1983, 186; and the Stansbury-O'Donnell reconstruction of Polygnotos' *Nekyia* (plate 14).

Kalypso herself, who never played an important role in Greek and Roman art, does not appear to have been represented before the fourth century B.C., see *LIMC* V, s.v. "Kalypso," (B. Rafn), 945–48.

97. Oakley and Sinos, 1993, 16–20 and esp. 64–72, figs. 23–40; 127–28, figs. 128–29.

98. Berlin, Antikensammlung (Charlottenburg) 2536, ARV^2 1287,1; $BAdd^2$ 358; *LIMC* IV, s.v. "Hélène," (L. Kahil), 517, no. 85, plate 306; Boardman, 1989, fig. 244.3. For the persuasion of Helen *LIMC* IV, s.v. "Hélène," 525–28, 557–58.

99. Berlin, Antikensammlung (Charlottenburg) 30036; ARV^2 1173,1; $BAdd^2$ 339; *LIMC* IV, s.v. "Hélène," 525, no. 140. For the allegorical interpretation of this vase painting, and the possibility that the composition might have derived from a lost monumental painting, see Shapiro, 1993b, 194–95 and n. 436; 260, no. 129.

100. Cf. Foley, 1978, 11; Murnaghan, 1986, 107; 1992, 262; Katz,

1991, 63; Murnaghan, Chapter 4, this volume; and Zeitlin, Chapter 7, this volume.

101. See Schein, Chapter 2; Foley, Chapter 6; and Zeitlin, Chapter 7, all this volume. Cf. Felson-Rubin, 1987, 66–67. On the relationship between Helen, Penelope, and Klytaimestra in the *Odyssey*, cf. Katz, 1991, with a discussion of earlier bibliography, particularly 183–87, 193; and Wohl, 1993, 35. On the handling of Helen's adultery in the *Odyssey*, see Zeitlin, Chapter 7, this volume.

102. Stanford and Luce, 1974, 52–53, illustration 35; Müller, 1913, 86–87; the relief was probably created as a pendant for the footwashing (cf. plate 58) in Augustan times. One of the maidservants has been associated with Melantho, *LIMC* VI, s.v. "Melantho," (O. Touche-Meynier), 412, no. 1. See also Havelock, Chapter 11, this volume.

103. *ARV*² 1300,1; *BAdd*² 360; Touchefeu-Meynier, 1968, 256, 479; see also Müller, 1913, 96–97. On the hair and clothing of maidservants, see n. 85 of this chapter. For the known depictions of the slaughter of the Suitors, see Buitron and Cohen, 1992, 169–75, with bibliography, 214; for the Campanian red-figure bell-krater from the last third of the fourth century attributed to the Ixion Painter, Paris, Louvre CA 7124, see Pasquier, 1992.

104. See the translation of Pausanias' description by Pollitt, 1990, 141. For this painting as a mythological evocation of the Persians' defeat at Plataea, see Francis, 1990, 74–84, 113; and Schefold and Jung, 1989, 323. On the possibility of maidservants having appeared in the Plataea painting, see Müller, 1913, 99. See Zeitlin, Chapter 7, this volume, regarding the treatment of the unfaithful maidservants in the poem.

105. Cf. the fourth-century frieze depicting the slaughter of the Suitors from the Heroon at Gjölbaschi-Trysa in Vienna, which includes Penelope as well as maidservants and thus telescopes different parts of the house for dramatic effect; Schefold and Jung, 1989, 323–24, figs. 281–83; and see Buitron and Cohen, 1992, 170–71. For the importance of women in Polygnotan compositions, see Simon, 1963, 57–61.

106. Cf. Simon, 1963, 61.

107. Foley, 1978, 10, 17, 21; also Marquardt, 1985. On the importance of the *oikos* in the poem, see Schein, Chapter 2, and Murnaghan, Chapter 4, both in this volume. For contrasting views of Penelope, cf. Winkler, 1990; Katz, 1991; and Felson-Rubin, 1993.

108. Pollitt, 1972, particularly 22–24.

1. *Odysseus and the Sirens.* Roman wall painting, from Pompeii, third
quarter of the first century A.D. London, British Museum 1867.5–8.1354.
Photo: Courtesy Trustees of the British Museum.

2. *Odysseus and the Sirens.*
Attic black-figure oinochoe,
Greek, late sixth century B.C.
New York, Collection of
Gregory Callimanopulos.
Photo: Jennifer Kotter.

3. *Sirens.* Detail of oinochoe in plate 2. Photo: Jennifer Kotter.

4. *Odysseus and the Sirens.* Paestan red-figure bell-krater, attributed to
Python, Greek, South Italian, ca. 350 B.C. Berlin, Antikensammlung
Staatliche Museen zu Berlin-Preussischer Kulturbesitz 4532. Photo:
Isolde Luckert.

5. *Siren.* Bronze askos in the shape of a Siren, Greek, South
Italian, first half of the fifth century B.C. H: 15.3 cm.; L: 18.7
cm. Malibu, J. Paul Getty Museum 92.AC.5 Photo: Collection
of the J. Paul Getty Museum, Malibu, California.

6. *Siren.* Profile view of askos in plate 5. Photo: Collection of
the J. Paul Getty Museum, Malibu, California.

7. *The Blinding of Polyphemos.* Fragment of a krater, from Argos, Greek, second quarter of the seventh century B.C. Argos, Archaeological Museum C 149. Photo: National Gallery of Art, Washington, D.C.

8. *Skylla and the Ship of Odysseus.* Detail of Etruscan ivory pyxis, from Chiusi, late seventh to early sixth century B.C. Florence, Archaeological Museum 73846. Photo: Soprintendenza alle Antichità-Firenze.

9. *Skylla.* Melian terra-cotta relief, Greek, ca. 460 B.C. London, British Museum B 374. Photo: Courtesy Trustees of the British Museum.

10. *Skylla.* Jasper scaraboid in gold finger ring, from Amathus. Greek, first half of the fifth century B.C. Limassol, Archaeological Museum T 286/32. Photo: Department of Antiquities, Nicosia, Cyprus.

11. *Skylla.* Impression of gem in plate 10. Photo: Department of Antiquities, Nicosia, Cyprus.

12. *Head of Athena (to right) in Attic Helmet, with Skylla Throwing a Stone.* Silver double stater of Thourioi, Greek, South Italian (Lucanian), ca. 400 B.C. American Numismatic Society 1905.57.39. Photo: ANS.

13. *Nike Crowning Winged Male Charioteer, and Skylla.* Silver tetradrachm of Syracuse, signed by Eumenes, and EY in the exergue, Greek, Sicilian, 415–405 B.C. American Numismatic Society 1967.152.518. Photo: ANS.

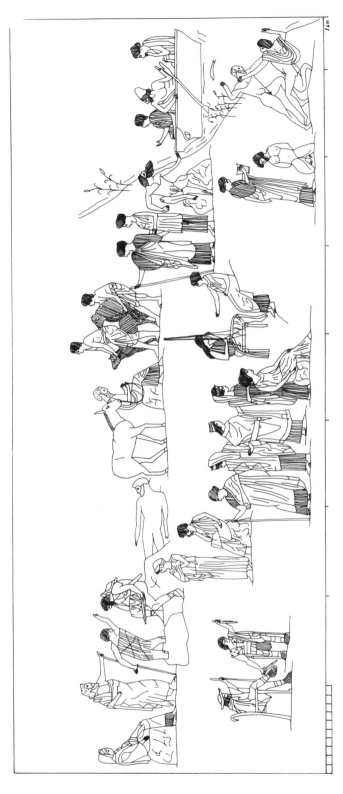

14. *North Wall of Polygnotos'* Nekyia. Detail of lost painting from the Lesche of the Cnidians, Delphi, Greek, middle of the fifth century B.C. Reconstruction drawing by M. D. Stansbury-O'Donnell. Photo: Courtesy Mark D. Stansbury-O'Donnell and *AJA* [94 (1990) 220, fig. 3].

15. *South Wall of Polygnotos' Nekyia*. Detail of lost painting from the Lesche of the Cnidians, Delphi, Greek, middle of the fifth century B.C. Reconstruction drawing by M. D. Stansbury-O'Donnell. Photo: Courtesy Mark D. Stansbury-O'Donnell and *AJA* [94 (1990) 221, fig. 5].

16. *The Underworld: Shades of Orion, Sisyphos, Tytios, and the Danaids.*
Detail of the *Odyssey* Landscapes. Roman wall painting, from the Esquiline,
Rome, middle of the first century B.C. Biblioteca Apostolica Vaticana. Photo:
Biblioteca.

17. *Telemachos, Penelope, and Her Loom.* Attic red-figure skyphos, attributed to the Penelope Painter, Greek, ca. 440 B.C. Chiusi, National Etruscan Museum 1831. Photo: Soprintendenza alle Antichità-Firenze.

18. *Penelope* (?). Fragmentary marble statue, from Persepolis, Greek, middle of the fifth century B.C. Teheran, Museum. Photo: Persepolis field negative number P-2446, Courtesy of The Oriental Institute of The University of Chicago.

19. *Head of Penelope.* Head from Roman marble copy of fifth-century B.C. Greek statue. Copenhagen, Ny Carlsberg Glyptotek 407. Photo: Glyptotek.

20. *Odysseus and Penelope.* Melian terra-cotta relief. Greek, ca. 460 B.C. New York, Metropolitan Museum of Art 30.11.9, Fletcher Fund, 1930. Photo: Museum.

21. *The Persuasion of Helen.* Attic red-figure pointed amphoriskos, attributed to the Heimarmene Painter, Greek, ca. 430 B.C. Berlin, Antikensammlung Staatliche Museen zu Berlin-Preussischer Kulturbesitz 30036. Photo: Isolde Luckert.

22. *The Slaughter of the Suitors: Odysseus and Maidservants.* Attic
red-figure skyphos, attributed to the Penelope Painter, Greek, ca. 440 B.C.
Berlin, Antikensammlung Staatliche Museen zu Berlin-Preussischer
Kulturbesitz F 2588. Photo: Antikensammlung.

23. *The Slaughter of the Suitors: the Suitors.* Reverse of skyphos in plate
21. Photo: Antikensammlung.

24. *Odysseus, Nausikaa, and Athena.* Attic red-figure neck-amphora, attributed to the Nausicaa Painter, Greek, ca. 440 B.C. Munich, Staatliche Antikensammlungen und Glyptothek 2322. Photo: Staatliche Antikensammlungen und Glyptothek.

25. *Odysseus, Nausikaa, Athena, and Laundresses.* Rollout drawing by K. Reichhold of neck-amphora in plate 24. Photo: Staatliche Antiken-sammlungen und Glyptothek.

26. *Odysseus and Nausikaa* (?). Attic red-figure covered kantharos,
Greek, ca. 440 B.C. London, British Museum E 156. Photo: Courtesy
Trustees of the British Museum.

27. *Odysseus, Nausikaa, and Athena.* Attic red-figure pyxis lid, attributed to
Aison, Greek, ca. 430 B.C. Boston, Museum of Fine Arts 04.18, H. L. Pierce
Fund. Photo: Courtesy Museum of Fine Arts, Boston.

28 and 29. *Poseidon Pursuing Amphitrite.* Attic red-figure pyxis, Greek, ca. 460–50 B.C. Athens, National Archaeological Museum A 1708. Photos: National Archaeological Museum.

30. *Satyr and Maenad.* Attic red-figure oinochoe, Greek, ca. 430–20 B.C. Basel, Antikenmuseum und Sammlung Ludwig BS 407. Photo: Claire Niggli.

31. *Boar-headed Companion and Nude Kirke.* Terra-cotta altar, from Sicily, ca. 550–30 B.C. Paris, Musée du Louvre CA 5956. Photo: PHOTO R.M.N.

32. *Kirke and the Companions, with Odysseus.* Attic black-figure cup, attributed to the Painter of the Boston Polyphemos, Greek, ca. 550 B.C. Boston, Museum of Fine Arts 99.518, H. L. Pierce Fund. Photo: Courtesy Museum of Fine Arts, Boston.

33. *Odysseus, Athena, the Companions, and Polyphemos.* Reverse of cup in plate 32. Photo: Courtesy Museum of Fine Arts, Boston.

34. *Odysseus, Monstrous Companions, and Kirke.* Attic red-figure calyx-
krater, attributed to the Persephone Painter, Greek, ca. 440 B.C. New York,
Metropolitan Museum of Art 41.83, Gift of Amelia E. White. Photo:
Museum.

35. *Odysseus and Kirke in Conversation.* Roman terracotta lamp, ca. 50–90 A.D. Munich, Staatliche Antikensammlungen und Glyptothek 5106. Photo: Christa Koppermann.

36. *Odysseus, Kirke, and Monstrous Companions.* Etruscan Alabaster Cinerary Urn, from Chiusi, second century B.C. Copenhagen, Ny Carlsberg Glyptotek H 299. Photo: Glyptotek.

37. *Odysseus, Alkinoos, and Kirke;
a Cock-headed Companion.* View
and detail of terra-cotta relief bowl,
"Megarian type," from Volos,
Hellenistic, late third century B.C.
Providence, Museum of Art, Rhode
Island School of Design 25.081
Ceramics. Photo: Museum.

38. *Odysseus, Kirke, Her Loom, Boar-headed Companion.* Black-figure Cabiran skyphos, Greek, Boeotian, late fifth century B.C. London, British Museum 93.3–3.1. Photo: After Touchefeu-Meynier, 1968, plate 18, 1.

39. *Odysseus and the Sirens, Kirke as Onlooker, Her Palace.* Late Corinthian black-figure aryballos, Greek, ca. 575–550 B.C. Boston, Museum of Fine Arts 01.81.00. Photo: After Weicker, 1902, 44, fig. 17.

40. *Odysseus and Hermes; Odysseus and Kirke; Odysseus, Kirke, and Monstrous Companions: Rondanini Tabula Odysseaca.* Eighteenth-century engraving after Roman marble relief of first century A.D. Warsaw, National Museum inv. 147975MN. Photo: After Touchefeu-Meynier, 1968, plate 20, 3.

41. *Skylla.* Parcel gilt silver emblema, possibly a pyxis lid, Hellenistic, third century B.C. New York Metropolitan Museum of Art 1981.11.22, Purchase, Rogers Fund, Classical Purchase Fund, Harris Brisbane Dick Fund and Anonymous, Mrs. Vincent Astor, Mr. and Mrs. Walter Bareiss, Mr. and Mrs. Howard J. Barnet, Christos G. Bastis, Mr. and Mrs. Martin Fried, Jerome Levy Foundation, Norbert Schimmel, and Mr. and Mrs. Thomas A. Spears Gifts, 1981. Photo: Museum.

42. *Odysseus Escapes from Charybdis*. Attic black-figure skyphos, Greek, late sixth century B.C. Palermo, Museo Archeologico. Photo: Deutsches Archäologisches Institut-Rom, Inst. Neg. 35–1515.

43. *Siren* (?). Late Geometric vase fragment from Pithekoussai, Greek, late eighth century B.C. Ischia. After Buchner, 1970–71, 67.

44. *Odysseus and the Sirens* (?). Middle Corinthian black-figure aryballos, Greek, ca. 590 B.C. Basel, Antikenmuseum Basel und Sammlung Ludwig BS 425. Photo: Claire Niggli.

45. Rollout drawing by I. Athanassiadi of aryballos in plate 44. After *AntK* 25, 1982, plate 1, fig. 3.6.

46. *Odysseus and the Sirens.* Attic black-figure oinochoe, Greek, late sixth century B.C. Berlin, Antikensammlung Staatliche Museen zu Berlin-Preussischer Kulturbesitz, ex Sammlung Brommer, Kat. Nr. 253. Photo: Antikensammlung.

47. *Odysseus and the Sirens.* Attic red-figure stamnos, attributed to the Siren Painter, Greek, ca. 475 B.C. London, British Museum E 440. Photo: Courtesy Trustees of the British Museum.

48. *Erotes.* Reverse of stamnos in plate 47. Photo: Courtesy Trustees of the British Museum.

49 and 50. *Odysseus and the Sirens.* Attic white-ground lekythos, attributed to the Edinburgh Painter, Greek, late sixth century B.C. Athens, National Archaeological Museum 1130. Photos: Museum.

51. *Orpheus (?) and Two Sirens.* Terra-cotta sculptural group, Greek, South
Italian, late fourth century B.C. Orpheus H: 104 cm.; Sirens H: 140 cm.
Malibu, J. Paul Getty Museum 76.AD.11. Photo: Collection of the J. Paul
Getty Museum, Malibu, California.

52. *Odysseus and the Sirens.* Etruscan alabaster cinerary urn, second century B.C. Volterra, Museo Guarnacci 278. Photo: Soprintendenza alle Antichità-Firenze.

53. *Rape of Europa, and Skylla.* Paestan red-figure calyx-krater, signed by Asteas, Greek, South Italian, ca. 340–30 B.C. H: 71.2 cm.; Diam.: 59.6 cm. Malibu, J. Paul Getty Museum 81.AE.78. Photo: Collection of the J. Paul Getty Museum, Malibu, California.

54. *The Footwashing of Odysseus.* Melian terra-cotta relief, Greek, ca. 460 B.C. New York, Metropolitan Museum of Art 25.78.26. Fletcher Fund, 1925. Photo: Museum.

55. *The Footwashing of Odysseus.* Fragmentary Melian terra-cotta relief, Greek, ca. 460 B.C. Athens, National Archaeological Museum inv. no. 9753. Photo: Museum.

56. *The Footwashing of Odysseus.* Reverse of Attic red-figure skyphos in plate 17, attributed to the Penelope Painter, Greek, ca. 440 B.C. Chiusi, National Etruscan Museum 1831. Photo: Soprintendenza alle Antichità-Firenze.

57. *The Footwashing of Odysseus.* Greek marble relief from Thessaly, ca. 350–300 B.C. Athens, National Archaeological Museum 1914. Photo: Museum.

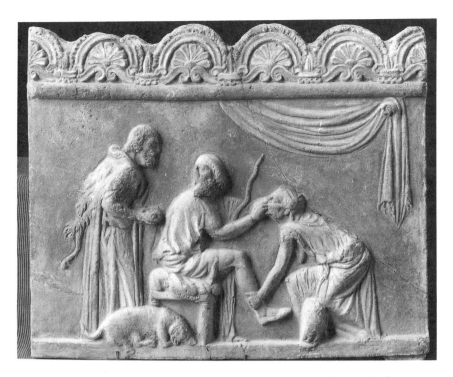

58. *The Footwashing of Odysseus.*
Roman terra-cotta plaque, first half
of the first century A.D. Rome,
Museo Nazionale delle Terme, Inv.
62 751. Photo: Alinari/Art Resource,
NY, Neg. No. 28367.

59. *Old Nurse with Baby.* Greek
terra-cotta figurine, from Tanagra,
ca. 350 B.C. London, British Museum
1911.4.16.1. Photo: Courtesy
Trustees of the British Museum.

60. *Penelope and Maidservants.* Roman terra-cotta plaque, first half of the first century A.D. London, British Museum 1951.11-23. Photo: Courtesy Trustees of the British Museum.

II

Female Representations
in the *Odyssey*

4

The Plan of Athena

Sheila Murnaghan

The *Odyssey* opens by dramatizing the Olympian negotiations behind its action, and the goddess Athena quickly emerges as the source and sponsor of the plot that follows. All of the gods except Poseidon are gathered in the halls of Zeus listening to his meditations on a story that is already concluded, the story of Agamemnon. Athena tactfully shifts Zeus' attention to the story that is on her mind, the still-unconcluded story of Odysseus. When Zeus allows that it is indeed time for Odysseus to return, she responds with a ready set of plans that constitute the two lines of action occupying the next twelve books of the poem: the adventures of Telemachos, initiated by her own visit to Ithaka in the guise of Mentes, and Odysseus' release from the island of Kalypso, initiated by Hermes sent as a messenger from Zeus (1.80–95). At the end of that phase of the action, Athena takes an even more direct hand in events, meeting with Odysseus as he reaches the shore of Ithaka in Book 13 and devising with him the plot that will control the second half of the poem.

The *Odyssey*, then, goes out of its way to identify the story it tells as Athena's project and, in doing so, signals both its concern with issues of gender and its finally conservative position on those issues. Athena has a distinctive role in the Greek mythological tradition as a figure who resolves conflicts between male and female powers. The resolutions she effects involve both the acknowledgment of female strength and the establishment of hierarchies in which the female is subordinated to the male. Through her own origins and nature and

61

through her interventions in human situations, Athena neutralizes the threats that the female is felt to pose for the male and enlists female figures as willing participants in stable, male-dominated social structures.

These characteristics are already expressed at the moment of Athena's birth. As we learn from the account of cosmic history given in Hesiod's *Theogony*, Athena's birth is the event that allows Zeus to become the supreme and permanent ruler of the universe. It represents his ability to halt the process of cosmic evolution whereby male gods are repeatedly displaced as their female consorts give birth to male heirs, who then usurp their fathers' powers. Zeus swallows Athena's mother, Metis, when she is pregnant and gives birth to Athena himself, through his head. He thus overcomes the threat of the female by preventing Metis from going on to bear him a son who could displace him, by gaining control of the normally female functions of generation, and by appropriating the potentially subversive cleverness that is associated with women and expressed in Metis' name, which can be translated "cunning intelligence."[1]

Athena's nature is true to her origins. Her unique combination of male and female traits makes her the ideal child for Zeus, one who resembles her father but does not threaten to displace him or to disturb the world order he controls. She is a warrior goddess who possesses the highly prized masculine qualities of strength and cunning in battle, but she lacks the brutality and irrationality of the male war god, Ares. Thus she is closely identified with civilization and with the victory of civilization over barbarism, as in the Greek victory over the Persians (from the Greek perspective), commemorated in Athens in the temple of Athena Nike. She is associated with the city as an institution and with civilized crafts, especially the male craft of shipbuilding and the female craft of weaving. How Athena's warrior identity is tempered by her femaleness can be seen in an anecdote about her birth, which forms the subject of the brief Homeric *Hymn to Athena*. When Athena bursts forth from Zeus' head fully armed and brandishing a spear, the gods are deeply alarmed and the cosmos reels in horror until she strips her armor from her shoulders, at which point Zeus rejoices.[2]

At the same time, Athena possesses none of the dangerous qualities typically associated with women—as this episode in which the uncovering of the female body proves entirely reassuring and unseductive makes clear. Above all, she is a virgin goddess who avoids the volatile realm of sexuality and the divided loyalties of marriage and motherhood. As an externalized version of her mother, Metis, whom Zeus has literally incorporated, Athena exercises her characteristically female cleverness through resourcefulness in carrying out the plans and projects of her father.

The literary text in which Athena plays out her role most explicitly is Aeschylus' *Oresteia*, a tragic trilogy of the fifth century that looks back to the older traditions reflected in Hesiod and recasts them in the context of the expanding city-state, in particular, the city of which Athena was patron, Athens. The trilogy tells a story of proliferating gender conflicts that issue, in the third play, the *Eumenides*, in a deadlock between Orestes, who has killed his mother, Klytaimestra to avenge her killing of his father, Agamemnon, and the Erinyes, or Furies, female spirits who demand Orestes' death on behalf of the dead Klytaimestra. This deadlock is broken by a jury trial in a court that Athena founds, in which she casts the deciding vote. She votes for Orestes' release from punishment for his matricide, making it clear as she does that she is carrying out the wishes of her father, Zeus, and expressing her ultimate allegiance to the male over the female. This allegiance causes her to value Agamemnon and his champion Orestes as military leaders over Klytaimestra, the mother whose role appears, from the perspective of Athena's own history, negligible. But Athena's role in concluding the action is not complete until she has won over Orestes' female adversaries, the Erinyes. Drawing both on her feminine powers of persuasion and her access to the weapons of Zeus, she convinces the Erinyes to accept her judgment in Orestes' favor and to take on an honored but subordinate role in the reconstituted social order that her decision has made possible.[3]

As she initiates and guides the action of the *Odyssey*, Athena similarly acts as the female upholder of male-dominated social structures, both Olympian and mortal, and of the value systems that support them. Thus she is a fitting emblem for a poem that at once acknowledges the power of women and equates the successful conclusion of its story with the enlistment of female characters in the male-centered project of the hero's Return. As several of the essays in this volume and other recent studies have shown,[4] the *Odyssey* is remarkably attuned to the nature of female experience and to the ways in which women can be powerful figures within the constraints of Homeric society, and it often uses female voices to show how its own values might be called into question; at the same time, it constructs a narrative in which female power is channeled into the reestablishment of a patriarchal order, and thus its own values are finally reaffirmed. Under Athena's watchful supervision, Odysseus overcomes the dangers posed by female figures and returns to restore Ithaka to a flourishing and ordered society with an authoritative husband and cooperative wife at its center. Like Athena herself, the *Odyssey* testifies to the importance of the female without departing from the prevalent male-dominated ideology of ancient Greek culture.[5]

By putting Athena in charge of a plot that leads to the triumph of the male hero and the regeneration of the society he leads, the *Odyssey* casts in a favorable light the very activity of plotting, an activity that is especially associated with women (whose cleverness often expresses itself in devious schemes) and that is often viewed with suspicion. The feminine associations of plotting are often expressed through metaphors of weaving, an activity pursued by women, ideally to the advantage of their households but sometimes in service of their own private and subversive schemes.[6] The *Odyssey* offers the paramount example of how these two activities intersect in its account of Penelope's concoction of a plot that literally depends on weaving, her scheme of forestalling her Suitors by weaving—and secretly unweaving—a shroud for Laertes. It also offers a particularly pointed use of the metaphor of weaving when in Book 13, as the action enters its final phase, Athena appears openly to Odysseus and announces that she is there to weave a plot with him ("*hina toi sun mētin huphēnō*," 13.303, cf. 13.386).

The plot that Athena metaphorically weaves in concert with Odysseus supersedes Penelope's plot with the shroud, which, by the time the *Odyssey*'s narrative begins, has outlived its usefulness and has been exposed. As the goddess in charge of weaving, Athena is able to perform both the literal handicraft and the more metaphorical devising of plots much more successfully than any mortal. The *Odyssey* highlights her success as a plotter through the structure of its narrative. With its famously nonlinear plot, the poem establishes a distinction between the events that take place in its own narrative present, which are narrated by the Muses operating through the poet, and earlier events, which are narrated by human characters in flashbacks within the poem. These earlier events include not only Penelope's temporary scheme to keep her Suitors at bay but also the entire history of Odysseus' adventures between his departure from Troy and the end of his seven-year stay with Kalypso, which is narrated by Odysseus himself in an extensive flashback spanning Books 9 through 12 of the poem.

Athena, who so prominently controls the narrative present, is markedly detached from Odysseus' cause during the earlier phase of the adventures, first because she is angry at all the returning Achaeans (3.135) and then because she is obliged to cede control of events to Poseidon, who is angry at Odysseus' treatment of his son, the Kyklops Polyphemos (13.339–43).[7] The division of the *Odyssey's* action into two phases, one controlled by Poseidon and the other by Athena, expresses an opposition between the two divinities that runs through the mythological tradition. This opposition is presented as an outright competition in the story of their contest for recognition as the patron deity of Athens. The contest is won by Athena when the olive tree she produces is judged to be more useful to the city—which is to say more conducive to the human control of nature—than the salt spring produced by Poseidon, and Athena's activities in the spheres where she and Poseidon overlap, such as navigation and horsemanship, generally involve the imposition of order on natural forces whose unruliness Poseidon leaves unchecked.[8]

Beginning as it does when Athena reasserts control over Odysseus' fate, the *Odyssey* represents another version of her ultimate victory over Poseidon. This victory is associated with civilization, as Odysseus both returns to civilization and restores civilized values on Ithaka, and with the cooperation of female figures in furthering the hero's goals. The phase of the action controlled by Poseidon is set in a fantastic and anarchic realm that lacks the familiar structures of human social organization and in which conventional gender roles are frequently overturned. This is a realm in which, as Schein points out, the unruliness of women seems to stand for the challenges of the sea itself, the element with which Odysseus must contend and over which Poseidon rules.[9] This is where Odysseus confronts the most powerful and menacing female figures: the terrifying, gigantic daughter and wife of the Laistrygonian king Antiphates; the voracious monsters Skylla and Charybdis. This is where we hear the most autonomous female voices: the voices of the Sirens and of the dead heroines who tell their stories to Odysseus in the underworld. And this is where the seductiveness of women—in particular of the two weaving, singing goddesses, Kirke and Kalypso—threatens to deflect Odysseus from his project of returning home to Ithaka and Penelope. This section of the narrative ends in an impasse with Odysseus trapped on the island of Kalypso. Subject to her desire for him, even though he does not reciprocate it, he is held there in a feminized state of passivity and grief.

Once Athena breaks this impasse and a new phase of the action begins under her guidance, the female figures whom Odysseus encounters are enlisted as willing helpers in his Return. Kalypso receives an Olympian injunction to release Odysseus and speed his journey, at which point he regains his male, heroic capacity for action.

Significantly, his first act is within the sphere of Athena: He builds a ship. From then on, Athena guarantees the cooperation of numerous female accomplices—Ino,[10] Nausikaa, Arete, Eurykleia, and Penelope—until Odysseus is restored to his allotted place in the social order, at the center of a flourishing household built around a harmonious, but asymmetrical partnership between Odysseus himself and his wife, Penelope (cf. 23.350–65).

Athena's methods for controlling the action of the *Odyssey* reflect her allegiance to the social order she is helping to restore. As she makes her first moves to spur Telemachos to action, she adopts the identities of male figures who stand in socially important relationships of solidarity to Odysseus and his family, first Odysseus' foreign guest-friend Mentes and then his loyal Ithacan ally and future battle companion, Mentor. In these disguises, she acts as wise advisor and surrogate father for Telemachos, anticipating the helpful bonds he will forge under her guidance with Odysseus' Trojan War comrades Nestor and Menelaos. As she stimulates the extension of mutually supportive relationships between aristocratic males from father to son, she activates the very process of heredity on which the aristocratic and patriarchal culture of the poem is based.

Athena's promotion of these socially important ties between men is complemented by the control she exercises over the volatile realm of female sexuality, which is perceived as a major threat to the social order. Athena intervenes at key points in the narrative by stimulating either women's own sexual feelings or men's anxieties about female sexuality. This mode of operation is in accord both with her traditional identity as a virgin who resists all sexual experience herself and with her traditional mastery of chaotic forces that often stand for sexuality, such as the sea or the wild spirit of horses, both significantly associated with Poseidon.

Probably the most memorable instance of Athena's working through a woman's sexuality is her role in bringing Nausikaa to the Phaeacian shore so that she can clothe and welcome Odysseus.[11] As Odysseus sleeps on the shore, recovering from his struggle with the sea, Athena goes to the house of Alkinoos "planning the Return (*noston*) of great-hearted Odysseus" (6.14). There she appears to Nausikaa in a dream in the form of her contemporary and close friend, the daughter of Dumas, and turns Nausikaa's thoughts to her impending marriage and thus to the laundry that must be done in preparation for it. Here Athena reveals the sympathy for women and for the bonds that they form among themselves that accompanies her allegiance to male interests. She works on Nausikaa through the kind of friendship among young women that is occasionally glimpsed in our surviving literary texts, most notably in the poems of Sappho. [12] To the extent that those friendships are portrayed, they tend to be treated mournfully and nostalgically, evoked in the context of their dissolution as the women involved are separated by marriage. In *Odyssey* 6, however, Athena uses this relationship as a way of promoting that separation, and in accord with its values, the *Odyssey* portrays only Nausikaa's eagerness for the socially central, male-oriented institution of marriage. [13]

Athena's immediate reason for awakening that eagerness is not, however, to promote Nausikaa's marriage, although that is certainly a byproduct of her efforts, but to further Odysseus' project of returning to Penelope. To do that, she deftly manipulates emotions that are both necessary to a young woman's successful transition to marriage and potentially disruptive in that the woman's newfound sexual feelings may complicate or compromise her safe placement in a approved union. Athena here pulls off the difficult task of exploiting Nausikaa's attraction to Odysseus so that she helps him achieve his own purposes without jeopardizing Nausikaa's eligibility as a wife for one of her many Phaeacian suitors. Not only does she send Nausikaa to the shore but she also sees that Odysseus wakes up in time to approach Nausikaa before she leaves (6.110–18), instills Nausikaa with the boldness necessary to face Odysseus when he appears to her (6.139–40), and enhances Odysseus' physical appeal as he dresses himself in the clothes Nausikaa lends him (6.229–35). Thus she creates an erotically charged situation that is nonetheless kept from leading to a dangerous entanglement through the civilized behavior of her protégés: Odysseus' careful diplomacy and Nausikaa's sense of modesty and propriety keep all thoughts of a union between them safely hypothetical. Odysseus' successful negotiation of the delicate situation in which he finds himself on Phaiakia transposes Athena's victory over Poseidon to the sphere of social life: Under her guidance he wins the confidence of a community of seafarers who are wary of outsiders and devoted to Poseidon (6.266; 7.27–36).

Athena also operates by manipulating men's anxieties about women's sexual feelings and especially about their ability to transfer their affections from one man to another. A good example is her intervention at the beginning of Book 15, where she sends Telemachos home from Sparta so he can help Odysseus regain his household. She appears to Telemachos as he sleeps in the palace of Menelaos and urges him to return home so he can catch up with his mother who, she claims, is being urged by her father and brothers to marry the richest of her Suitors, Eurymachos. Athena is noncommittal about Penelope's own response to this supposed pressure (of which we hear nothing elsewhere in the poem), but makes sure that Telemachos is worried by alluding in general terms to the mobility of women's feelings.

> You know what sort of heart is in the breast of a woman;
> she wants to help the household of whichever man marries her,
> and no longer remembers her earlier children or her beloved husband
> now that he is dead, nor does she think about them.   (15.20–24)

As the effectiveness of this strategy shows, the poem presents Penelope's response to her Suitors and to the competing pressures that she faces as crucial to the successful outcome of its plot. The *Odyssey* stresses the importance of Penelope's frame of mind by generating a certain degree of mystery about it, at times leaving her thoughts opaque and inaccessible. At other times, however, Athena becomes actively involved in making sure that Penelope's thoughts are properly under control and not veering in directions that might undermine Odysseus' success.

Her first such intervention occurs at the end of Book 4, where she responds to an anxious prayer from Penelope by sending her a dream. Penelope has just learned of both Telemachos' absence and the Suitors' plot to ambush and kill him on his return, and she is distraught with worry about his safety. Eurykleia urges her to pray to Athena, which she does before falling asleep. Athena responds by fashioning an image of Penelope's sister Iphthime, once again working through those bonds between women that are necessarily sacrificed to marriage. In this case, that sacrifice is poignantly evoked as Penelope addresses the image with amazement: "Why have you come here, sister? Never before this / did you come, since you inhabit a house that is very far away" (4.810–11).

Penelope then goes on to rehearse her troubles, first the loss of her husband, and now the risky journey undertaken by her inexperienced son. As she does so, she also gives priority to her concern for Telemachos: "For this one I grieve even more than for that one" (*Odyssey* 4.819). Penelope here voices an overriding maternal concern that is understandable in her circumstances and yet is potentially dangerous from the point of view of Odysseus' interests, to which Athena is wholly dedicated. Early Greek poetry expresses a recurrent concern that a mother's tie to a son can prove troublesome for her mate, most dramatically in the Succession Myth of Hesiod's *The-*

ogony, where in each generation sons unite with their mothers to overthrow their fathers—until Zeus contrives, in the episode previously described, literally to contain the power of his mate and to limit her offspring to Athena. In the *Odyssey,* the growing crisis that makes Odysseus' Return urgently necessary centers on Telemachos' maturity and the pressure it brings on Penelope to serve his interests—at the expense of Odysseus—by marrying one of the Suitors.

Through her surrogate, Athena works to counteract these pressures. The dream image offers Penelope complete reassurance about Telemachos, informing her that he has the company and guidance of none other than Athena herself. But when Penelope then asks her for information about Odysseus, she remains tantalizingly mysterious: "Where that one is concerned, I won't tell you the whole story / whether he lives or has died. It is bad to speak idly" (4.836–37). In this way, Athena redirects Penelope's interest and concern away from her son and toward her absent husband, discouraging her from giving him up for lost and preparing her to reassume, rather than abandon, her role as wife.

When the action of the *Odyssey* enters its most intense phase in Book 13, with Odysseus' arrival on the shore of Ithaka and Athena's more overt involvement on his behalf, Athena makes use of Penelope in a more complicated way. The plot that she concocts with Odysseus centers on concealing Odysseus' identity, and Penelope—along with the Suitors—is a target of that disguise. In encouraging Odysseus to conceal himself from Penelope, Athena operates much as she later will with Telemachos when she inspires him to return from Sparta. Without claiming that Penelope is inclined toward the Suitors—in fact, while assuring him that she is entirely loyal—she nonetheless encourages Odysseus to exercise his characteristic wiliness in relation specifically to Penelope (13.335–38), playing on his generalized anxieties about the possible treachery of women. Odysseus shows how susceptible he is to these anxieties when his first response on hearing about the Suitors is to think of the death of Agamemnon, which was brought about by the paradigmatic disloyal wife, Klytaimestra (13.383–85).[14]

Keeping Penelope in the dark allows Athena and Odysseus to use her in a particularly daring and masterful way, exploiting for Odysseus' advantage the growing willingness to marry one of the Suitors that Penelope feels as time marches on and Telemachos' needs become more pressing. This is a brilliantly successful strategy, which culminates in the bow contest when Penelope's decisive step toward remarriage brings about Odysseus' triumph over the Suitors. It is also risky; there is always the possibility that Penelope herself will experience that shift of loyalty to a new husband that Athena evokes to Telemachos, with damaging consequences both for Odysseus' goal of regaining his place as Penelope's husband and for Penelope's reputation for fidelity.

One consequence of Athena's firm control over the *Odyssey's* plot is that, although this risk is occasionally evoked in provocative ways, most notably in Penelope's trick with the marriage bed, it is never realized.[15] Before their plan is launched, Athena offers Odysseus authoritative testimony to Penelope's fidelity (13.336–38). When she most blatantly exploits Penelope's attractiveness to the Suitors, in the episode in Book 18 in which Penelope appears in the hall and extracts gifts from them, the narrative makes it clear that Athena is working not with Penelope's own inclinations, as in almost all cases of divine intervention in Homer, but against them.

The incident is clearly masterminded by Athena; the account of it begins with the statement that Athena put it in Penelope's mind to appear before the Suitors "so that she might especially stir up / the hearts of the Suitors and appear more precious / to her husband and son than she had been before" (18.160–1). But Penelope herself is portrayed as repeatedly resisting the sexual dimension of Athena's plan even as she carries it out. When she registers the impulse to appear before the Suitors in a speech to her servant Eurynome, she expresses great surprise at it and immediately reinterprets it as a desire to speak to Telemachos and warn him against the Suitors (18.164–68). Here her maternal concern for Telemachos, although implicated in her growing willingness to accept one of the Suitors, nonetheless serves as a far more acceptable screen for an impulse to engage the Suitors sexually. When Eurynome responds by encouraging her to beautify herself, Penelope refuses to hear of it, and Athena has to put Penelope to sleep and do it herself; when Penelope awakens, she offers a spontaneous avowal of loyalty to Odysseus, expressing a wish to die so she could stop her perpetual grieving for her lost husband.

Once Penelope has arrived in the hall, she ignores the Suitors and their strong erotic response to her presence and speaks only to Telemachos. When Eurymachos draws her into conversation by praising her beauty and attractiveness, she brusquely denies that she possesses these qualities and launches into the account of how Odysseus instructed her on his departure to remarry once Telemachos was grown, which makes it clear that any move she makes in that direction should be interpreted as loyalty to Odysseus rather than attraction to any of them. Her demand for gifts comes only after this extensive series of refusals to enter into the sexual atmosphere of the encounter, and it is hardly surprising—even if it is not strictly logical—that Odysseus rejoices and concludes, even as she enchants the Suitors' hearts, that "her mind had other intentions" (18.283). Athena's control over female sexuality here takes the form of creating and exploiting a sexual dimension to Penelope's behavior that Penelope herself resists and denies.

Athena's management of Penelope, which is both unusually manipulative and unusually at odds with the inclinations of the human character involved, contrasts markedly with the extraordinary partnership she establishes with Odysseus in Book 13. While Athena is notable for her tendency to stand by the heroes she favors,[16] and both Homeric epics include references to her special attention to Odysseus at Troy (e.g., *Iliad* 23.783; *Odyssey* 3.377–79), the openness and completeness of her support for Odysseus in the second half of the *Odyssey* are unparalleled. The encounter between Odysseus and Athena in Book 13 dramatizes the formation of a partnership unlike any other, either between a god and a human or between a female and a male.

In this episode, Athena and Odysseus carry out an extensive negotiation of their relationship in which the tensions between female and male that run through the poem are addressed and resolved. Her first act is to trick him by disguising Ithaka itself with a transforming mist. By doing this, she exercises the power associated with the female of making things seem other than they really are and appears to fulfill the threat, also associated with the female, of depriving the hero of what he most desires, in Odysseus' case, his Return. When she reveals herself and offers him reassurance, he responds by charging her with what he fears most from women: abandonment of his cause and seduction (13.312–28). He complains that, although she was "gentle" (*ēpiē*) toward him at Troy, she was nowhere to be seen once he embarked on his homeward journey. He goes on to say that he doubts that he has really come to Ithaka as she claims: "For I think you are teasing me / when you say that, so that you may seduce my mind" (13.326–27).

The verb used here for "seduce," *ēperopeuō*, has general connotations of deception and cajoling, but is especially associated with sexual seduction. Odysseus is responding to the muted but evident sexuality of Athena's approach to him, which involves her transformation out of her first disguise as a young shepherd into a beautiful woman, a smile (which can denote sexual allure, as in Aphrodite's epithet *philommeidēs*, "smile-loving"), and the intimate gesture of stroking him with her hand (13.286–88). She, in turn, counters his fears by explaining her absence during his journey as necessary deference to Poseidon and revealing to him that he really is on Ithaka; the appearance of his longed-for native land becomes the token of her continuous good faith.

Athena's Olympian stature, which means that her designs are endorsed by Zeus himself, makes her a more reliable and confident ally than any of the other female figures on whom Odysseus must depend in the course of the poem, and her prominently deployed partnership with Odysseus eclipses all other such relationships, even that between Odysseus and Penelope. Thus the poem's most emphatic account of *homophrosynē*, "like-mindedness," the defining characteristic of a successful marriage (6.180–85), comes in Athena's declaration to Odysseus in Book 13.

> Only a sly and thievish one could outdo you
> in all sorts of tricks, even if a god were to encounter you.
> Scoundrel, clever-minded, full of tricks, you were not about,
> even in your own land, to give up deceptions
> and treacherous words, which are dear to your nature.
> But come, let's not say any more about that, since we both are versed
> in sharp dealings, for you are by far the best of all mortals
> at laying plans and spinning tales, and I among all the gods
> am renowned for cunning and sharp dealings.   (13.291–99)

Shortly afterward, she makes it clear that this like-mindedness is the basis for her unwavering devotion.

> Always such thinking is in your heart!
> That is why I cannot abandon you, wretched as you are,
> because you are alert, and quick-witted, and careful.   (13.330–32)

Athena explicitly presents herself as a better ally for Odysseus than Penelope. Complimenting him on his instinct to test his wife before revealing himself to her, she adds,

> Yet she all the same
> stays in the great hall, and always bitter nights
> and days wear her away as she weeps.
> But I, on the other hand, never doubted, but in my heart
> I knew that you would get home. . . .   (13.336–40)

Penelope's limited mortal knowledge leads her to despair, and although that despair is a sign of her emotional commitment to Odysseus, it is also implicated in her growing willingness to consider remarriage, which threatens Odysseus' success.

With her Olympian power and omniscience, Athena need have no doubts about the wisdom of complete loyalty to Odysseus. Not only does she make a point of announcing her own constancy but she also goes out of her way to accentuate Penelope's relative unreliability, playing an especially aggressive role in assuring that Odysseus never joins forces with his wife until the danger of the Suitors has been overcome. We learn in Book 13 that her purpose in obscuring Ithaka from Odysseus is to assure that he not reveal himself to Penelope, among others (13.189–93). When Odysseus taxes Athena with her seeming abandonment of him and expresses doubt that he really is on Ithaka, Athena supplies as the motive for his wariness that "it doesn't suit you to expose yourself by asking questions / until you test your wife" (13.335–36). If Odysseus is here directing against Athena the general complaints that male Homeric heroes have about women, Athena is encouraging Odysseus to apply those general complaints to Penelope: She urges him to treat Penelope as if she were disloyal even though she is not. Following her allegiance to a male perspective, Athena reinforces the misogynistic assumptions of which Penelope is, in effect, a victim.

As the narrative progresses, Athena makes sure that Penelope does not recognize Odysseus until the Suitors are defeated. To this end, she again intervenes more crudely than usual for a Homeric god: In the footwashing scene in Book 19, when Eurykleia wants to let Penelope know that the stranger is Odysseus, Athena simply makes it impossible for her to get Penelope's attention (19.476–79). Once she has set the contest, Penelope, as a mortal woman, has no role in the battle against the Suitors, and she is sent from the hall by Telemachos and put to sleep by Athena (21.343–58). Of course, Athena, in her divine androgyny, plays a vital role in the battle. As the archery contest is followed by a full-scale spear battle, she appears first as Odysseus' ally Mentor, then as a swallow perched on a roof beam; from this vantage point, she directs Odysseus' triumph, causing the Suitors' spears to go astray and finally imposing on them a wild mania that contrasts with the purposeful onslaught of her favorites (22.297–309). Only when the Suitors have been eliminated does Athena promote an open reunion between husband and wife, restore Odysseus to his youthful appearance so that Penelope can recognize him (23.156–63), and hold back the night so that they can enjoy at leisure their return to their marriage bed (23.241–46).

The reunion of Odysseus and Penelope echoes many of the themes of the Book 13 encounter between Odysseus and Athena, and, in the course of it, Penelope emerges as a partner who shares many of

Athena's qualities. Her trick with the marriage bed reveals that she too is endowed with *mētis* and resembles Athena's disguise of Ithaka as a sign of seeming betrayal that is really a proof of constancy. Penelope's *homophrosynē* with Odysseus is also stressed, although less directly in a simile: It is experienced by the characters, but it is not articulated between them (23.233–40).

On the other hand, although Odysseus' reunion with Penelope has an undeniable emotional power, its strategic significance is relatively small; the role of Odysseus' active female partner in his recovery of his home has been taken over by his divine patron. Moreover, although both episodes end with a scene of plotting, in which the alliance that has just been renegotiated is acted out, the hierarchies operating in each are different. Athena is clearly Odysseus' superior, and she is the one who dictates their plot, announcing that she will disguise him and that he must go first to the hut of the swineherd Eumaios while she fetches Telemachos back from Sparta (13.397–415). With Penelope the balance of power is reversed, so that Odysseus presents her with a plan that expresses a classic gender asymmetry: He will go out and attend to matters beyond the house, while she must remain quietly inside (23.350–65).

Despite the hint of flirtatiousness in her dealings with Odysseus, Athena's efficacy in managing the *Odyssey*'s plot—as in her other mythical exploits—rests on the fact that she is a virgin as well as a goddess. Her aloofness from marriage detaches her from a relationship that inevitably involves divided and shifting loyalties; a wife's loyalties shift from father to husband and possibly again from one husband to another, as various characters in the *Odyssey* fear will happen with Penelope. Athena's undivided loyalty to her father, Zeus, gives her the influence with him that enables her to bring about Odysseus' triumph over Penelope's Suitors. Having no sexual designs on Odysseus, Athena lacks the reluctance to let him return to Penelope found in Kirke and especially in Kalypso; having no sexual designs on anyone else, she lacks the motives for betrayal found in Helen and Klytaimestra, whose behavior colors the *Odyssey*'s presentation of Penelope.

In addition, Athena's virginity detaches her from the other relationship that comes with marriage and female sexuality, namely, motherhood, which entails a further division of loyalty between father and son.[17] Athena's difference from Penelope in this respect is expressed in the way her actions, especially her orchestration of their reunion in Book 16, promote harmonious cooperation between Odysseus and Telemachos, while Penelope is portrayed as painfully torn between her duties as Odysseus' wife and as Telemachos' mother (e.g., 19.512–34).

The advantage of Athena's lack of motherhood can be seen by comparing her relationship to Odysseus to the closely parallel relationship between the goddess Thetis and her mortal son, Achilles, in the *Iliad*. In both poems, the goddess's advocacy of her mortal protégé effectively structures the plot. Like Athena in *Odyssey* 1, Thetis sets the plot of the *Iliad* in motion by appealing to Zeus on behalf of Achilles and gaining Zeus' assent to a plan to restore to Achilles what he has lost, in his case the honor that went with his war prize Briseis. Each goddess also appears at the end of the poem to bring the story to a close: Thetis is sent from Zeus to tell Achilles he must return Hektor's body to Priam, while Athena makes a concluding epiphany to construct a truce between Odysseus and the Suitors' relatives.

The similarity of these goddesses' supportive roles is underscored by the parallel construction of the key episodes in which each comes to her hero's aid. In Book 1 of the *Iliad*, Achilles, desperate over his mistreatment by Agamemnon, goes alone to the shore and prays to his mother, at which point she emerges from the sea to console and help him. In Book 13 of the *Odyssey*, Athena appears to Odysseus as his open and unconditional supporter when he too is wandering unhappily along a shore. Despondent over his seeming failure to reach Ithaka, Odysseus is slapping his thighs (a sign of mortality[18]), bemoaning his fate, and dragging himself along *thina poluphloisboio thalassēs*, "the strand of the much-echoing sea" (*Odyssey* 13.220).

The solicitude that Athena displays toward Odysseus, both in *Odyssey* 13 and elsewhere in the Homeric epics, is reminiscent of a mother's care as well as a lover's. Indeed, during the funeral games in *Iliad* 23, when Athena causes Ajax to lose to Odysseus in the running race, Ajax ruefully refers to her as the goddess who "like a mother stands by Odysseus and brings him help" (*Iliad* 23.783). But, for all the eloquence of this simile in measuring Athena's devotion to Odysseus, her ultimate success in helping him depends on the fact that she is not his mother or anyone else's mother.[19] Despite the structural similarities between the roles of Thetis and Athena, Thetis is not able to secure for Achilles the happy outcome to his struggles that Athena achieves for Odysseus, and this failure is closely tied to Thetis' maternity.

In the mythological tradition that lies behind the *Iliad*, Thetis is a double for Athena's mother, Metis.[20] She is a powerful and alluring sea goddess with whom Zeus is eager to mate until he learns that she is destined to bear a son who will be stronger than his father. As with

Metis, Zeus forestalls this threat, in this case by marrying Thetis off to a mortal, Peleus, to whom she bears Achilles, the mortal hero who is indeed greater than his mortal father, but who cannot challenge Zeus. Zeus secures his sovereignty by depriving Thetis and Achilles of the greater glory that might have been theirs, and this is the source of their power over him, of the ability to enlist him in their plan that is dramatized at the beginning of the *Iliad*. This power cannot, however, offset the pain that Zeus' manuever costs each of them, in Achilles' case the pain of mortality and in Thetis', the pain of seeing her own son suffer and die.

As generative mother and challenging son, Thetis and Achilles remain troublesome figures for Zeus, in contrast to Athena, in whom—as a virgin rather than a mother and as a daughter rather than a son—the threats posed by those roles have been neutralized. Thus Zeus' agreement with Thetis at the beginning of the *Iliad* has a wholly different character from his agreement with Athena at the beginning of the *Odyssey*. He enters into Thetis' plan only reluctantly and secretly, and his acquiescence causes him trouble with both his legitimate consort, Hera, and his beloved daughter, Athena (e.g., *Iliad* 8.438–84).

Furthermore, although the outcome Athena negotiates for Odysseus is straightforward and clearly beneficial, the plan to which Thetis wins Zeus' agreement is murkier and full of unexpected consequences. With Athena's help, Odysseus manages to transcend a hero's normal limitations, adding a successful homecoming (*nostos*) to the winning of glory (*kleos*). But, for all of Thetis' advocacy, Achilles' achievement remains circumscribed by the necessity of choosing between homecoming and glory (*Iliad* 9.410–16) and Thetis' plan of having Achilles win glory through Trojan victories during his absence from battle bears the unforeseen cost of Patroklos' death. The stark limits on what Thetis can do for Achilles are highlighted at the end of the *Iliad* when Zeus summons Thetis to Olympos and instructs her to tell Achilles he must return Hektor's body, imposing on Achilles an action that acknowledges his mortal limitation and subjection to divine will.

Thetis' fulfillment of Zeus' command brings formal symmetry to the *Iliad*'s plot, echoing and reversing her actions in Book 1, where she induces Zeus to act on Achilles' behalf. Her action also promotes a return to civilized values, as Achilles is forced to give up his savage and pointless punishment of Hektor's body. That return to civilization, however, brings with it a check on the personal aspirations of the human hero Achilles and has a limited impact; the brief and fragile truce between Achilles and Priam has no effect on the ongoing course of the war.

Like the *Iliad*, the *Odyssey* ends with the goddess who has initiated the poem's plot bringing it to a close. But, in accord with her closer and more comfortable relationship with Zeus, Athena's role at the end of the *Odyssey* is both more prominent and more happily effective than that of Thetis in the *Iliad*. The *Odyssey*'s conclusion, like its beginning, is worked out in a conversation between Zeus and Athena that Athena initiates. As the Suitors' relatives begin their vengeful attack on Odysseus, Athena turns to her father and asks him his intentions: whether he will bring about war among the Ithacans or a harmonious alliance.

Zeus responds to Athena's characteristic deference by reminding her that this story has so far been her project and ceding control to her: "Did not you yourself devise this plan, / by which Odysseus, returning, took vengeance on those men? / Arrange things as you wish." But he also goes on to tell her what outcome would be fitting (*hōs epeoiken*), and it is typical of the relationship between Zeus and Athena that what is fitting to him is also what is most pleasing to her: lasting peace and prosperity among the Ithacans, continuous rule for Odysseus, and a miraculous forgetting of the slaughter of the Suitors (24.482–86).

Authorized by Zeus to carry out what she already desires (24.487), Athena orchestrates a brief, final episode in which Odysseus' paramount good fortune is rehearsed. She allows the war between Odysseus and the Suitors' relatives to proceed just long enough for the superiority of Odysseus' side to be put on display. What is particularly stressed here is the power of the aristocratic, patriarchal family as Odysseus enjoins Telemachos to live up to the glory of his forefathers, Telemachos assures his father that he will do so, and Laertes rejoices that his son and his grandson are competing in valor. The power of the family is bound up with the favor of Athena, who appears as Mentor to encourage them and, in that role, urges Laertes to pray to herself. He duly does so and is rewarded when she causes his spear to hit Antinoos' father, Eupeithes, the leader of their opponents. But when Odysseus and Telemachos move in to follow up on this success, Athena brings the war to an abrupt halt, sending the Ithacans into terrified flight and preventing Odysseus from going after them. With the backing of her father, she insists that the quarrel be ended and arranges the truce between the sides, in accord with her identity as a goddess of war who nonetheless upholds civilization and peaceful order.

Athena's final intervention in this plot that she has created and guided throughout constitutes an endorsement of the Homeric *oikos*, the hereditary extended household to which Odysseus has made his arduous, glorious Return. The *oikos* is identified as the basis of Odysseus' power, as Athena creates an invincible fighting force out of three generations of his family. Athena's action also reveals the *oikos* as the sphere in which Odysseus can enjoy the unqualified success that distinguishes him from other heroes; she assures a happy ending to his story by cutting it short just as he begins to move aggressively beyond the boundaries of his estate.[21] Yet if Odysseus' story, like Achilles', ends with the gods imposing limits on the individual hero, Zeus' proposal to Athena makes it clear that that limitation will be painless: Odysseus will retain his preeminence in Ithaka, and the entire population will flourish. The hero's violent obliteration of his rivals will go unavenged for the sake of peace.

The image of the *oikos* celebrated in this final episode is dominated by men; it is encapsulated in the unbroken male heritage represented by Laertes, Odysseus, and Telemachos. Through a plot constructed around the danger posed by Penelope's Suitors, the *Odyssey* presents the *oikos* as having to be protected by force, and that means that it can function properly only with a male hero at its center. Although the poem has done much to indicate the importance of women to the functioning of the *oikos* and to its preservation, women are notably absent from its concluding pageant. Even Penelope—who has contrived to preserve Odysseus' household in his absence and who has helped to create the biological tie between Odysseus and his son—is hidden from view in the inner part of the house. Instead, Odysseus has at his side the one female figure on whom a male hero can most surely depend: the goddess Athena, who devotes to his cause both her masculine ability as a fighter and her feminine skill as a weaver of plots, devising an end to his story that is at once the restoration of society and the fulfillment of his desires.

Notes

This essay is dedicated to Jane Espy Gordon, whose early arrival prevented it from being finished on time. My thanks to Beth Cohen for the good grace with which she tolerated the delay and for helpful editorial comments.

1. The definitive study of *mētis* in Greek thought is Detienne and Vernant, 1978.

2. For a concise survey of Athena's various attributes, see Burkert, 1985, 139–43.

3. On the sexual politics of the *Oresteia*, see Zeitlin, 1984.

4. Schein, Chapter 2, and Doherty, Chapter 5, both in this volume; Felson-Rubin, 1987; Foley, 1978; Winkler, 1990, 129–61.

5. I am extending here an argument I have made elsewhere in connection with Penelope. See Murnaghan, 1986; 1987, 118–47; 1994. On the sexual ideology of the *Odyssey*, see also Wohl, 1993.

6. Among the many discussions of this metaphor, Bergren, 1983, 71–73, has been especially influential.

7. For the argument that Athena's failure to help Odysseus during his adventures stems from anger at him personally, see Clay, 1983.

8. On the interactions between Athena and Poseidon in these realms, see Detienne and Vernant, 1978, 187–258.

9. Schein, Chapter 2, this volume.

10. Ino appears to Odysseus in the form of an *aithuia* or sea crow, a bird identified with Athena in her capacity as navigator. See Detienne and Vernant, 1978, 218.

11. For the way fifth-century vase painters depicting the meeting of Odysseus and Nausikaa emphasized both the involvement of Athena and the sexual dimension of the encounter, see Shapiro, Chapter 8, this volume, who also includes bibliographical references to the main discussions of the episode. The prominence of Athena in representations of this scene is especially notable because, as Buitron-Oliver and Cohen point out (Chapter 3, this volume), she is otherwise rarely included in depictions of scenes from the *Odyssey*.

12. For other examples, see the portrayal of Persephone and her companions in the Homeric *Hymn to Demeter*, Alkman's first *Partheneion*, and the surviving fragment of Erinna's *Distaff*.

13. For an outright admission that marriage promotes primarily the interests of men, a situation that is implicit throughout ancient Greek literature and cultural institutions, see Athena's comment at *Eumenides* 737 that her refusal to marry is the only respect in which she does not automatically side with the male.

14. For further discussion of the paradox that Athena and Odysseus exclude Penelope from the disguise plot even though she is loyal to Odysseus, see Murnaghan, 1986; 1987.

15. For a thorough account of the marriage bed and its role as a symbol of fidelity, see Zeitlin, Chapter 7, this volume.

16. Otto, 1954, 46–50, 53.

17. For the wary attitude toward motherhood expressed in Homeric poetry, see Murnaghan, 1992.

18. Lowenstam, 1981, 56–60.

19. Athena does undergo a reluctant, deflected, and virginal version of motherhood through her role in the origins of the legendary Athenian king

Erichthonios. Hephaistos attempts to rape Athena but she resists and his semen falls on her thigh; she wipes it off with a piece of wool, which she throws to the ground; at the place where it falls, Erichthonios springs from the earth. See Frazer, 1979, 2:90–91 for Apollodoros' account of this story and references to other versions.

20. For the comparison, see Detienne and Vernant, 1978, 59–61. On Thetis' role in the *Iliad,* see Slatkin, 1991.

21. On Athena's association with boundaries, see Detienne and Vernant, 1978, 230.

5

Sirens, Muses, and Female Narrators in the *Odyssey*

Lillian Eileen Doherty

To judge by the frequency with which it has been evoked or adapted in ancient and modern works of art,[1] the episode of the Sirens is one of the most compelling in the *Odyssey*— one of those passages that are most likely to resonate in the imaginations of readers. It can be a shock, then, even to one who knows the epic well, to be reminded that Odysseus' account of the episode takes just thirty-five lines—less than a page and a half in the Oxford Classical Text edition[2]—and that the snatch of the Sirens' song we are allowed to hear is only eight lines long. The evocative power of the passage, then, seems to stand in inverse proportion to its length. I would like to examine this paradox in light of the narrative strategies of the *Odyssey* as a whole. At the same time I will explore the implications, for the poet and his audience, of attributing to female figures the power to tell stories in epic form—the power, that is, to manipulate the traditional and culturally sanctioned discourse of the poet's own medium.

The Sirens episode distills in a particularly potent set of images the dynamics of male-female interaction that prevail in the *Odyssey*.[3] Insofar as female figures constitute a series of threats or false goals for the male hero, the Sirens, like Kalypso and Kirke, must be relegated to the margins of the human world and resisted with all available means. Yet because the Sirens also represent the lure of poetry, indeed of *epic* poetry, their power is intertwined with that of the

Odyssey itself. For this reason Odysseus must desire to hear them and must inspire his own audience with the same desire. Their female power must be contained so that Odysseus may achieve his homecoming; their narrative power must be contained so that the *Odyssey* may run its course. Yet this power, once evoked, is like the genie that cannot be put back into its bottle. As Schein argues in his introduction to this volume, the *Odyssey* "tempts its audience" to accept the male-focalized values of its hero; at the same time, it portrays other figures who offer conflicting perspectives.[4] At some points the epic narrator allows mutually contradictory accounts to stand without suggesting that they can be reconciled. In its vividness, the Sirens episode offers one of the most striking examples of a subversive voice that cannot be fully contained by the normative patterns of the poem as a whole.

One long-standing critical approach to the Homeric Sirens has been to dwell on their folkloric dimension and to stress their similarities to mermaids, underworld *daimones,* or other monstrous creatures the Greeks thought of as dwelling far outside the settled human world.[5] Pollard summarized this approach when he located Sirens with Sphinxes and satyrs in what he called "the great No-man's land of folk belief."[6] That the Homeric Sirens were linked in the popular imagination with such marginal creatures seems confirmed by the portrayal of Sirens in visual art, where allusions to the *Odyssey* episode are rare at first and influenced by earlier depictions of hybrid forms—part human, part animal—unconnected with the Homeric text.[7] Laurence Kahn's sensitive reading of the *Odyssey* scene[8] shows how much is to be gained by situating it in a mythological "semantic field" where femaleness evokes social marginality and perilous transitions (especially that from virginity to wifehood).[9] But as Kahn and others have noted, the Sirens cannot simply be relegated to the margins because they also wield the language of culture par excellence: the discourse of epic poetry. In so doing they claim a competence equal to that of the Muses.[10] I would like to expand on this comparison and link it to the ambiguous portrayal of another female narrator in the *Odyssey:* Helen.

We owe our most vivid description of the Muses to Hesiod's *Theogony,* that is, to a source distinct from the Homeric epics yet close to them in time. Although we cannot assume that all details of Hesiod's account would have been accepted by the poet of the *Odyssey,* there are no outright contradictions and enough common elements that we may assume a degree of continuity between the Hesiodic and the Homeric views of the Muses.[11] Thus in both traditions they are the daughters of Zeus and closely associated with Apollo as singers and inspirers of song.[12] They perform as a chorus at the feasts of the gods,[13] but they are also described as encountering individual human bards: In the *Theogony,* they appear to Hesiod on Mount Helikon; in the *Iliad,* they are said to have confronted Thamyris as he traveled from Oichalia to Dorion near Pylos (2.594–600). They are credited with an extraordinary breadth of knowledge: of past, present, and future in Hesiod (38); of the Greek experience at Troy in the *Odyssey* (8.488–91); of "all things" in the *Iliad* (*panta,* 2.485). Another point common to both Homer and Hesiod is the double-edged quality of the Muses' gifts. This doubleness takes two forms: truth versus falsehood and benefit versus harm. Hesiod's Muses emphasize their ability to speak truths *or* lies that resemble truths (27–28); in the *Odyssey* the Muses are said to have given "both good and evil" (*agathon te kakon te,* 8.63) to Demodokos, depriving him of his sight while granting him the gift of "sweet song" (8.63–64).[14]

On the basis of this composite portrait, we can identify a number of similarities between the Muses and the Homeric Sirens. The Sirens, too, are divine females[15] whose primary activity is song. They are encountered outside settled territory by human males whom they address individually, yet they claim full knowledge of what happens in the world (*hossa genētai, Odyssey* 12.191) and promise to convey that knowledge to their male protégés—Odysseus and Hesiod—who in turn will report the encounter to a wider human audience. Hesiod's Muses are described as themselves admitting their ability to speak truths or falsehoods resembling truths. In the case of the Sirens, the question of truth or falsehood is raised by the contradiction between their *own* claim that their listeners "depart" or "return home" (*neitai* can mean both, 12.188) and the warning of Kirke that those who pause to listen do not reach home (41–43).[16] The uncertainty about truth in turn is linked to the doubleness of benefit or harm: If Odysseus could believe them, the Sirens' offer of knowledge and pleasure would be a clear benefit, but if their claim to let listeners go is misleading, as Kirke's warning suggests, great harm can come of listening to them. The dual number used twice of the Homeric Sirens may serve as a metaphoric reflection of their essential doubleness.[17]

These similarities between the Muses and the Sirens have serious consequences for the truth claims of epic discourse.[18] Even for Hesiod, an overtly didactic poet, there is danger in the admission that narrative can be seductive, plausible, and yet harmful. This danger is still greater in the *Odyssey,* which portrays a variety of bards and other storytellers as a way of inviting reflection on the act of epic narration. Taken to its logical conclusion, the equation between Sirens and Muses would have the effect of subverting the poet's authority by hinting at the seductive aspects of his own activity.

Yet the *Odyssey* poet, like Hesiod, seeks to contain this threat to his authority, and one of the ways he does so is to portray the Sirens as differing in some crucial ways from the Muse who inspires his own song. Whereas the Muses invoked in the *Iliad* are, with two exceptions, plural like the Sirens, the *Odyssey* poet always refers to a singular Muse.[19] This insistence on the singular may be a way of minimizing the Muses' potential ambiguity by contrasting "the" Muse of the *Odyssey* with the plural Sirens. A second contrast involves the relations of Muses and Sirens to the *kleos* (fame) of heroes. As Charles Segal has argued,[20] the Sirens, by causing their victims to perish far from the human world, destroy instead of preserving heroic *kleos;* this makes the Sirens anti-Muses whose aims are altogether opposed to those of the true Muses and of the poets they inspire. Third, the Sirens' choice of epithets for Odysseus, and their diction more generally, may be traced to the Iliadic tradition, as Pietro Pucci has shown.[21] This makes it possible for an audience to equate the Sirens with the Muses of a different epic tradition, which the *Odyssey* poet portrays as a rival tradition and seeks to discredit. In this view the Muses of the *Iliad*, given their way, would keep Odysseus in thrall to his past and prevent his earning the *kleos* of homecoming, which the *Odyssey* poet claims for him.

Although all of these contrasts are significant, I would like to focus on a further one that has not yet been developed. It has to do with the relations between these female deities and two groups of males: the humans to whom they address themselves and the gods who are above them in the divine hierarchy.

The choir of Muses in the *Theogony*, though described as lovely and desirable, have no husbands or lovers; they seem to be cast in the mold of the maiden chorus and are closely linked to their father's house (*Theogony* 36–74).[22] The Muses invoked in both the *Iliad* and the *Odyssey* are virtually sexless. By contrast, the Sirens have a decidedly ambiguous sexual status. Like Kalypso, they occupy a flowery meadow (5.72; 12.159), a setting connected elsewhere in archaic poetry with sexual encounters.[23] Their song is said to delight (*terpein*, 12.189) and to charm (*thelgein*, 12.44) an exclusively male audience of sailors, who are thus prevented, according to Kirke, from returning to their wives and children (12.41–43). Whereas *terpein* and *thelgein* are commonly used of the pleasure given by poetry, they are also associated with sexual pleasure and help to link the Sirens with other seductive females in the *Odyssey*,[24] including Kirke herself. At least one strand in the history of the Sirens' visual representation also associates them with erotic passion and seduction.[25] Thus the virginal or sexless Muses may be contrasted with the seductive Sirens. Moreover, like proper virgins, the Muses are clearly identified as daughters of Zeus, whereas the Homeric Sirens are given no lineage.[26] The Muses perform not only on the peaks of Helikon but in the halls of Zeus on Olympos; the Sirens, on their far-flung island, do not associate with the Olympians in any way. Unlike the Muses, whose narrative authority derives from Zeus, the Sirens appeal to no authority but their own knowledge.[27] Rather than addressing an entire human community through the medium of male bards, they address males as individuals and may even prevent them from returning to the communities they have left. Thus in contrast to the Muses' song, which is said to coincide with epic narrative ("Sing, goddess, the wrath," "Tell me, Muse, of the man"), the Sirens' song is portrayed as threatening the *Odyssey* narrative and must be cut short by it. I think this is not so much because the Sirens are Muses of the *Iliad* as because they are unauthorized Muses, seductive rather than dependent females who command the language of poetry for their own inscrutable purposes.

This ambiguous power of the Sirens resembles, and should be compared with, that of other female narrators in the *Odyssey*, that is, with female characters who are portrayed as telling stories to other characters in the poem. In contrast to the male storytellers, many of whom address large audiences, all the female narrators but three[28] address only individual male listeners. In most cases, this single male listener is the hero himself. Because the narration takes place outside any communal setting, in a tête-à-tête between female and male, a potential for seduction exists in almost every case. (Here the sole exception is Athena, whose virginal status is a given of the tradition.[29]) Of course, Odysseus is himself portrayed as exercising a kind of seduction over many of these females, including most obviously Nausikaa and Penelope. Yet because of the narrative structure, which uses the figure of Odysseus as primary focalizer of the action, seduction figures in the epic plot primarily as a *threat* to the hero that must be deflected and manipulated by him. In most cases he succeeds in this deflection, and the potentially dangerous female narrators—Kalypso, Ino, Kirke, Nausikaa, and Penelope herself—are enlisted in support of the hero's own goals. Only the Sirens and Helen remain permanently inscrutable and potentially hostile. Virtually all the poem's female figures—including Penelope, Eurykleia, and even, for a time, Athena[30]—are portrayed as posing threats to the hero's safe homecoming. But the threat posed by female narrators is more specific: They would usurp the hero's privileges as narrator and focalizer of his own story. In the final portion of my paper I explore the ways in which the epic narrator contains this threat and the ways in which nonetheless it lingers to lend power to the Sirens episode.

In Book 4, Helen administers a drug to her exclusively male audience before regaling them with a tale of Odysseus and herself at Troy. She claims to have seen through Odysseus' beggarly disguise when he came to Troy as a spy; she further claims to have conspired with him because by then she had had a change of heart and come to desire a Greek victory. Thus Helen, while ostensibly telling a story in praise of Odysseus, also seeks to revise her own story, to promulgate a new *kleos* for herself. But just as the Sirens' song is balanced by Kirke's warning to resist it, so Helen's tale is balanced by a contradictory tale offered by Menelaos. On the very last night of the war, according to Menelaos, Helen had come to the Wooden Horse and called out to the hidden Greek chiefs one by one, simulating their wives' voices. Odysseus had saved the situation by restraining the Greeks until Helen went away. The clear implication of Menelaos' story is that Helen's story was false—that her "change of heart" is an invention not only for her present audience but also for Odysseus, her audience in the story (when she protested to him in Troy that she was his ally). Odysseus may have been fooled once, Menelaos implies, but when Helen attempted her second ruse Odysseus was able to resist her and to maintain the "disguise" of the Horse for himself and his comrades. As a number of scholars have recently shown,[31] the juxtaposed tales of Helen and Menelaos offer contrasting models of the male hero's response to female seduction—a seduction that relies partly on sex but largely on plausible speech. In the episode itself, Menelaos' tale is given somewhat greater weight than Helen's by its position: It serves as an implicit rebuttal, which Helen has no chance to contest. In the framework of the larger epic plot, the model of resistance, of opposing seduction with disguise, is clearly endorsed by the epic narrator. By maintaining his beggarly disguise in Ithaka, Odysseus triumphs over the Suitors, in a kind of reprise of the trick by which he raised the siege of Troy. Thus Helen's attempt at an epic narrative is presented in an elaborate frame that serves to contain its teller's subversive ambition to revise her own *kleos* and link it with that of Odysseus.

A similar narrative frame encloses the Sirens' song; indeed, here the frame is still more elaborate, perhaps in recognition of the greater power of the Sirens to subvert the hierarchy of narrative control. The Sirens are described three times, always within the context of Odysseus' tale to the Phaeacians and thus under his control as internal narrator. Yet the first of these three accounts is ascribed to Kirke, herself an immortal female with dangerous seductive powers that have already been contained. Having successfully resisted Kirke's drugs—which bear an interesting resemblance to Helen's—Odysseus has made of her a loyal ally, one who will entertain him only as long as he wishes and then help him on his way. In this helping role she warns him against the Sirens, whose song shares her own (now chastened) ability literally to enthrall men.[32] Odysseus' resistance to Kirke thus not only foreshadows but makes possible his resistance to the Sirens. At the same time, it should not be forgotten that both these episodes are narrated by Odysseus to an internal audience who *also* have the power to delay him. Thus he can be seen as using his tales to model the behavior of the Phaeacians, his audience in the poem, who are to follow Kirke's example by entertaining him and letting him go. I do not think it merely fortuitous that his audience for this tale includes a woman, Arete, whose power to delay or speed his homecoming is specially emphasized by Athena (7.53–77).[33]

The framing devices and overall shape of the epic plot thus work to circumscribe the narrative power of its dangerous females, that is, those who threaten the *kleos* of its hero. Yet these circumscribing effects are by no means definitive: They are balanced by a number of openings in the narrative structure that allow, and to some extent invite, a less negative view of Helen and the Sirens.

In the first place, the epic narrator never puts his own authority, or that of his narrator-hero, behind the most damaging charges of Menelaos and Kirke. The account of the Wooden Horse that Odysseus hears from Demodokos, whose previous Trojan song he has praised for its accuracy (8.487–91), does not include the episode of Helen's treachery (8.499–520). In fact, Odysseus himself tells the story of the Wooden Horse to Achilles in the underworld, and there again Helen plays no part (11.523–32).[34] It is true that Helen's story receives no external validation either, but at least she and Menelaos are even on that score. Likewise, the description of the moldering bodies of the Sirens' victims is given by Kirke alone; Odysseus does not repeat it in his firsthand version of the encounter. Of course, it is unlikely that under the Sirens' spell he should have noticed these grisly details, but again a damning charge is left without confirmation. What is more, neither Helen nor the Sirens are punished, at least in the *Odyssey*, for their alleged treachery. This impunity is due, at least in part, to the quasi-divine status both seem to enjoy. Although the poet does not call them immortal, he implies as much: Helen, like Athena and the Muses, is the daughter of Zeus, and Menelaos will enjoy eternal life because he is her husband (4.561–69); the Sirens claim a breadth of knowledge that implies supernatural capacity. Both Helen and the Sirens, then, assume the privileges of divinity. Like the Muses, they also assume the authoritative stance that belongs to epic discourse, but they use the language of authority for purposes of their own. Their independence is suggested at both ends of the chain of command, so to speak, in their lack of divine male inspiration and in their refusal to speak through male bards.

They address male audiences, to be sure, and in this respect they do reproduce a central feature of epic performance, at least as portrayed in the *Odyssey*.[35] But instead of addressing groups of males *as* groups, in such a way as to reinforce the bonds among them (as a good bard does), they appeal seductively to individuals: Helen to Telemachos, the Sirens to Odysseus. By applying the model of female seduction to the act of narration, they make it their own, if only momentarily; the effect, Homer suggests, is irresistible.

Ann Bergren has argued that the notion of a female Muse can be seen as an "appropriation by the male of what he attributes to the female."[36] In a tradition that acknowledges no female bards, both the attribution of narrative power to one or more Muses and the claim to inspiration by these figures are masculine initiatives. I believe female readers of the *Odyssey* need to be aware that the epic evokes images of ostensible female power that in fact serve to reinforce a male-dominated gender system. But it is equally important for female readers to locate images that can elude or subvert this kind of co-optation.[37] I see the Homeric Sirens as one such image, precisely because in contrast to the Muses they are unaligned with any male authority, human or divine. They are potentially sexual, but narrative, not sex, is the true source of their power. Thus they can elude the assimilation of femaleness to "nature" and sexuality, for their language is impeccably that of culture. In the very act of containing and cutting short their song, the *Odyssey* poet implicitly acknowledges their power to take over his narrative and to substitute for it one of their own, which Odysseus himself is eager to hear.

In a recent study of Homeric poetics, Andrew Ford has argued that the Sirens' song must be cut short precisely because they are *like* the Muses, whose divine and complete knowledge must be simultaneously invoked—as the "ground" of epic discourse—and banished—because in its very completeness it threatens to overwhelm the individual poem.[38] "The text constantly makes us aware of other stories that cannot be told, other parts of the stories that are told, so that we feel there is a great exterior in which all is supported and fits together. . . . But this whole must always be put outside the text, for the text cannot at once contain it and rely on it as basis and ground." Paradoxically, in order to evoke a totality, the poem must exclude certain voices. In the epic genre, where plots are traditionally focalized by masculine heroes and narrators, it makes a kind of poetic sense that the excluded voice that guarantees wholeness should be feminine. Yet, as Ford wisely adds, the poet's evocation of excluded voices, however brief, is an opening that makes interpretation possible.[39] For me, it is this opening—this space in which a female voice claims the authority of an epic poet—that makes for the enduring power of the Sirens episode.

Notes

I am grateful to Marylin Arthur Katz, Beth Cohen, and the anonymous readers for their helpful comments on earlier drafts of this paper. I would like to dedicate the paper to the memory of A. K. Ramanujan, poet, scholar, and teacher.

1. See Buitron and Cohen, 1992, 14, 109–11.
2. Allen, 1917, 3: 218–19 (Book 12, lines 165–200). The total comes to forty-seven lines if Odysseus' introductory speech (12.154–64) is included and to sixty-three if Kirke's warning speech (12.39–54) is added.
3. See Schein, Chapter 2, this volume.
4. Ibid. Among other scholars who have taken related positions are Felson-Rubin, 1987 and 1993, and Murnaghan, 1986.
5. This approach is represented by, e.g., Roscher IV, 602–39; Buschor, 1944; and Page, 1973.
6. Pollard, 1965, 144.
7. Buitron and Cohen, 1992, 109.
8. Kahn, 1980, 121–34.
9. Compare Brilliant's observation that "the hybrid monster exemplifies the very fact of the transgression of boundaries" (Chapter 9, this volume).
10. An explicit comparison between a Muse and a Siren is first preserved in a fragment of the poet Alkman (frag. 30, Campbell, 1988, quoted by Aelius Aristides, *Orations* 28.51). In the modern critical literature, the comparison has been explored at length by Pucci (see n. 18, this chapter), and Kahn, 1980 and 1982. See also Segal, 1983, esp. 40; and Thalmann, 1984, 129 and 150. Buschor, 1944, also saw a resemblance between Muses and Sirens, but he did not explore the implications of this resemblance for the status of epic narrative.
11. This is not to deny the possibility, carefully outlined by Svenbro, 1976, 46–73, that the source of poetic authority that the Muse represents was understood quite differently by Hesiod and the poets of the Homeric tradition.

12. Daughters of Zeus: *Iliad* 2.491–92, 598; *Odyssey* 1.10, 8.488; *Theogony* 25, 29, etc. Associated with Apollo: *Iliad* 1.603–4; *Odyssey* 8.488; *Theogony* 94–95.

13. *Iliad* 1.601–4; *Theogony* 36–43.

14. In the case of Thamyris, they inflict a twofold punishment when the bard dares to rival their singing: He is physically maimed *and* deprived of his poetic gifts, which presumably he owed to the Muses in the first place (*Iliad* 2.599–600).

15. Although the *Odyssey* does not explicitly identify the Sirens as divine, their portrayal implies as much. Alkman's *Louvre Partheneion* (frag. 1.98, Davies, 1991), a seventh-century work, identifies the Sirens as goddesses.

16. *Hos tis aïdreiēi pelasēi kai phthongon akousēi / Seirēnōn, tōi d' ou ti gunē kai nēpia tekna/ oikade nostēsanti paristatai oude ganuntai* ("whoever approaches in ignorance and listens to the voice of the Sirens, that man's wife and infant children do not meet him coming home or celebrate his return") 12.41–43.

17. The dual is used at 12.52 (Kirke, quoted by Odysseus) and 167 (Odysseus' narrative). Elsewhere in the Homeric text, the Sirens are referred to in the plural. The notion that there were two Sirens may of course have been traditional (one sixth-century aryballos, plate 46, portrays two of them; see Neils, Chapter 10, this volume), but such a tradition might enhance the metaphoric potential of the dual number applied to them here.

18. This position has been most fully argued by Pucci, 1979; 1987, 209–13. See also Pucci 1977, 8–14, on Hesiod's portrayal of the Muses.

19. Muses in the plural: *Iliad* 1.604; 2.491, 594, and 598; 2.484 = 11.218 = 14.508 = 16.112. The exceptions are at 2.761 and at 1.1, where the Muse is addressed as *thea*—an important exception because it stands first and parallels the usage of the *Odyssey* proem. Singular Muse in the *Odyssey:* 1.1; 8.63, 73, 481, and 488; 24.62. Although the *Odyssey* poet never *invokes* Muses in the plural, he does portray Agamemnon as describing a threnody sung by the nine Muses at Achilles' funeral, 24.60.

20. Segal, 1983, 40.

21. Pucci, 1979. For alternative views of the relationship between the traditions represented by the monumental *Iliad* and *Odyssey*, see also Nagy, 1979; Redfield, 1973.

22. Noted by, e.g., Arthur, 1983, 98–99; Tyrrell and Brown, 1991, 20–21. Stehle, forthcoming, chapter 2, analyzes the subtle ways in which Alkman's *Louvre Partheneion* handles the paradox of the maiden choral performance as authorized public speech by a group whose gender should exclude them from such speech. An important element of this paradox seems to be the performers' denial of their own sexual attractiveness, which their performance is designed to display. Especially interesting in light of my own argument is the maidens' apparent claim that their age-mate Hagesichora does not sing as sweetly as the Sirens (frag. 1.96–98, Davies, 1991).

23. Noted by Schein, Chapter 2, this volume, who cites Motte, 1973. Gresseth, 1970, 208–9, cites similar examples and adds evidence for the (paradisiac) underworld associations of flowery *leimones*.

24. Schein, Chapter 2, this volume.

25. See Neils's account of their association with Erotes in vase paintings, Chapter 10, this volume. Their portrayal on mirrors and perfume vessels is also suggestive of erotic connotations.

26. It is ironic, in light of the contrasts cited here, that some later authors describe the Sirens as daughters of Melpomene, one of the Muses (cf. Apollodoros, *Library* 1.3.4). An alternative tradition (also preserved in Apollodoros, *Library* 1.7.10) makes the Sirens children of a mortal woman, Sterope, and the river god Acheloos.

27. The relationship of the Muses to their father, Zeus, is clearly meant to authorize their utterances; it should be compared to the similar relationship between Athena and Zeus, discussed by Murnaghan, Chapter 4, this volume.

28. The three exceptions are Helen in Book 4 (235–64), Arete in Book 11 (336–41), and Penelope when she addresses the assembled Suitors in Book 21 (68–79). Note that in other scenes involving Penelope and the Suitors, she ostensibly addresses herself to individuals among them (18.251–80; 21.311–19, 331–42). I count a total of thirteen female narrators whose direct speech to individual males is reported. These include Athena, Penelope, Eurykleia, Helen, Eidothea, Kalypso, Ino, Nausikaa, Kirke, Antikleia, the nymph Lampetie, Eumaios' Phoenician nurse, and the slave Melantho.

29. Murnaghan, Chapter 4, this volume, who basically shares this position, nonetheless points to a "hint of flirtatiousness in [Athena's] dealings with Odysseus."

30. In Nestor's tale of the aftermath of the Trojan War (3.135), treated at length in Clay, 1983.

31. E.g., Olson, 1989a; Katz, 1991, 75–76.

32. It should be noted that while Menelaos seeks to discredit Helen's story, he has apparently accepted a life with her that resembles the life of immortal ease Odysseus refused to share with Kalypso and Kirke (cf. also 4.561–70).

33. See Doherty, 1991.

34. For a fuller comparison of these versions, see Andersen, 1977.

35. See Doherty, 1992, for a fuller version of this argument.

36. Bergren, 1983, 71.

37. In light of the late-twentieth-century awareness of audiences and their role in the production of artistic meaning, it is especially unfortunate that so little evidence survives for the composition of early epic audiences. This problem extends to the "audiences" for visual representations of the Sirens, which must have been understood quite differently by different groups and individuals in the range of artists, purchasers, and users of the surviving objects. The sheer numbers of Siren images on a wide variety of

objects suggest the adaptability of the motif, and the fact that these objects included gems, amulets, and perfume bottles makes it unlikely that the Sirens were always imagined in purely negative terms. As Cohen writes of one such gem, "This siren's charms must have had some personal amuletic significance for her owner either in life or during the passage from life to death" (Buitron and Cohen, 1992, 127).

38. Ford, 1992, 86–87.

39. Ibid., 89.

6

Penelope as Moral Agent

Helene P. Foley

In his *Poetics*, Aristotle defines tragic character in relation to tragic choice. Character, Aristotle argues, reveals a *prohairesis* or a process of undertaking moral commitment in which a person chooses to act or to abstain from action in circumstances where the choice is not obvious (*Poetics* 1450b8–10).[1] The central moral decision on which the action of the *Odyssey* turns is Penelope's. She must decide whether to stay in Odysseus' house, continue to guard it, and wait for her husband's return or to marry one of the Suitors. Yet she must make this decision in ignorance of Odysseus' identity; that is, she does not know who the beggar is and hence whether Odysseus is alive or dead. Thus, as in Aristotle's exemplary tragedy *Oedipus Tyrannos*, Penelope's choice entails the tragic dilemma of a person faced with the need to act without critical knowledge of the circumstances.

A closer look at Aristotle's assumptions about women as moral agents, however, makes clear that one cannot generalize so easily from Oedipus to Penelope. In his *Politics* and *Ethics*, Aristotle defends the view, against his teacher, Plato, that women are by nature morally inferior to men. Woman's natural function is to reproduce the species and care for the daily needs of her household; man's is to live a life in the polis that offers him opportunities for rational activity, higher learning, leisure, and the exercise of the virtues suitable for political activities. Men are good absolutely, women are good for their function; women's virtues fit them to be ruled, men's to rule (*Eudemian Ethics* 7.1237a). A woman's capacity for moral deliberation is

93

without authority (*akuros; Politics* 1.5 1260a13), hence she benefits
from the protection and supervision of a *kurios* or guardian. Man, as a
naturally superior being, thus has a permanent constitutional rule
(*politikōs*) over the naturally inferior woman (*Politics* 1.5 1259b1–2).
As free citizens, women must be educated to be virtuous (*Politics* 1.5
1260b13–21). Both sexes have *sōphrosynē* or self-control, supple-
mented in the male by courage (a virtue largely useless in women) and
in the female by industrious habits, free from servility (*Rhetoric*
1.1361a).[2] Yet the virtues of women differ in kind and not in degree
from those of men (*Politics* 1.5 1260a21–24). Women have need only
of right opinion, not of a genuine practical wisdom. Aristotle thus
quotes with approval the popular view that "silence brings glory to
woman" (*Politics* 1.5 1260a32).

We should emphasize here that Aristotle's assumption that
women are fundamentally different as moral agents from men is not
idiosyncratic to himself but derives from popular Classical perceptions. Plato and some provocative passages from drama to the contrary, most Classical writers assume that any nonreligious public activity performed by a woman violates the silence, invisibility, and
moral dependence appropriate to a virtuous wife. Even in private life,
the wife's virtues entail obeying and serving the interests of her
spouse. Biologically, as is clear from both the work of Aristotle and the
Hippocratic medical texts, women's unstable bodies make it impossible to rely on their ability to make rational judgments in a consistent
and reliable fashion. Legally—and this is the most telling point—Attic
women were in most circumstances not permitted to undertake significant actions without the supervision of a *kurios* or guardian.[3]

Given his views, it is not surprising that female characters in
drama often—seemingly more often than male characters—violate
Aristotle's assumptions about what they should be like. According to
the *Poetics*, tragic characters should be good, traditional (or like),
consistent, and appropriate. To give just one example of deviance, it is
not appropriate for female characters to be manly or clever like Euripides' philosophical Melanippe.[4] The case of Melanippe makes clear
the depth of Aristotle's potential difficulties with female tragic figures,
for to eliminate manly or clever heroines would be to purge much of
Euripidēs, to say nothing of Aeschylus' brilliant and androgynous
Klytaimestra.[5]

Yet what about Penelope? To what degree does she meet Aristotle's standards for a serious (*spoudaios*) literary character undertaking a deliberate moral commitment? To what degree does the world of
the *Odyssey* prefigure popular Classical Athenian assumptions about

women as moral agents? In this chapter I will examine the complex interrelation between female moral capacity and female social role that conditions and is articulated in Penelope's critical choice, as well as speculate briefly on why the poem gives that central decision to a woman.

On the surface at least, the *Odyssey's* women *are* endowed with the same moral *capacities* as men. Both men and women are praised for *eidos*, physical appearance; *megethos*, stature; and *phrenas endon eisas*, a balanced capacity for thought and feeling within (18.249 of Penelope, 11.337 of Odysseus, etc.). The same formulas are used to describe the way that they reason about questions of strategy or moral dilemmas.[6] The *thumos* (heart) of both sexes can deliberate, be divided,[7] and then decide in a rational fashion that one alternative is better than another. Both can subdue emotion through reason or bring desire into line with rational goals. Both Penelope and Odysseus are singled out for their ability to be hard-hearted and enduring in the face of suffering. Homeric women are expected to display moral responsibility in their own sphere of the household and to enforce moral standards, such as those relating to hospitality, in the absence of their menfolk.

More important, both sexes can publicly demonstrate *aretē* (excellence or virtue) and achieve *kleos* (fame) for their actions, although they exercise their capacities for virtue in different contexts and achieve fame by different routes. Odysseus wins *kleos* for his skills in battle and counsel in the Trojan War (9.20, which includes his reputation for *dolos* (trickery); 16.241; see also 8.74), for his role as king (1.344; 4.726, 816), and ultimately for his journey and his revenge against the Suitors (implied by the *kleos* of Telemachos' journey, 1.95, 3.78, 13.415 and the *kleos* won by Orestes and others for revenge, 1.298; 3.204). Penelope wins praise for her *kleos aretēs* from the shade of the dead Agamemnon in Book 24 (196–97). Men will sing songs of praise for her because she remembered Odysseus (*hos eu memnēt' Oduseōs*, 195). Although Agamemnon means here to celebrate Penelope's chastity (198, *echephroni Pēnelopeiēi*; 194, *agathai phrenes*), the explicit emphasis on her remembering Odysseus has, as we shall see, far larger implications in the poem.[8]

In Book 2, 116–28, the Suitor Antinoos argues that Penelope knows in her *thumos* (heart) that Athena endowed her with the knowledge of beautiful works (weaving), *phrenas esthlas* (good sense), and *kerdea* (clever counsels) such as no other Achaean woman had before—not Tyro, Alkmene, or Mykene. No other woman was capable of *homoia noēmata* (similar ideas). For this, says Antinoos, she is at this very moment winning *kleos*. As the Suitor Eurymachos later adds, the Suitors thus sensibly compete for Penelope on account of her *aretē* instead of marrying other women (2.205–7). Penelope herself thinks that she will win *kleos* or good report for her correct treatment of guests, and she chastises Telemachos for permitting the mistreatment of the beggar Odysseus (18.215–25). As she says at 19.325–26 to Odysseus, disguised as a beggar, "How shall you know if I excel other women in mind (*noos*) and thoughtful good sense (*epiphrona mētin*)," if a beggar sits unwashed in the halls? In praising men for their good sense (19.349–52) or in chastising the Suitors for their violation of hospitality or their mode of wooing in Odysseus' house (16.409–33, 21.331–33), Penelope repeatedly shows that she shares the value system of her men (see also the chastising of the immoral maidservant, Melantho, 19.91–95). In recognition of her capacity for moral responsibility, Odysseus entrusted the care of his household, his son, and his parents to Penelope on his departure for Troy (18.266).[9] Most important, in Odysseus' mind the ideal couple shares the same mental outlook (6.180–85). *Homophrosynē* (like-mindedness) is the quality most to be desired in a marriage. A husband and wife *homophroneonte noēmasin* (like-minded in their thoughts) are a grief to foes and a delight to well-wishers.

Although women in the *Odyssey* (even Klytaimestra and Helen) are generally viewed as ethically responsible for their actions,[10] they do not have the same degree of moral autonomy and self-sufficient virtue as men. All characters in Homer are subject to social constraints and divine intervention. Yet although women's ethical capacities are apparently the same, they are notably less free to ignore moral pressures from others or to define themselves and to act apart from their families, and there are many fewer areas in which they can make an independent show of virtue.[11] Penelope's beauty and *aretē*, she twice repeats, were destroyed on Odysseus' departure for Troy (18.251–53, 19.24–26; see also 18.180–81). Similarly, Zeus takes away half the *aretē* of a man on the day of his slavery (17.320–22). If Odysseus were to return, Penelope's *kleos* would, she says, be greater and better, and she would give the stranger Theoklymenos or the disguised Odysseus many gifts (17.163–65; 19.309–11; Helen gives them in the presence of Menelaos). In short, Penelope is not fully herself without her husband. A woman must also defer to the master of her household. In Book 1 (345–59), for example, Telemachos for the first time attempts to claim authority (*kratos*) over his house and tells Penelope to leave the choice of themes for song at the banquet to himself. Although the theme of the Achaeans' return from Troy is wounding to Penelope, Telemachos finds it appropriate. Penelope should go within; speech will now be a care to men. The amazed Penelope returns in silence to her quarters and lays the wise saying of her son to her heart. Virtually the same thing happens when Telemachos reclaims Odysseus' bow from Penelope in Book 21 (343–53).

Finally, the poem continually expresses doubt that even wives of basically good character, when unsupervised by a husband or his surrogate, will make decisions in the interests of their marital family. Before Penelope makes her decision in Book 19, both Helen and Klytaimestra have served as examples of what happens when wives make decisions in the absence of their husbands; in Book 15 (20–23), when Athena appears in a dream to Telemachos, she warns Telemachos about the *thumos* in the breast of a woman. She tends to forget her previous marriage and children when she weds another (yet Penelope asserts at 19.581 that this will never be the case with herself). Overall, women are vulnerable to seduction in the absence of their husbands and endowed with deceptive intelligence that can be used to destroy them if they decide on another man.

As the recent and formidable studies of Murnaghan, Winkler, Felson-Rubin, and Katz, among others, have argued, the narrative context in which Penelope acts has made both her decision to establish the contest for her hand and her behavior leading up to that decision appear ambivalent, opaque, and/or contradictory to critics from antiquity on.[12] The books of Katz and Rubin make clear that these problems deserve a book-length discussion; it is neither possible nor desirable for me to go over the same ground in detail once more in this essay. Instead, I shall take the position, at the risk of oversimplification, that although the text does not give us full access to Penelope's thoughts and feelings, her well-articulated dilemma and her stated reasons for establishing the contest make it possible to judge and make ethical sense of her decision. The first two books of the poem examine Penelope's dilemma from the perspective of the goddess Athena disguised as Mentes, the Suitors, and Telemachos. Books 18 and 19 at last give us Penelope's own views on the issue. Finally, Penelope reluctantly makes a decision to set up the contest of the bow for her hand, ironically in the presence of Odysseus disguised as a beggar. My discussion will stress the moment at which Penelope chooses to act, to establish the contest for the bow.[13]

Because we see her situation first through the eyes of others, the text emphasizes from the start the social constraints that Penelope faces. In Book 1 (274–78), Athena, disguised as Mentes, gives advice to Telemachos. He should let the Suitors depart. If Penelope's *thumos* bids her marry, let her go back to the halls of her powerful father. Her family will prepare a feast and make ready gifts that should go with a *philē pais* (beloved daughter). Shortly afterwards, Athena offers a second piece of advice on the same issue. She urges Telemachos to find out if Odysseus is dead. If he is, Telemachos should heap up a mound for his father, perform over it appropriate funeral rites, and give his mother to a husband (1.289–92). While Odysseus lives, Athena advises Telemachos to let Penelope choose to return to her father's house and to remarry. If he is dead, she advises Telemachos to act for her.

In Book 2 (50–54), Telemachos complains to the assembled Ithacans that the Suitors beset an unwilling Penelope with their wooing and shrink from going to her father, Ikarios, so that he might dower her (give her *hedna*) and give her to whomever he wishes.[14] Not so, replies Antinoos the Suitor. Penelope, not the Achaeans, is to blame in this case, for she knows wiles beyond others and has been deceiving the Suitors for almost four years (85–110). Send her back to her father, he advises Telemachos, and command (*anōchthi*) her to marry whom her father bids and whoever is pleasing to her. Penelope knows, Antinoos says, how superior she is to other women. And the *noos* (intelligence) that the gods are putting in her breast will bring great *kleos* to her, but want of livelihood to Telemachos. Thus, Antinoos concludes, the Suitors will wait until Penelope marries the Suitor whom she wishes (2.113–14, 116–28). Telemachos replies that he will not thrust from the house the mother who bore and reared him. If he willingly (*hekōn*) sent his mother away, he would have to pay back her dowry and suffer retribution from her father, Ikarios; his mother would invoke the hateful Erinyes (spirits of revenge) on her departure; and there would be *nemesis* (moral disapproval) from men (2.130–37). Eurymachos, another Suitor, then again urges Telemachos to command (*anōgetō*) his mother to return to her father for marriage and dowry. Until then, the Suitors will compete for her on account of her *aretē* (2.195–97). Telemachos, defeated, asks for a ship. If he finds his father is dead, he will give his mother to a husband (198–223). In Book 15 (16–23), Athena warns Telemachos in a dream that Penelope's father and brothers bid (*kelontai*) her wed Eurymachos, who surpasses the other Suitors with his gifts and now increases them. Athena advises Telemachos to look to his possessions because Penelope may decide to marry and take Telemachos' goods with her.[15] (This dream does not correspond to what the audience hears elsewhere about Penelope in Telemachos' absence.) In Book 20 (341–44), Telemachos reiterates to the Suitors the point he made in

Book 2. Insisting that Odysseus is now dead (although he now knows that he is not), he bids (*keleuō*) Penelope marry whomever she wishes and offers to provide a dowry, but is ashamed to force her to depart unwillingly from the house.[16]

The text thus identifies the factors conditioning Penelope's decision in a somewhat confusing fashion. Sometimes the choice to remarry is said to be Penelope's alone; sometimes it lies in the hands of her son or father; sometimes the decision is a joint one in which Penelope will decide in conjunction with her son or father. After his return to Ithaka, Telemachos is willing to play a more active role by urging Penelope to remarry if Odysseus is dead, but he is consistently unwilling, even though the delay continually threatens first his livelihood and then his life, to force her to leave the house and remarry; Odysseus' parting instructions to Penelope reported at 18.257–70 also place the choice to remarry in Penelope's hands.

I am avoiding the use of the later term *kurios* or guardian to describe the authority male figures have over women in this context because these passages raise considerable doubt about the exact parameters involved in male guardianship of a wife in the *Odyssey*.[17] Fathers generally arrange first marriages for their virgin daughters in Homeric epic, although even here (as in the case of Helen and her suitors) the daughter's preference may play a role; this is an option in Penelope's case. Yet Telemachos suggests that a wife or widow can invoke strong sanctions against being forced to remarry against her will. Clearly, Penelope cannot create the economic conditions of a proper marriage, like the preparation of a wedding feast or the presentation of a dowry; and male relatives can play a major role in urging her to make a choice, even a particular choice. So her decision is not fully her own. Nevertheless, despite minor inconsistencies, it appears that her preference plays an essential role in the process, a role sufficiently important that she can delay the marriage and even incur from the Suitors a mixture of public calumny and grudging praise for her crafty behavior. After Book 2, because no one claims the authority to force her to remarry, Penelope is apparently left free to choose if and when she will do so. In Book 19, she herself does (after acquiring the approval of Odysseus in disguise) make the decision to set up the bow contest for her hand. Thus the *Odyssey* gives its audience the opportunity to observe a mature female moral agent making a critical and autonomous ethical decision.

When the poem returns to the issue of Penelope's marriage in Books 18 and 19, the focus is on Penelope, and we discover that she views her dilemma more or less in the fashion that Telemachos has reported to Eumaios and Odysseus in Book 16 (73–77). Here Telemachos says that Penelope's heart is divided over whether to stay with him and respect her husband's bed and the voice of the people or to follow the best of the Achaeans who offers the most gifts of wooing.

In Book 18 (257–70) Penelope reports to the Suitors, Telemachos, and the disguised Odysseus on Odysseus' parting instructions to her as he left for Troy. Odysseus put his right hand on her wrist, in a gesture that echoes the initial appropriation of a bride by a husband in marriage. This same gesture appears on the fifth-century Melian relief in the Metropolitan Museum (plate 20), where Odysseus, disguised as a beggar, takes the wrist of the mourning Penelope. Uncertain as to whether he would survive the war, Odysseus entrusted the care of the household to her and bid her wed whomever she might wish and leave when her son is bearded. Penelope asserts that all that Odysseus predicted is being brought to pass. She thus represents the timing of her remarriage as powerfully conditioned by Odysseus' parting instructions.[18]

Before the Suitors, whom she then provokes into offering new gifts of wooing, Penelope mentions only one reason why she must soon remarry. In Book 19.124–61, Penelope describes her dilemma more fully to the disguised Odysseus. The Suitors have discovered her deception with the web; she can no longer unweave each night the shroud she was weaving for Odysseus' father, Laertes. Now she cannot escape marriage or devise a new trick; her parents press her to act, her son frets, the Suitors are devouring Telemachos' livelihood, and Telemachos is a man. Later in Book 19 (524–34), Penelope gives the beggar a precise statement of her moral quandry. She says that her heart is divided over whether to stay by her son, guard the house, revere the bed of her husband, and respect public opinion (for this important influence, see also 16.75 and 23.149–51) or to marry (literally, follow a husband). Her child, who previously would not permit her to marry, is now grown and vexed over his loss of livelihood. She then tells Odysseus about a dream in which her pet geese are slain by an eagle who goes on to say that he is Odysseus (19.535–53). Odysseus affirms the dream. Penelope doubts his interpretation; in her view the dream was a false one. But, she laments, the day is coming that will divide her from the house of Odysseus and she decides to appoint the contest for her hand with the bow. Later, when she gets the bow from the storeroom, she weeps (20.55–60). She also wishes to die and dreams of Odysseus as he looked when he left for Troy (20.61–90; see also 18.202–5). Although she clearly regrets her decision to remarry,

Telemachos' maturity and the threat to both his livelihood and his life make it imperative for Penelope to act.

In Book 19, then, Penelope gradually arrives at the point where she is willing to make a (at least in her own view) socially responsible decision to move toward remarriage—in contrast to expectations that the poem generates about the behavior of wives in the absence of their husbands, who generally surrender to seduction.[19] In full recognition of the suffering it will bring her, she moves to subordinate her own desires to the needs of her son and the parting instructions of her husband. Yet critics have argued that because Penelope has received repeated signs that Odysseus' return is imminent, her decision to remarry is both ill-timed and an inadvertent betrayal of her husband, who is in fact alive and present without her knowledge.[20] Her behavior has also been categorized as intuitive, irrational, passive, contradictory, indicative of a moral collapse, and even unintelligent.[21] Nevertheless, it should be stressed again that critics' questions about the decision have, often by their own admission, arisen above all from the narrative context in which her choice is made.

In my concern with the nature of Penelope's moral choice, I wish to stress the following points. First, she is facing a dilemma that she defines clearly and rationally. Penelope's moral stance is in itself, as both the poem and Aristotle make clear, intelligible, commendable, and appropriate to her role as wife. As in Aristotle's *Oikonomika* and *Politics*, the Homeric wife's virtue apparently consists in her ability to obey with intelligence and self-control the instructions of her husband, even when he is absent. Indeed, the pseudo-Aristotelian *Oikonomika* 3.1 not only asserts that Penelope fits the wifely ideal that has just been defined in these terms but also adds that she is especially to be commended for proving herself faithful (like Alkestis) to her husband in adverse circumstances. The *Odyssey* repeatedly acknowledges Penelope's virtue and casts no *explicit* doubts on her action. Even Agamemnon in the underworld of Book 11 (444–46) thinks Penelope is an exception to the general danger of women's infidelity; Odysseus' mother (11.177–79) and Athena (13.379–81) earlier affirm her fidelity; at 20.33–35, shortly after Penelope's decision, Athena again affirms the worth of Odysseus' wife and child. Finally, the shade of Agamemnon praises Penelope in Book 24. Later Greek tradition simply makes Penelope the paradigm of the virtuous wife. The disguised Odysseus twice endorses Penelope's decision to abandon her customary retirement and approach the Suitors. In Book 18 he approves Penelope's showing herself to the Suitors (18.281–83) and winning wedding gifts while her mind intended other things (see overall 18.158–303; also 2.87–92 and 13.379–81, where Antinoos and Athena interpret her intentions in other contexts in the same terms);[22] in Book 19 he approves her choice for the contest for her hand.[23] Given Telemachos' situation and Odysseus' instructions reported by Penelope in Book 19, both to remarry and not to remarry are potentially acts of moral fidelity to Odysseus.[24] Because of her ignorance of both Odysseus' identity and his fate, the critical problem for Penelope is the timing of the decision, not the decision to remarry itself.[25] Let us turn briefly, then, to the issue of timing and circumstances.

Penelope could not in good conscience have continued to delay her remarriage much longer. After Telemachos returns from his journey and recognizes Odysseus, he demonstrates his ability to take charge of the household for the first time; pretending he thinks that Odysseus is dead, he takes a more active role in encouraging Penelope to remarry (see esp. 19.159–61, 530–34; 20.339–44); at the same time, he is under threat from the Suitors. In Book 19, where she begins to move explicitly toward the decision to remarry, Penelope consistently expresses pessimism about Odysseus' Return and rejects the signs and dreams that presage it (19.257–60, 313–16, 560–68; 20.87–90; 23.59–68).[26] Even when she has reliable evidence from Eurykleia of Odysseus' Return in Book 23, Penelope refuses to recognize her husband until she has tested his knowledge of their bed. Here she apologizes to Odysseus for her insistence on testing to the last.[27] She was always afraid, she tells him, lest some man would come and beguile her with his words, for there are many men who plan such evils (23.215–17). Earlier she remarks to the disguised Odysseus in a similar vein that she pays no attention to strangers, suppliants, and heralds (19.134–35). The swineherd Eumaios, who apparently receives a positive appraisal for being equally cautious, tells us in Book 14 that Penelope repeatedly questions beggars, but that no wanderer with reports about Odysseus could persuade his wife and son (122–28). In a poem that registers with admiration an equal wariness in Odysseus himself (see especially 13.330–38), is Penelope's skepticism—a vigilance that logically increases as the temptation to give way to hope becomes more pressing—really as contradictory as many critics would have it?[28] Or does the timing of Penelope's choice seems questionable only from the perspective of a privileged access to the truth?

In my view Odysseus' approval of Penelope's choice to establish the contest is perfectly intelligible. Logistically, it creates the opportunity (heretofore missing) for him to take on the Suitors, and it is a contest in which he knows he has a chance of success. It has been argued that the plot simply demands from Odysseus a reaction that does not account for the full complexities of the situation.[29] Yet from an ethical perspective, in a context where Odysseus has chosen to test his wife rather than revealing his identity, he observes her following his own previous instructions (reported by Penelope in his presence) and maintaining a heroic and crafty defense against seductive evidence to hope and delay. From this perspective, Penelope's choice is less dubious or irrational than tragic (by Aristotle's standards): the dilemma of a good person attempting to act correctly without full and, in this case, critical knowledge of the circumstances (Odysseus' identity and fate). As in tragedy, the consequences of both alternatives are unavoidably at least partially and potentially negative.[30] For Aristotle, tragic irony of the kind created in this scene appropriately evokes pity and fear.[31] One could even argue that *it is precisely by proposing to establish the contest for her hand with such evident regret that Penelope passes the test of the faithful wife.*

Telemachos, complaining that his house is overrun with enemies who waste his livelihood, remarks that his mother neither refuses hateful marriage nor is able to make an end (16.121–28). The poem might have rescued Penelope from a decision by having Odysseus return and dispose of the Suitors while she still delayed, or it could have staged an earlier recognition between husband and wife (what the Suitor Amphimedon imagines actually occurred in Book 24.120– 90). Yet in my view Penelope's fidelity to Odysseus would be far less effectively demonstrated if the poem had simply taken the painful choice out of her hands. After the recognition in Book 23, Penelope raises the puzzling exemplum of Helen in relation to herself; it is certainly possible to interpret this exemplum as a recognition by Penelope that she inadvertently flirted with adultery in setting up the contest of the bow.[32] And public opinion has apparently always been on the side of waiting, although the public is neither privy to the complex events within the palace nor able to defend Telemachos. Insofar as the text does endow Penelope with desire (e.g., her sudden urge—produced by Athena and resisted by Penelope—to show herself to the Suitors in Book 18) and ambivalence (her weeping over the geese slaughtered by the eagle Odysseus in her dream in Book 19) and offers general warnings about women's vulnerability to seduction, Penelope's acceptance of the less palatable choice in Book 19 demonstrates—however ironic the scene, given the audience's knowledge of the truth—a greater moral fidelity to her spouse.[33]

Finally, although Penelope's distress makes it clear that she views the contest with the bow as the critical step on a path toward remarriage, the narrative indicates that her choice of a contest of skill and strength leaves open, in a fashion characteristic of Penelope, several possibilities. The Suitors may demonstrate that none of them is the equal of Odysseus; although Penelope has put her fate into male hands by establishing the contest, she has at least tried to ensure that the victor will be like her former husband. The contest with the bow has the potential to serve, like the web, as a tricky device to delay the remarriage. The text has led us to expect that Penelope would choose to marry the Suitor who offered the most gifts of wooing, as her family advised; the surprise choice of the contest may thus suggest that Penelope has this in mind. If all the signs and portents prove reliable, Odysseus will return and Penelope will not have to abide by the consequences of her choice. The beggar insists that Odysseus himself will be there before the Suitors have shot the arrow through the iron (23.585–87), and Penelope acknowledges, even after her choice, how pleasurable this outcome would be to her (23.587–90). In addition, the audience knows at the time Penelope makes her decision that she will be rescued from her suffering (and hence that it will have no negative consequences).

The *Odyssey* ultimately locates significant action within a social context that threatens to destroy the household of Odysseus from many angles. Ithaka does not readily submit to the returning Odysseus' authority. Odysseus' men have been destroyed during the journey home in large part over their refusal to listen to and obey Odysseus; the Suitors persistently violate the laws of hospitality. Both groups submit too readily to their appetites. Telemachos cannot imitate Orestes in avenging his father, and he could not in Book 2 mobilize public opinion for his just cause in any effective fashion; Odysseus' subjects seem to have forgotten his paternal form of kingship, his fairness and gentleness. Even when the Suitors recall Odysseus' generous leadership, it has no effect on their actions. At 16.442–44, for example, Eurymachos recalls Odysseus' hospitality to himself as a child and promises to protect Telemachos for this reason, but he is lying. At 16.424–33 Penelope reminds Antinoos, to no effect, of how Odysseus saved his father's house (see also 4.687–95, where Penelope chastises Medon, and by extension the Suitors, for not remembering Odysseus as king). The poem predicates survival on intelligence and social cooperation within the family group. Even Odysseus cannot achieve his Return without his son, wife, and servants. In making the action turn on Penelope's decision, the poem seems to privilege and celebrate the importance and even the heroism of social responsibility in a moral agent, as well as the contingencies that make taking moral responsibility problematic.[34] In Penelope's domestic world on Ithaka, there is no legitimate room either for the wrath, withdrawal, or honor from Zeus alone temporarily espoused by Achilles in the *Iliad* or for the freely chosen immortal obscurity offered by Kalypso to Odysseus.[35] The forces driving her to remarry leave little place for self-interest or for the nearly godlike freedom to shape a human destiny offered to the two Homeric heroes. She can only attempt to serve her son's interests and to obey her husband's parting instructions. The potentially notorious *kleos* Penelope won during the period of wooing, which threatened to destroy Telemachos' livelihood, becomes the permanent *kleos* won by her devotion to her husband, a *kleos* that now enhances the household of Odysseus. (See her point that *kleos* can be achieved by being *amumōn*, blameless, at 19.333.)

A poem that urges the value of conformity to certain basic social norms like hospitality in an Ithaka represented as either indifferent to them or afraid to act on them needs to make its case in a subtle fashion. As in later Greek literature, the *Odyssey* deploys to its advantage a female figure, whom no listener could imagine escaping from social encumbrance without great damage to her family and to the reputation of all women (see *Odyssey* 24.199–202). Penelope's sophisticated moral choice thus forms a key part of the *Odyssey*'s emphasis on ethical norms such as justice and on the quieter values that promote social cohesion. In Book 19, the disguised Odysseus compares Penelope to a king whose benevolence brings fertility and order to his kingdom. I suggest that Penelope's ethical behavior in part prefigures that of the restored Ithaka in a context where the paternal king Odysseus cannot as yet display his full character as leader. As was mentioned earlier, in Book 24 Penelope is awarded *kleos* in part for remembering her husband (*hos eu memnēt' Oduseos*, 195); she elsewhere insists that even if she remarries she will, unlike other women who tend to forget the previous marriage and children (15.20–23), remember Odysseus' house in her dreams (19.581). In remembering Odysseus and reminding others to conform to the standards that he once enforced—and we should recall how important a theme memory is in the poem as a whole—the beleaguered Penelope continues to live by the standards of that vanished kingdom, and through her actions we can begin to glimpse what it might be. The reestablishing of order in the household—a smaller institution in which roles and responsibilities are relatively well defined—can be symbolically extended to the fragmented public arena. The poem can also stress through Penelope the heroism of social responsibility without compromising to the same degree the greater autonomy of its hero, Odysseus. Odysseus' ethical responsibilities as king are in partial conflict with his ambitions to win fame and to protect his household as hero and avenger, roles that involve in each case a dramatic destruction of his male subjects. Penelope's choice allows the returning Odysseus to retain both the heroism he won as an individual for his journey and his revenge and his future fame as a just and benevolent king.

When major Homeric characters deliberate, reasoning generally provides the basis for a course of action to be taken in a specific case. In the majority of cases, the choice to be made is narrowly strategic: how best to survive in a situation of war or danger, and how best to win a desired goal (e.g., honor).[36] The most elaborate decision of this kind is faced by Odysseus at the beginning of Book 20. First, he debates whether to punish the unfaithful maidservants immediately or to delay the punishment to a more strategic moment; then he turns to worrying over how to punish the Suitors or to escape from the consequences if he does kill them. Sometimes, although rarely in the *Odyssey*, gods intervene to influence the choice.[37] Odysseus' choice to leave Kalypso and Achilles' choice about whether to return to battle are unusual because the hero has already been told the major outlines of his fate. Penelope's critical and elaborated choice has been incomprehensibly neglected in the general literature on Homeric decision making.[38] Penelope makes a fully conscious and autonomous decision that entails rejecting hope and desire for obedience to social responsibilities; there is no question of divine intervention in the critical moments in 19 (or 23; in 18 Athena intervenes, and Penelope resists).[39] Certainly, the question of contingency is notably operational in this instance. Indeed, if I am correct, Penelope's decision best prefigures those singled out by Aristotle as particularly effective on the tragic stage and thus gives an as-yet-unrecognized depth to Homeric philosophy.[40] Most important, by forcing Penelope to make a choice so conditioned by both critical responsibilities and uncertainties, the epic takes a leap into a complex moral territory that it normally avoids (Achilles' complex decision in *Iliad* 9 is a very different matter).[41]

In my discussion, I have also tried to emphasize the ways in which the *Odyssey* defines and makes use of subtle differences between men and women as moral agents. Even when men and women share the same values and moral capacities and deliberate about ethical issues in the same fashion, as they do here, they act under different constraints and with different priorities. Contemporary feminists have also begun to try to understand such moral differences in a modern context, and this debate served as a catalyst for this paper. The sociologist Carol Gilligan, for example, has argued for the validity of what she calls a different moral voice. For Gilligan, moral problems often arise for women "from conflicting responsibilities rather than from competing rights."[42] "The morality of rights" often adopted by men "differs from" this "morality of responsibility in its emphasis on separation rather than connection, in its consideration of the individual rather than the relationship as primary."[43] As moral agents, women tend toward self-sacrifice and are, in Gilligan's view, often "suspended in a paralysis of initiative."[44] No Homeric character deliberates in terms of competing rights in the modern sense, and decisions by Homeric male as well as female characters are always heavily determined by communal standards. Moreover, as a result of the formulaic nature of oral epic, all characters tend to deliberate about moral issues in the same terms. Although I agree with recent critics of Snell such as Williams that Homeric characters are convincing moral agents, they are not ethical individuals in a post-Kantian sense.[45] Hence, even if her controversial formulation of the relation between gender and ethics proved a reliable basis for discussion of the modern context,[46] Gilligan's distinctions, to which I cannot do justice here, are not applicable in any simple sense to the *Odyssey*.

Nevertheless, the *Odyssey* makes important distinctions about male and female moral agents that correspond to some degree with— even while they also deviate from—those established by Gilligan. Relatively speaking, for example, Penelope operates more fully than any male character in the poem within a web of relationships and responsibilities from which she neither can nor wishes to withdraw. This is not simply the result of a distinction between public and private worlds because in the household of a king no such clear boundaries can be consistently drawn. Penelope's actions can affect and be celebrated by the world beyond her household and thus have public implications, yet her choices, unlike those of a male hero, are limited to defending her present household and those within it or commiting herself to follow another husband. Sex roles, then, are critical to defining gender differences in moral agency in this poem. Penelope makes a choice to sacrifice her own desires in establishing the contest with the bow, and she is placed in a paralyzing position in which she can take no action that is without negative consequences. Positive actions by women in Greek literature (whether virgins or wives like Alkestis) typically involve such sacrifice and self control. Penelope is apparently the only character in either of the two Homeric epics who faces a choice between two responsibilities to others, and it may be significant that she is never, like the male heroes, permitted an ethical soliloquy, but always debates her alternatives in dialogue with other characters. There are no discussions comparable to those about Penelope's remarriage in *Odyssey* 2 over whether a male agent has or should have the autonomy to make a critical decision. Similarly, Klytaimestra's betrayal of Agamemnon is said in *Iliad* 24 to tarnish the reputation of *all* women, even those who, like Penelope, act appropriately (*kai hē k'euergos eēisin,* 199–202); the *kleos* of a Homeric hero does not depend in part on the presence or actions of another person, as does Penelope's (17.163–65, 19.309–11). Penelope wins *kleos* as wife, as a person powerless to act except in relation to another, not as a powerful warrior-leader defending his reputation.

Nevertheless, the particular limits under which a female agent in Homer is ideally meant to operate make giving Penelope moral autonomy in this instance an attractive opportunity to the *Odyssey* poet.[47] On the one hand, her social role makes it dangerous for a woman to claim full moral autonomy. Furthermore, feminization, or a breakdown in gender boundaries, is a fate repeatedly feared by the typical male hero; warriors taunt their opponents by associating them with women; the bodies of male heroes, lying helpless and without armor on the battlefield, are viewed as feminized;[48] Hektor in *Iliad* 6 insists on sex-role differences between men and women as a defense against Andromache's plea that he adopt a more defensive role in the battle (490–93). On the other hand, choices made from a marginal, relatively powerless position can also serve to set a new moral direction for the dominant male agents of Homeric poetry.[49] Because Penelope shares Odysseus' values and is both constrained and willing in a situation of hopeless uncertainty to sacrifice her own needs for the benefit of others, her female difference contributes to rather than undermines the social order. Indeed, this willingness to abide by the social standards of her world ultimately separates her from Odysseus' disruptive enemies, the Suitors, and makes her the figure for a future order in which respect for such standards will be the basis for a community united under the leadership of her husband. Insofar as tragic choices of the kind identified and praised by Aristotle are symptomatic of a social world in which obligations to promote civic welfare have acquired a greater ideological interest and resonance, it is not surprising that the *Odyssey*'s most nearly tragic choice is made by a character whose social role is defined so pointedly in terms of responsibilities.

Notes

A portion of this essay was presented at Vassar College, in spring 1992. I wish to thank the audiences at Bard, at Vassar, and at a conference on Women in Antiquity in St. Hilda's College, Oxford, in September 1993, as well as Richard Seaford and Laura Slatkin, for their comments on an earlier draft.

1. Here I accept the view of Chamberlain, 1984, that *prohairesis* entails a process of choosing a course of action and sustaining commitment to that course of action. Perception (*aisthēsis*), reason (*dianoia* or *nous*), and desire (*orexis*) play roles in the process.

2. At *Politics* 1.5 1260a21–24 Aristotle says that the *sōphrosynē* of men and women differs, and that women need courage only for obedience.

3. For a recent discussion of the legal position of Attic women, see Just, 1991.

4. Melanippe's speech seems to have contained a knowledge of science and philosophy inappropriate for a woman (*Poetics* 15.8–9, 1454a). Apparently Aristotle disapproves of behavior in a tragic character that he would have disapproved and/or found to lack verisimilitude in a real woman.

5. I address these issues in tragedy in a forthcoming paper.

6. One exception, addressed later in this chapter, is that Penelope does not have any moral soliloquies. See Russo, 1968, 280–94 on the way that the *Odyssey*'s typical scenes of deliberation depart in certain respects from those in the *Iliad*; in particular, decisions in the *Odyssey* are only exceptionally resolved by divine intervention.

7. See, e.g., 16.73 and 19.524 of Penelope, 9.299–306 and 20.9–13 of Odysseus.

8. See further Schein, Chapter 2, this volume.

9. It is also said that Odysseus left Mentor to oversee his *oikos* (2.226), but Mentor has apparently not exercised whatever authority he may have in this circumstance. As the assembly in Book 2 makes clear, the community is in general helpless to oppose the Suitors.

10. For a discussion, see Katz, 1991, on both Klytaimestra and Helen.

11. Adkins, 1960, 37, remarks that *aretē* in Homeric women is defined by men and entails the "quiet" or cooperative virtues. Because they are not called on to defend the household, they do not need competitive virtues. "As a result, Homeric women may be effectively censured for actions which Homeric heroes have a strong claim to be allowed to perform." The women of the *Odyssey* are self-conscious about such public opinion. Nausikaa seeks to compromise between her social obligations to the shipwrecked Odysseus and her reputation; she would chastise an unwed girl who consorted with men (6.286). Public opinion is a factor in Penelope's decision concerning remarriage (16.75; 19.527), and the people criticize her when they think she has chosen to do so (23.149–51).

12. Murnaghan, 1986, 1987; Winkler, 1990; Felson-Rubin, 1987, 1993; and Katz, 1991. See further, Schein, Chapter 2, this volume. In this essay I shall, except for a few brief notes on critical issues, refer the reader to extensive discussion of these questions in Katz and Felson-Rubin, 1993. My own focus on Penelope as a moral agent leads me to adopt a different interpretation of Penelope's decision to establish the contest of the bow from that of these recent critics.

13. As was said earlier, by Aristotelian standards at least, character (*ēthos*) reveals *prohairesis*, the sort of thing a person avoids in circumstances where the choice (and the resulting commitment to carry through on the choice) is not obvious; speeches in which the speaker does not commit him or herself or avoid something convey no character (*Poetics* 1450b8–10).

14. Recent discussion has made clear that the word *dowry* may be misleading in a Homeric context. What is important is that at marriage gifts were exchanged among the men aiming to marry or to give in marriage a particular woman. See with full earlier bibliography Morris, 1986; and Leduc, 1992.

15. For further discussion of this passage, see Murnaghan, Chapter 4, this volume.

16. This last speech comes after Penelope has decided on the contest, but it is clear from what Penelope says in Book 19 that Telemachos has made similar statements to her earlier.

17. For further discussion, see Finley, 1955; Lacey, 1966; Vernant, 1980; Mossé, 1981; Morris, 1986; and Katz, 1991.

18. Doherty, Chapter 5, this volume, stresses the unreliability of female narrators in the *Odyssey*, but here Penelope's story is told before the teller, and he does not question it.

19. See above all Helen, Klytaimestra, and the behavior of the unfaithful maidservants.

20. See Katz, 1991, 93–113, for a summary of previous views.

21. Those critics who view Penelope as unintelligent think that she ought to have recognized Odysseus. (I am here rejecting the views of critics like Harsh, 1950, and Winkler, 1990, who argue ingeniously that Penelope has recognized Odysseus.) Critics such as Amory, 1963, and Russo, 1982, who think that Penelope has subconsciously recognized Odysseus, view her as a positive example of feminine intuition. Those who view her as irrational object to her resistance to the signs indicating an imminent return for Odysseus. For a full summary of earlier views, see Katz, 1991; Murnaghan, 1987; and Felson-Rubin, 1993. These last three critics, in different ways, view the constraints of the narrative as responsible for Penelope's multivalence in the eyes of the reader. I agree with Katz, 92–93, that the audience's knowledge of Penelope's moral dilemma as reported by Telemachos in Book 16 helps to give coherence to the scene in Book 18. Penelope has no character beyond what the poem gives her, hence we cannot fill in the gaps in her motivation. Yet a divided self can still in a strictly limited sense be psychologically and

characterologically coherent, and the narrative has established the terms by which an audience—particularly an audience whose expectations are shaped by the conventions of oral narrative—can and (despite textual ambiguities) inevitably will construct a plausible agent from Penelope (for this position, see Felson-Rubin, 1993).

22. Does the text at the same time represent Odysseus as repeatedly deceived by Penelope? In Book 18, it is clear, as critics have pointed out, that Penelope's motives for appearing before the Suitors are not quite as clear-cut as Odysseus imagines. Athena intends her to excite the Suitors and win greater honor from her husband and son. Penelope herself resists the impulse Athena instills in her. She laughs *achreion* ("pointlessly," 163) as she tries to explain the sudden urge to show herself to her wooers, although they are hateful to her. Eurynome interprets Penelope's move here as one toward remarriage, yet Penelope refuses to beautify herself as Eurynome suggests, denies her beauty, and wishes for death. She says she wants to warn Telemachos, and she actually does chastise him over the treatment of the beggar (at 16.409–33 Penelope similarly decides to appear before the Suitors and chastise them because of her fear for Telemachos). Showing herself to the Suitors is no decision to remarry, although it prepares for her later moves to do so; in Book 19, she represents herself as still struggling with the decision in the terms that Telemachos laid them out in Book 16, where he represents Penelope as continually divided between staying and remarrying. In 18, Penelope acts the part of a prospective bride, but her mind is still divided over the gesture (she is also still playing the mother to Telemachos). Hence, she can be said to be intending simultaneously things other than those that are apparent to the Suitors, and Odysseus is not incorrect in interpreting her actions in the light of what he has heard from Athena and Telemachos. Furthermore, because Penelope represents the move toward remarriage in the light of Odysseus' original instructions and denies her beauty even as it is melting the Suitors, he has no reason to be other than delighted with her actions. He knows that the Suitors' gifts will remain his and that Penelope is attempting to be faithful to his intentions. For extensive discussion of this scene, see especially Katz, 1991; Emlyn-Jones, 1984; and Felson-Rubin, 1993, with full bibliography.

23. The ambivalence that Penelope shows in the dream with the geese (19.535–81, weeping over their slaughter) goes unregistered. Katz, 1991, 119, sees Odysseus' approval as a patriarchal maneuver that denies Penelope a set of meanings and interests separate from those of her spouse and makes the couple appear more compatible than they are. At the same time, in her view, feminist readings like Felson-Rubin's, 1987, give Penelope an autonomy that the text does not support. In my view both Penelope and Odysseus subscribe to a patriarchal ideology; the text makes a point of giving Penelope the autonomy to make a nevertheless severely circumscribed choice; in judging Penelope as a moral agent, what is important is what action she takes and the role that reason and emotion play in that choice. (See

Murnaghan, Chapter 4, this volume, on the male-dominated ideology of the poem.)

24. Thornton, 1970, 109–10, 113, argues that Penelope's choice is appropriately conditioned by Odysseus' instructions, although her overall discussion does not come to terms with the full complexity of the circumstances.

25. See, e.g., Katz, 1991, 148, who argues that Telemachos' coming of age on the one hand legitimates the decision to remarry, yet in the light of the surrounding narrative the decision also becomes a form of (unintentional) betrayal (153; Murnaghan, 1987, Felson-Rubin, 1987, 1993; and others take a similar position) that is forestalled only by Odysseus' interpretation of Penelope's choice as faithfulness (147). It is true that Penelope comes close to inadvertent adultery, but in my view this does not make her morally suspect. As long as we accept her lack of trust in the portents as rational, her behavior is not incoherent.

26. The earlier portents to which Penelope reacts are as follows. In Book 17, Telemachos reports on the account of Proteus to Menelaos. The news rouses the heart in Penelope's breast (17.150). Theoklymenos says Odysseus is already there and planning evil for the Suitors (17.157–59). Penelope wishes it might come to pass (17.163). At the end of 17, Penelope hopes Odysseus might arrive and avenge the violence of the Suitors (17.539–40). Telemachos sneezes. Penelope interprets the sneeze as a sign the Suitors will meet their fate (17.545–47). The text repeatedly stresses that Penelope wishes to believe in the portents, but resists that wish, either at once or by the time we next return to her in the text. Her momentary optimism in 17 does give way to the desire (which puzzles Penelope herself) to approach the Suitors in Book 18. Yet the continuing dilemma as defined by Telemachos in Book 16 has not evaporated in 18, nor has there been any direct sign of Odysseus' return. I endorse the view of Emlyn-Jones, 1984, 3, that, by and large, Penelope's skepticism rarely wavers, "only occasionally straying into the optative in the face of a particularly convincing prediction." Moreover (5), it "enables the poet to exploit dramatic irony."

27. Penelope's final decision about whether to test Odysseus or fall into his arms (23.85–87) parallels Odysseus' concerning Laertes in 24. Both decisions have raised questions in the minds of readers, but the poem seems overall to offer a positive appraisal of seemingly hard-hearted caution. See Athena on Odysseus' exceptional caution at 13.330–38. Eurykleia displays hardness of heart over Odysseus' secret about the scar (hard as stone or iron, 19.494). At 19.209–12 Odysseus pities Penelope, but refuses to lament as she does—his lids are of horn or iron. Although Penelope is criticized for her hardness of heart in 23 (72, 97, 103), she gives a good explanation for her resistance during the recognition.

28. See Zeitlin, Chapter 7, this volume, on how Penelope's bed trick serves to test the heroine as well as Odysseus; Penelope here proves that she never gives in too easily.

29. As Murnaghan demonstrates, Athena plays a large role in setting up and directing this plot.

30. In the *Poetics*, ignorance concerning the identity of a relative (or of one's own identity) is the typical tragic error. This is part of the issue here. But in the *Nichomachean Ethics* (2.1.15–17, 1110b–1111a), when Aristotle is discussing by what standards one may treat an act as voluntary (blameworthy) or involuntary (to be pitied and forgiven), he broadens the ways in which an agent may be considered ignorant of his or her interests. One may be ignorant concerning the agent (one's own identity), the act, the thing or person affected by the act, the instrument, the effect of the action, and the manner. In 2.6.11–12 1108b, when discussing the emotions that moral agents feel, he argues that time, occasion, purpose, and manner are critical. It seems likely that Aristotle would have wanted these broader standards to apply to tragic ignorance as well.

31. One might argue—from the perspective of critics who think that the narrative denies coherence to Penelope's actions and feelings—that tragic irony is blurred in this case because clear lines between what the character and the audience know do not exist. From a strictly ethical perspective, I have tried to demonstrate that this is not the case.

32. On the complex issues raised by Penelope's use of Helen as an exemplum in this scene, see especially Katz, 1991; Murnaghan, 1987; and Felson-Rubin, 1993, with further bibliography.

33. The text clearly takes a risk, given these cultural preconceptions, on giving Penelope what amounts to sexual autonomy. At the same time, by acting, Penelope becomes a far more convincing example of the faithful wife. The fact that Penelope's desire for marriage (and / or the disguised Odysseus) is gradually reawakened in Books 18–23 at the same time that she resists it does not compromise her as a moral agent. Desire is a legitimate part of the ethical process in the views of most Greeks, including Aristotle, as long as it serves the dictates of reason. Indeed, knowing that Penelope has complex emotions of grief and desire simply makes her decision to suppress her own wishes more impressive.

34. Murnaghan, 1987, 128–29, 134, 146, rightly stresses that the plot makes Penelope far more vulnerable to contingency and less able to control her circumstances than the disguised Odysseus. In her view Penelope is "defeated . . . by the incompatibility between her fidelity to her husband and her social position"; hence she forces "us to acknowledge the element of chance that turns the contest of the bow into Odysseus' triumph" (1986, 113). Because I view Penelope's final decision as an act of loyalty to Odysseus, I find her choice less disturbing. Nevertheless, I agree with both Murnaghan and Felson-Rubin, 1987, 1993, that Penelope's ignorance is central to our understanding and judgment of her situation and actions in Books 18–23.

35. See further, Schein, Chapter 2, this volume.

36. For examples, see Sharples, 1983; Gaskin, 1990. The implications of

these decisions may, as in the case of Achilles' choice in *Iliad* 9, entail larger issues concerning the quality of a hero's life.

37. Athena intervenes in a decision-making scene only in this instance. See further, Russo, 1968, 292–93.

38. The debate, inaugurated by Snell, 1960, 1–22; and Voigt, 1933 (see also Fraenkel, 1975; Adkins, 1960), has concentrated largely on the nature of the Homeric moral agent and whether such agents can be understood to act as integrated beings (see most recently Sharples, 1983; Gaskin, 1990; and Williams, 1993). Most of the more detailed discussion has justifiably centered on Achilles in *Iliad* 9 (the bibliography is too extensive to cite here). Williams recognizes that the case of Penelope is more complex and hence decides not to address her decision in detail (1993, 48). Surprisingly, Nussbaum, 1986, did not turn to Penelope in a study that makes the problem of moral contingency in Greek literature a central concern.

39. As Murnaghan, Chapter 4, this volume, points out, Homeric characters rarely resist divine suggestion. Penelope's defiance of convention in this respect may serve to underline her self-control.

40. Gaskin, 1990, 14, thinks that Penelope comes close to tragic *amēchania* in 4.787–94, where she helplessly debates over the threat to Telemachos' life by the Suitors. He argues that most decisions in epic lack the complexity of the tragic dilemmas facing an Agamemnon or Orestes: "While Achilles' decision in the *Iliad* to avenge his friend is to be sure tragic, it is so in a different and much simpler sense than Agamemnon's. . . . Achilles has no difficulty reaching his decision; he faces no insoluble moral dilemma, with disaster threatening him on either side of the choice. All that is required of him is courage, and that is a virtue he can unproblematically supply" (14). By these standards, Penelope's decision to approach remarriage is more deeply tragic.

41. Williams, 1993, 41–42, notes that duty in the modern sense has not been thought to play a role in Homeric decision making. The term does not occur in Homeric vocabulary, but Penelope's choice perhaps comes closer than any other Homeric decision to invoking what we might call duty as a basis for her choice. Hektor, whose representation is so closely linked with that of his city, is the male character most similar to Penelope. In his decision about whether to stay outside the walls and fight Achilles or to retreat into the city, as his parents wish him to, Hektor weighs the taunts of those who will accuse him of ruining his people by his mistaken strategies if he goes into the city and his fear that Achilles would not negotiate with him against risking death with glory (*Iliad* 22.98–130). Even here, however, Hektor's own honor as warrior ultimately takes precedence over his responsibility to protect his city or at least to delay its fall.

42. 1982, 19.

43. Ibid.

44. Ibid., 82.

45. Williams, 1993, esp. 21–29, is the most recent of the critics of Snell.

46. Gilligan's work has been criticized on multiple grounds. For a representative critique with further bibliography, see Porter, 1991, 142–93. In the case of the *Odyssey*, the differences between male and female moral agents arise from differences in socially defined sex roles, not from differences in the moral capacities and proclivities of the agent. In this respect, the present study may have something to contribute to the modern debate, in which Gilligan has been accused of essentialism, or of being insufficiently attentive to the contexts (e.g., public or private) in which decisions are made. In addition, the difficulties encountered by scholars in defining Penelope's character may result in part from the inextricable embedding of female characters in their social role.

47. For a recent general discussion of sexual ideology in the *Odyssey*, see Wohl, 1993.

48. See Vermeule, 1979, esp. 101–3, 105.

49. The role played by the marginal figure Thersites in the *Iliad* also serves to reshape our perspective on the ethics of Homeric heroes. In tragedy also, female experience can be educative to the male. See, e.g., Foley, 1992, for Penelope and Odysseus serving as a paradigm in this respect for Helen and Menelaos in Euripides' *Helen*, as well as Zeitlin, 1985, on Phaidra and Hippolytos. In its use of reverse similes, which often assimilate male and female experiences, the *Odyssey* similarly plays with dissolving gender role boundaries. See further, Foley, 1978.

7

Figuring Fidelity in Homer's *Odyssey*

Froma I. Zeitlin

The *Odyssey* has an extraordinary capacity for creating memorable visual objects, signs, and symbols as focusing elements of a highly complex narrative structure. In a world ruled by uncertainty, suspension, disguise, and dimmed perception, such apparent tokens of a tangible reality emerge at critical interpretative junctures in the plot, often serving as means of prediction, identification, or proof.[1] Generally speaking, all material objects in both the *Iliad* and the *Odyssey* are invested with psychological and cognitive resonances that go far beyond the details of their mere description to exemplify a typical and indispensable mode of charting social and mental experience. As M. I. Finley remarks, the "heroic world is unable to visualize any achievement or relationship except in concrete terms. The gods are anthropomorphized, emotions and feelings are located in specific organs of the body, even the soul was materialized. Every quality or state," he concludes, "had to be translated into some specific symbol, marriage into gifts of cattle, honor into a trophy, friendship into treasure."[2] Jasper Griffin takes another view of this well-known epic feature, judging it "not as just a matter of literary style, but [one that] arises from the way the Homeric poet sees the world itself." "Symbolic and significant objects and gestures," he suggests, "developed out of those which were originally conceived as magical and charged with supernatural power," even if such distinctions are not always absolutely clear.[3] What accounts in part for this sense of compelling presence is an aesthetic quality that heightens the value of articles primarily designed for practical use. Homeric epic, observes Kenneth Atchity, is "a treasure house of beautiful objects of art: swords, cups, robes, bows, beds, shields,"[4] outstanding specimens of craftsmanship that elicit the amazed awe of the spectators (*thauma idesthai*), an experience that often comes close to an epiphanic viewing.[5]

The result is that such objects are often talismans of power: They can be circulated and exchanged, transmitted as precious heirlooms, and endowed with certain active values that inhere in the genealogy of their ownership as well as in the beauty of their manufacture. In some instances, like the shield and spear of Achilles, they may belong wholly to particular individuals, functioning like personal attributes or as inalienable signs of identity that no one else, *oude tis allos,* can appropriate. An item can also belong to several categories. Odysseus' bow, for example, although ultimately reserved for his use alone, was originally a gift from a guest-friend and, like many such items, constitutes a tangible link of memory that connects the hero to the world of other heroes and whose evocation in the text provides the occasion for a tale that integrates it fully into its epic setting.

Of all these signifying objects, however, the most famous by far is the bed in Book 23 of the *Odyssey* whose owner and maker are one and the same. This is the sign by which Penelope comes to test Odysseus' identity following the slaying of the Suitors, and the revelation of its existence is the necessary prelude that leads directly to their long-awaited reunion. Situated between the identifying signs in Book 19 (the mantle and brooch described to Penelope, the scar recognized by Eurykleia) and Book 24 (Odysseus' identification of the trees in the orchard), the scene of the bed is the centerpiece in the unfolding drama of recognition at home—so much so that already in antiquity, we may recall, Alexandrian scholars promoted the idea that the poem actually ended, not with the close of the work as we have it, but with the immediate aftermath of this striking moment.[6] Anything else would seem to some to be an anticlimax—a disappointing follow-up to that most satisfying of all romantic closures: "and so to bed."

And so to bed—after twenty years of waiting—not just any bed, but one that is *sui generis,* a single and unique artifact, in that we know of no other like it in all of Greek tradition. Some have looked for affinities with a species of world tree or axis mundi or have suggested mythic or ritual parallels, whether of Indo-European or Near Eastern provenance.[7] But the power of its significance lies (if you will pardon the pun) in its embeddedness within the narrative, a sign-symbol made to order only for the purposes of this poem, its manufacture assigned to the only one who could have made it.

The bed is an object of value, artfully crafted with remarkable skill, as we are told in the combined description and narrative, when Odysseus in his own words recalls its special properties and retraces the steps of its making:

> What man
> has put my bed in another place? But it would be difficult
> for even a very expert one, unless a god, coming
> to help in person, were easily to put it in another place . . .
> but of men there is no other living mortal, not even in the full
>   strength of his youth,
> who could have easily moved it away, since a great mark (*mega sēma*)
>   is wrought
> into the artfully fashioned bed. It is I who made it and nobody else
>   (*oude tis allos*).
> There was the bole of an olive tree with long leaves growing
> in full flowering in the courtyard, and it was thick, like a column.
> I laid down my chamber around this, and built it, until I
> finished it, with close-set stones, and roofed it well over,
> and added the compacted doors, fitting closely together.
> Then I cut away the foliage of the long-leaved olive,
> and trimmed the trunk from the roots up, planing it with a brazen
> adze, well and expertly, and trued it straight to a chalkline,
> making a bed post of it, and bored all holes with an auger.
> I began with this and built my bed, until it was finished,
> and skillfully embellished it with gold and silver and ivory.
> Then I lashed it with thongs of oxhide, dyed bright with purple.
> In this way I proclaim and make manifest the sign / token (*sēma*
>   *piphauskomai*). But I do
> not know now whether the bed is still firmly in place (*empedon*), o
>   woman / wife (*gunai*)
> or if some man has cut underneath the stump of the olive and moved
>   it elsewhere.   (23.184–204)[8]

The bed is an integral part of the bedchamber itself, which Odysseus had built at the time of his marriage. But unlike other such constructions as we know, for example, from the reference to Paris' house in Troy (*Iliad* 6.314–17), the most distinctive feature of this particular bed is its immobility. Oddly fixed in place for all time, it is located at the center of a widening set of circles that constitute a social topography of habitation in accord with fixed conventions of property and propriety, a focal point that dictates its privileged position in the architecture of the house. If the bed is curiously stationary, however, it is hardly a static symbol. Rather, in the circumstances in which its "discovery" is staged, it is the site of a dynamic and two-sided operation, one that involves a complex interplay between two characters, whose knowledge of one another is made to inhere both in the shared secret of its existence and in the surprising reversal of roles that brings it into the light of day. Above all, the bed is a *sēma*, and this in the two senses of the word: first, some exceptional mark or aspect in its own right, as in this instance, the *mega sēma* that is wrought into this unusual bed (188–89), and second, as a sign or token of something else (that is, of the stranger's true identity).[9]

The tempting allure of a sign, any sign, is its implicit invitation to be deciphered and its message interpreted, even appropriated, by those who can discern its meaning. Like a wonder or *thauma*, as Raymond Prier suggests, a symbol-sign is "a phenomenon made to be seen or recognized." It is something wrought or "created" (*teuchomai*) that produces a quality "of affective signification" in the eye and the mind.[10] This is especially the case when the suggestiveness of a *sēma* expands in so many symbolic and psychological directions and so far exceeds the express reactions of the actors within the text. The bed belongs to both Penelope and Odysseus: The divulgence of its concrete reality, unchanged and unmoved through all these years, is enough to overcome the last impediment to their reunion. As a double-sided sign—of identity for him, fidelity for her—it is meant to be the visual proof of a private and unique relationship.[11] The bed is there, we might say, because it is made to be there; it needs to be located in this place and at this time. We want more. The urge to enter the sacrosanct *thalamos* once more is irresistible, and many others before me have ventured there.

Much indeed has been written and continues to be written on the many possible implications (and satisfactions) of this scene of *anagnōrisis*. It is taken to exemplify the complementary relation between Odysseus and Penelope—the sign of their *homophrosynē*, or likemindedness, by which she shows herself a match for her husband in clever quick-wittedness when she pretends at first that the bed has been moved. As the mark of Odysseus' identity, the bed he made matches him to his characteristic skill as an artisan, and through the sharing of a marital secret recalled from the distant past, is an especially appropriate means to reclaim his role as a husband, which he "reconstructs" in the process of recalling how he first "constructed" it.[12] Hence, the delay in Penelope's recognition as her need to "adjust past to present" in the demand that "Odysseus prove himself her husband now as he was then."[13] Or, beyond the personal story of this notorious couple, the bed, in its allegiance to both nature (living tree) and culture (its craftsmanship), is an emblem of the desired solidity of the house and the place of marriage within it. As Katz has put it most recently, "the bed . . . retains a connection with the natural world from which it came, and thus represents the institution of marriage itself, which, centered on the biological realities of sexuality and procreation, nevertheless is configured in space and time as a social artifact."[14] In particular, the fixed position of the bed is understood as a figure of marriage itself: permanent, durable, stable, and inalienable. Even the ancient scholiast on this passage underscores this point in observing that the bed's "immovable" (*akinēton*) quality is a riddling way of stating that the nuptial couch (the conjugal bond) is "indestructible," "indissoluble" (*adialuton*).[15]

I am not going to controvert these interpretations. Indeed, I am generally in accord with them. But I want to drive a small wedge between text and interpretation to open a space for exploring the nature and uses of this singular bed as the master sign in the *Odyssey*'s emplotment, and to do so, I aim to ground the scene more fully in the cultural context as well as in the narrative, semantic, and symbolic structures of the poem itself.

At first glance, it should not perhaps seem strange that masculine identity should be intertwined with feminine fidelity in the dynamics of this scene or that the idea of marriage between a man and a woman should rely on two such unequal modalities of self-definition. Even beyond the obvious social disparities in the institution of marriage, both configurations resemble one another in one important sense: Each is ultimately open to doubt. After all, he may not be who he says he is, and she, in not conducting herself as the rules prescribe, may not be what she appears to be. Only if these two quite disparate "truths" are made to converge, we might say, as two divided halves of a *sumbolon*, only if husband and wife match their knowledge of the secret *sēmata* (23.107–9) in the one artifact they both share (and agree to recall), can this marriage be recreated, reconstructed, and finally resumed.

Yet a certain paradox remains in the unequal symmetry between identity and fidelity that dictates to each sex its defining terms—a relation first challenged in the reversal of roles and an apparent shift of power between male and female before the scene reaches its expected conclusion in reaffirming the social norms. That challenge gives rise to certain questions I would like to explore further. What is at stake in this elaborate backhanded game? Why, for example, should moving the bed be instantly construed as a sign of infidelity? What more may be implied by Penelope's action in initiating the test of the bed, or, more precisely, how does her ruse address the inherent dilemma of the poem, which assures us of Penelope's fidelity, while also keeping it in doubt? The further unraveling of these various strands in what follows will, I hope, help us to decipher the underlying logic of this scene that requires (and reinforces) the ideological need to resort to the external and externalizing sign of the bed as the requisite "foreplay" to the "real thing."

Penelope is the first to set the terms of an *anagnōrisis* as a testing of her husband. Refusing the evidence of the scar and the assurances of Eurykleia and Telemachos in her initial encounter with him after the slaughter of the Suitors, she maintains that

> If he is truly Odysseus,
> and he has come home, then we shall find other ways, and better,
> to recognize each other, for we have signs (*sēmata*) that we know of
> between the two of us only, but they are secret (*kekrummena*) from
> the others. (23.107–8).

Odysseus, however, is the one who actually gives the cue. Freshly bathed and marvelously restored by Athena's handiwork, he again takes his place opposite an unyielding Penelope, and, as if resigned to her stony attitude, he orders the nurse to make him up a bed (23.171–72). Now it is her turn, and although not denying she knows what he looked like long ago when he sailed for Troy, she takes him at his word and instructs Eurykleia to set up a bed outside the well-built chamber. Not just any bed, such as the kind regularly offered to guests in the house, but "that very bed he himself had made," she adds, and the text forewarns us that this is the means she has chosen to "test her husband" (23.181). It is a clever ruse, for it catches Odysseus offguard, and by eliciting his spontaneous indignation, her trick succeeds far better than any direct interrogation[16] to guarantee the authenticity of his knowledge and hence of his identity.

But the ruse works in two directions, because in raising the awful possibility that his bed has been moved, her testing of *his* identity raises the far more important question of *her* sexual fidelity to him. This is the principal anxiety that hovers over the whole poem. It conditions Odysseus' entire strategy once he has returned to Ithaka and accounts for Penelope's belated position in the sequence of his several self-revelations to others at home. At this, the moment of reckoning, the crucial issue is never directly stated. Yet its presence is instantaneously grasped through a series of oblique and symbolic moves. The secret existence of this particular bed, which only the two of them (and a trusted maidservant) are permitted to know, suggests the intimacy shared by the couple and the husband's sexual monopoly of his wife, whereby it is understood that mere divulgence of the bed's existence would be equivalent to an irrevocable betrayal. To move it, however, would mean to undermine the entire cultural ideology that supports the bed in its "natural" grounding of the house in the institution of marriage. Immobility is equated with the desired permanence of the conjugal bond, which would be fatally undermined by the ax's blow. So much is clear. The symbolic values hold.

But does representation fully replace reality? After all, in principle, Penelope could have made love with another man in the very same bed or, for that matter, anywhere else she chose.[17] Yet the fact of not moving the bed becomes a decisive and incontrovertible proof. Why should this be so? She could not, of course, have moved it by herself. The effort, says Odysseus, would have required the strength of some remarkable man (with a god's help) to accomplish it. Moving the bed is represented as a heroic feat, a task beyond the capacity of most mortal men. It requires exceptional physical prowess, such as only a worthy virile rival might display. Hence the man who moved the bed has done more than violate the idea of a stable marriage, but in unmaking what Odysseus had previously made, he will have proved himself Odysseus' sexual equal, even superior, who could rightly claim the title of "best of the Achaeans" in his stead (16.74–77; 19.525–29). To displace the bed, therefore, suggests another male's entitlement to displace him, an entitlement exercised by the first encroachment into the bedchamber that is followed now by this permanent and irreversible sign of mastery.[18]

Merely to enter the bedroom is to gain access to the innermost region of the house, its protected core. This is the domain the woman inhabits, once she has been brought into the household as the lawfully wedded wife, and whose benefits she enjoys because of her relationship with her husband that is symbolized, above all, in her sharing of his bed.[19] Then again, if the marital bed cannot be alienated from its maker without destroying its integrity (and his), its place of honor in the spatial arrangement of the house signifies that the woman, for her part, has ceased to be an object of exchange among men in the protocols of betrothal and matrimony. She, too, like the bed, is expected to be fixed in place from then on, and her continuing fidelity to him finds its direct correlative in the object that has remained in place through all these years as a secret no one else knows. Its lasting condition then must depend on a corresponding steadfastness of mind in the wife, who, in her husband's absence, agrees to guard the privacy (and exclusivity) of both her body and their bed. In her role as the custodian of his rights to exclusive possession of her and hence as the mainstay of the social system in which both spouses are awarded their respective positions, Penelope is faced with a situation that gives her unaccustomed power in the right to determine what man will finally share that bed and, in so doing, to grant or withhold from her errant husband the stability of a safe anchorage at home. As Suzuki puts it, "refusing to become an object of exchange between the Suitors and either her son Telemachos or her father Icarius [in remarriage], Penelope" is more than "a sign that is exchanged among men; instead, she insists upon her status as a [speaking] subject, a generator of signs," a role that reaches its climax in the sign of the bed.[20]

The bed, of course, is the place for sex and therefore the central and virtually indispensable feature of any description of sexual activity in Homeric narrative. In Hera's deception of Zeus in *Iliad* 14, he is so overwhelmed by desire that although he utters the conventional formula, "let us go to bed and turn to lovemaking" (*en philotēti trapeiomen eunēthente*), he cannot wait to return to their well-fitted bedchamber, as propriety demands. But a bed is needed, and the god therefore creates its equivalent in a grassy meadow he magically causes to grow on the mountain, as thick (*puknon*) and soft (*malakon*), as any cozy boudoir, and he ensures their privacy from prying eyes in the golden cloud he lowers around them (*Iliad* 14.312–53).

An invitation to lovemaking may or may not begin with a formal move to the bedchamber (*es thalamon t'ienai*), but a constant feature of such scenes is an explicit mention of mounting a bed (*eunē*: e.g., 10.333–34, *nōi d'epeita eunēs hēmeterēs epibēsomen*), followed by some version of the formulaic expression "they mingled together in" *eunē* and *philotēs*: (*ophra migente eunēi kai philotēti*, 10.340, 334–35).[21] Claude Calame translates this phrase to mean "unite in amorous exchange in a bed" and suggests that each term is properly placed to designate the three components of a sexual act: a bed (*eunē*), commerce or interchange (*meignumi*), and a fiduciary aspect (*philotēs*) that signifies the reciprocal nature of the erotic relationship.[22] *Eunē*, however, has a richer valence. In its lexical range, the word corresponds most closely to our own verbal noun "bedding" in that it literally refers to the bedcoverings as well as the act of bedding down. From these two meanings, the term may extend to indicate the actual bed itself or the activity conducted there, be it sex or sometimes just sleep. But when it comes to designating the bed as a material object, an article of furniture, then *lechos* (or sometimes *lektron*) is the standard word,[23] just as in the case of the bedstead Odysseus has fashioned in his chamber (23.171, 177, 179, 184, 189, 199, 203).[24]

Unlike *eunē*, the word *lechos* has an institutional meaning. The *lechos* is the basis of a woman's legitimate status as a wife, signified by their "mingling together in *eunē* and *philotēs.*" She is her husband's *alochos*, one who shares the same bed, and the adjectives that some-times accompany the word (*mnēstē, kouridiē* = "lawfully wedded") confirm that she has been brought into the household under the proper social and ritual protocols.[25] It is only one short step further from bed to marriage, and *lechos* can stand in for the institution of matrimony itself (*Iliad* 8.291), as it does more regularly in later poetic texts, where it may even be taken as a synonym for the wife herself.[26] Thus, while, strictly speaking, *lechos* remains a visual and concrete artifact, a practical necessity in the house, it also means something more. Both object and idea, both artifact and symbol, the bed stands for itself and also for something larger than itself, which Homeric idiom can fully put into play.[27]

There are no precise terms in Homer either for sexual adultery or for marital fidelity. True, women may deceive their husbands and elicit Agamemnon's pessimistic remark that there is nothing trustwor-thy (*pista*) among women (11.456). But *pistos* as a qualifying adjective refers only to comrades (*hetairoi*), and the negative form *apistos*, used both of Odysseus and Penelope, points rather to a quality of sus-picious caution that both of them share (14.150, 391; 23.72). In tradi-tional diction, terms for *adultery* and *fidelity* focus around the state of the marital bed, defined between the two poles of "shaming" (*aischu-nein*, 8.269) or "respecting" (*aidomenē*) its sacrosanct qualities. Yet fidelity assumes still another dimension, expressed in the phrase "to stay in place by one's child and keep everything safe" (*menei para paidi kai empeda panta phulassei*). This is how Odysseus' mother, Antikleia, describes Penelope's behavior to him in the underworld (11.178) and how first Telemachos and then Penelope herself charac-terize one of the two alternatives facing her: "either to remain beside her child and keep everything *empeda*, her possessions, maidser-vants, and high roofed house, respecting the bed of her husband (*eunēn t'aidomenē posios*) and the opinion of the people (*dēmoio te phēmin*)—or to follow after that one, the best of the Achaeans who is wooing her in the halls, and offering her gifts" (16.74–77; 19.525–29).

Empeda is the key word. Translated as "steadfastly," "with firm stand" or "fixedly," even "safe and secure," it literally means to be grounded in the earth (*en pedōi*), precisely the issue at stake for Odysseus in regard to his bed: "I do not know whether the *lechos* is still *empedon* or whether some man has put it elsewhere, having cut under the stump of the olive tree" (23.203). *Empedos* as an adjective is a highly prized trait of human behavior. In the world of warriors, it characterizes a man's strength (*bia*), vigor (*menos*), wits (*phrenes*), heart (*ētor*), mind (*noos*), feet (*podes*), and limbs (*guia*), as well as his shield (*sakos*) and spear (*egchos*), and denotes any purposeful activity. Often *menō* (remain) and *empedos/on* are coupled together in literal fashion to describe troops on the plain firmly awaiting the onslaught of battle (*Iliad* 5.526; 15.405, 622) or horses who wait patiently for their master's return (*Iliad* 13.37). The obverse is a man who is past the flowering of his youth and can no longer count on such steadfast strength, and its negation is fear and timidity as opposed to courage. Helen in the *Iliad* resigns herself to the fact that Paris will never conform to the proprieties, a man whose *phrenes* will never be *empedoi* (*Iliad* 6.352–53), preferring always bed to battle and taking his pleasures as he can with charming insouciance.

In the *Odyssey*, *empedos* recurs, typically again as a masculine trait, and it covers the same spectrum of meaning that includes physical valor as well as mental resolve. The minds of Odysseus' men remain *empedoi*, as they always were, even though Kirke has changed their human forms into swine (10.240).[28] In the underworld Teiresias is granted the special capacity to keep his mind *empedos* (10.493), unlike the strengthless dead, such as Agamemnon, who mourns the fact that his power and strength (*is, kikus*) are no longer *empedos* (11.393). Most often the word describes Odysseus himself. In the underworld, he is twice depicted as waiting *empedos*, first in hope of conversing with his mother and then with some of the shades of his Iliadic comrades (11.152, 628). When passing the island of the Sirens, he needs to be bound to the mast so that he may hear their seductive song but still remain *empedos* (12.161), and in facing the dangers of Skylla and Charybdis, he searches in vain for a foothold to brace himself *empedos* on the rock (12.434). When one of the Suitors pelts him with a footstool, now he is the rock that faces the attack *empedos* (17.464), and in stringing the bow, he rejoices that his *menos* is still *empedon*, as it once was in the past (21.426; cf. 14.468, 503; 22.226). Only once does *empedos* apply directly to a woman, and she is Eurykleia, who, when enjoined on pain of death to keep his identity a secret, assures her master of a *menos* that is likewise *empedon*, unyielding (*oud' epieikton*), and she promises she "will hold as stubborn as stone or iron" (19.493–94).

Penelope too has just such a resolve, but it is initially a cause for reproach in this scene, when she refuses to accept her husband, although others have assured her of his identity and he sits in her presence. Telemachos speaks of her "hard heart" (*apēnea thumon*, 23.97) and her "stubborn" or "steadfast" spirit (*tetlēoti thumōi*,

23.100), more firmly fixed than stone (23.103), and Odysseus echoes his son's sentiments in almost the same terms (*kēr ateramnon*, 23.167–68). But all through these years, precisely because of her "stubborn heart" (cf. 11.181; 16.37), a phrase characteristic too of Odysseus (9.435; 18.135; 24.163),[29] Penelope has "remained by her child and kept everything *empeda.*" To be literally *empedos* is to be fixed in the earth, like the wall the Achaeans built (*Iliad* 11.9, 12) or a funeral stele that remains planted in the ground (*Iliad* 17.434), a *sēma* that will permanently endure, just like the bed of Odysseus. The fixity of the marriage bed may enact the principle of fidelity itself that, like the trunk of the olive, sustains the institution on which it is founded, but reciprocally it must be matched by a psychic correlative in the characters and actions of the partners who share it, each of them marked by the same quality of endurance, the capacity to be, or keep, everything *empedos.*

Yet the symmetry between the couple in this respect may be more apparent than real. Penelope's position, as she outlines it to Odysseus in disguise when they first exchange confidences in the firelight, exemplifies the dilemma in which she is placed by the circumstances of the poem: either wait steadfastly for Odysseus, who may no longer be among the living, or go off with one of the Suitors as his wife and leave her husband's house forever. Indeed, the latter is continually presented as a legitimate choice. Her son has come of age and is impatient now for her to make a decision so that he can assume his rightful place and resolve his own ambiguous status as heir to his father's title and possessions. She has exhausted her own strategies of delay in the ruse of the loom, and time has brought her custodial function to an end. The Suitors have become still more dangerous, plotting to kill Telemachos on his return from his voyage, and the impoverishment of the household's resources through the Suitors' insolent feasting increases day by day. She is ready to initiate a bride contest in the trial of the bow to find a replacement for Odysseus, someone who may openly replace him by duplicating his special feat with his own weapon. Yet her perfectly legitimate choice, urged upon her from every side, to go home to her father or accept one of the Suitors, is continually undermined by the intimation that to do so would constitute a betrayal of Odysseus, whose fate is still unknown. She would have failed in reverence for both the bed of her husband and the public opinion of the townsfolk.[30]

But if the bed had been moved (we know not when or by whom), then an entirely different issue is raised. To accept a second marriage is not, after all, equivalent to adultery, despite the wanton conduct of her Suitors. There is a distinction, after all, between acquiescence to courtship, no matter how unwelcome, and actually sleeping with the enemy—between publicly considering the choice of another mate and a furtive coupling on the side with some unknown partner.

The *Odyssey* is noticeably reticent about addressing acts of adultery. The question of Helen's infidelity is raised only obliquely in Book 4 when she and Menelaos offer their respective tales about Helen's behavior at Troy (4.242–89). Both stories avoid any direct mention of their marital relationship to focus instead on the larger matter of her allegiance to or betrayal of the Greeks. In any case, the primary motive for telling these tales is to recall the cunning feats of Odysseus, with the aim of reviving memories of a lost friend and of edifying his son, Telemachos, who, coming to Sparta to find news of his father, learns instead about Odysseus' heroic past at Troy. We may take the cues of these two stories as offering possible alternatives for Penelope herself. Will she, as in Helen's version, receive Odysseus as a stranger in disguise and give him welcome? Conversely, following Menelaos' tale, will her deportment with the Suitors resemble Helen's provocative temptation of the Greeks hidden inside the Wooden Horse? For now, everything is pure innuendo. The erotic undertones at the banquet in Sparta run deep and strong, to be sure, but even so, only as whispers of seduction—the foreplay, perhaps, but not the "real thing."[31]

Avoidance is one strategy. Euphemism is another. The adulterous act is called an *ergon aeikes*, an unseemly act. This is how Penelope, after the scene of *anagnōrisis* in Book 23, describes Helen's action in going off with Paris (23.222), and Klytaimestra too is charged with performing an *ergon aeikes*, which at times refers to her sexual miscreance but more often is elided with its outcome in the murder of Agamemnon (3.265; 11.429). One scene, however, tells a tale of adultery, complete with a guilty couple and an outraged husband, and it is the only one, in fact, that does not hesitate to speak plainly (8.332).[32]

This scene is none other than the song of Ares and Aphrodite, performed in Book 8 by the bard Demodokos at the Phaeacian court (8.266–366), a song that so scandalized ancient commentators that, along with some of their modern counterparts, they wanted to athetize it from the text.[33] But not least among its virtues is the fact that the tale provides some important parallels and contrasts with our scene in Book 23 for their mutual elucidation. Its significance is all the more enhanced by the fact that Demodokos presents it in the very episode of the *Odyssey* that, as we shall see, is carefully framed in a number of ways to foreshadow and ultimately validate the dramatic reunion of Odysseus and Penelope.

The song of Ares and Aphrodite occupies the central position in the triad of the bard's performances at the court of Alkinoos, situated between two others that each refer to Odysseus at Troy: a quarrel between Odysseus and Achilles, on the one hand (8.75–82); on the other, Odysseus' role in the sack of Troy through the ruse of the Wooden Horse (8.493–520). The contrasts are striking: a tale about gods, not mortals; about sex, not war; and, instead of relations between men, about those between male and female. Although all three are constructed around themes of antagonism and conflict, the lay of Ares and Aphrodite also markedly differs from the other two in its ribald tone and comic outcome.

A bed, the marital bed, plays the starring role in this erotic triangle that recounts the *philotēs* between Ares and Aphrodite, how "they first mingled (*migēsan*) secretly in the house of Hephaistos," when he "shamed" the *lechos . . . kai eunēn* of the lord Hephaistos" (8.266–70). This bed, too, is an unusual exemplar of its kind, not in its unusual mode of manufacture or position in the bedroom, but in what its owner devises for it after Helios observes the guilty couple "mingling in *philotēs*" and tattles to the cuckolded spouse (8.270–73). The craftsman god is not at a loss for skillful tricks. The stratagem he chooses is to construct an invisible net, finer than a spider's web, which he suspends over the bed to catch and hold fast the adulterous pair, so they may be exhibited in all their shame to the prurient and ridiculing gaze of the assembly of gods (except for the virginal goddesses). His plan was to "hammer out unbreakable bonds that cannot be loosed," so that when the lovers next indulged in *philotēs*, they would remain there *empedon*—fixed fast (*menoien empedon*, 8.275), with no hope of escape. Hephaistos indeed succeeds in this literal version of entrapment: "neither of them could stir a limb or get up and now they saw the truth and they could not escape" (8.298–99). By his clever device, Hephaistos reverses the balance of power between his all too virile rival and himself, one he could maintain in perpetuity, if he so wished, as he ironically remarks:

> But you shall see how the two of them have gone into my bed and lie there
> making love. I am sickened when I look at them, and yet
> I suppose they would not like to lie this way even a moment more,
> much though they are in love. Nor will they soon want to
> sleep, but my ruse and my bonds will contain them. . . .
> (8.313–17)[34]

In the private chamber of Odysseus and Penelope, the bed remains fixed in the interplay between husband and wife as the private
site and condition of their marital reunion and the enduring permanence of their conjugal bond. Adultery, on the other hand, answers to
these same principles but is configured in their parodic and sinister
inversion. Here the issue at stake is not the status of an immovable
bed but rather the lovers themselves who remain locked in a perpetual embrace, neither able to separate from one another nor together enjoy the pleasures of sex and sleep. In an erotic context, the
quality of steadfastness is represented as shifting between a positive
and a negative pole—between a virtuous ideal and an unimpeachable
emblem of shame, between stability and constancy on the one hand
and detainment and even imprisonment on the other—as signifying
the difference between licit and illicit sexuality, the latter threatening
to become an unbearably permanent state of being, if Hephaistos
were not persuaded finally to let the errant couple go.[35]

Once viewed mainly as an embarrassing if not interpolated di-
gression, which reflects well on neither the gods nor the poet,
the tale of Ares and Aphrodite has more recently undergone a satisfying rehabilitation at the hands of critics. The effect of this renewed interest extends from situating the song in the immediate
context of the framing events in Phaiakia to the larger implications
that bear on the sexual ideology of the poem, with particular emphasis
on the situation of Odysseus himself. The distancing effects of "a poem
within a poem," along with its tone of bawdy humor and shift to the
realm of the gods, may seem to divide it sharply from the two other
songs that directly address the exploits of Odysseus at Troy. But these
same features also enhance the symbolic values of the story as a suggestive and complex sign, a *sēma* in its own right, we might say,
which, accordingly, solicits efforts to determine what and how it
might mean. The immediate setting furnishes one parallel in both
content and form: the ultimate reconciliation between the two erotic
rivals is matched by the amicable settlement of the strife between
Odysseus and Euryalos in the matter of athletic competition, whereby
Odysseus is exonerated and his burly opponent shamed.[36] At the
same time, the air of comic burlesque also works to the same effect:
Male rivalry on the playing fields is recoded into sexual joking, and
the shared laughter of the male audience, including Odysseus, at the
laughter of the gods repairs the previous tensions for all concerned.
Yet, as already observed by ancient commentators,[37] the pertinence
of a theme of sexual infidelity extends beyond the context of the
present performance to address the central concern of the poem itself

in advance of Odysseus' return to Ithaka to reclaim his wife and his bed.

The objective of this pivotal book of the poem is precisely to reestablish Odysseus' identity through his active participation in events as well as in the songs of the bard. The narrative is cunningly fashioned to construct that identity through a complex layering of past, present, and future with the aim of merging the Iliadic and Odyssean facets of his character into a composite and convincing portrait of this uncommon hero. Only when the current deeds and reactions of the unknown stranger are matched up with the past history of Odysseus through the two tales of the hero's experiences at Troy[38] is he finally empowered to take the last step toward self-revelation when he finally launches the first-person narration of his own story under his own name. In this dense texture of reenactment and recall, the love song of Ares and Aphrodite moves to another plane of relevance in the forging of that identity by its staging of a conflict between two wholly other adversaries and in supplying an erotic context that obliquely looks ahead to future events, while also recasting them in a more problematic way.

True, the defense of a husband against adultery conducted in his own bed and the resort to trickery in outwitting a male rival hint both at the theme of the entire poem (if not its facts) and the characteristic quality of *mētis* that Odysseus shares with Hephaistos, the master builder.[39] This is the salient point of identification to which we will return. On the other hand, if Hephaistos' honor is restored through his exposure of the lovers and his successful demand for retribution, the rest of the tale implies that the model does not fully hold. Beyond the generic embarrassment of a cuckolded husband is the singular unattractiveness of this lame and ugly spouse, as Hephaistos himself acknowledges. As a result, he cannot claim a full virility, according to the prevailing standards of judgment; more significant still, he never actually reclaims his wife because, once released from his trap, she conveniently finds refuge in her distant sanctuary at Cyprus, where she may restore her sexual allure for another occasion of lovemaking. The erotic mismatch between this married couple therefore compromises the analogy, which is further undermined by a quasi-exoneration of Ares when Hermes declares that he too would desire "to sleep by the side of Aphrodite the golden" even if "there could be three times this number of endless bonds, and all you gods could be looking on and all the goddesses" (8.339–41). Manliness is measured by a fine male body and evidence of physical prowess, as even here, when Athena transforms Odysseus at the beginning of the episode "so that

he might be loved by all the Phaeacians, and to them might be wonderful and respected, and might accomplish many trials of strength by
which the Phaeacians tested Odysseus" (8.17–23). For the situation on
Ithaka, Odysseus will need this strength; he must exercise *bia*, after
all, as well as his resourceful *mētis* to overcome the Suitors, even if the
cunning of *mētis* is essential to prepare the way for his retributive
victory over them.[40]

Nevertheless, the ostensible triumph of Hephaistos in the tale
offers significant parallels for the future. These not only align Odysseus with his Hephaestean attributes but also keep the narrative context of the song in mind at the reunion of Odysseus and Penelope in
Book 23. In an illuminating essay, Rick Newton focuses on the corre-
spondences between these two masters of ruse and practical skills,
who both possess the qualities of *mētis* and *technē*, and he notes the
fact that allusions to Hephaistos increase toward the latter part of
the poem, until they culminate finally in echoes from the scene at the
Phaeacian court in the *anagnōrisis* of Odysseus and Penelope.[41] The
first clues, however, pertain to physical appearance. Hephaistos is, of
course, noted for his limping gait. Odysseus, for his part, when extoll-
ing his various competitive skills to the Phaeacian men, specifically
excludes any strength of foot, claiming that life at sea has put him out
of practice (8.230–33).[42] On Ithaka, too, we note that in his beggar's
disguise, he requires a staff to assist him in walking (17.196, 203, 338),
and, like Hephaistos, he seems to be continually at risk of being
hurled out of doors by his foot (17.478–80, 18.10; cf. *Iliad* 1.590–91;
15.18–24; 18.395). But more notable are the interests the two share in
carpentry and also in metallurgy.

Odysseus' credentials as a craftsman are established elsewhere in
the poem before he arrives among the Phaeacians: first, when he
builds his raft on the island of Kalypso (5.228–61), and then in the
simile of the blacksmith's art that Odysseus chooses to describe his
blinding of the Kyklops with the heated point of the sharpened log
(9.391). Newton cites the parallel between Hephaistos' departure for
his forge to devise his means of entrapment (8.273) and its later echo
in Ithaka in the jeering suggestion made to Odysseus that he get out of
the house and find a smithy somewhere as lodging for the night
(18.328).[43] Both figures are also associated through their house-
building skills. In *Iliad* 1, when the gods disperse for the night, we are
told that "strong-handed Hephaistos had built a house [for each] by
means of his craftsmanship and cunning" (*Iliad* 1.607–8), and it is not
an otiose detail that Odysseus' first glimpse of his house leads to an
approving assessment of its excellent handiwork.

Surely this is the handsome house of Odysseus.
Easily it is singled out and seen among many,
for one part is joined on to another, and the courtyard is worked on
with wall and copings, and the doors have been well made, with
   double
panels. Nobody could belittle this house.   (17.264–68)[44]

Finally and above all is the shared emphasis on marital beds as the site
of lovemaking—beds that each of them had made and prove to have
special devices for testing wifely fidelity. Newton looks back still earlier in the poem for a "possible analogy between Hephaistos's net and
Odysseus' actual bed." The scene is Telemachos' return from his journey in Book 16, where he "wonders whether his mother is still at
home or whether she has married one of the Suitors, and Odysseus'
bed lies in want of bedclothes or occupants (*eneunaiōn*), collecting
foul spider webs" (16.33–35). It was Athena, as Newton observes, who
had first "plant[ed] the suspicion in his mind" when he was tarrying at
the court of Menelaos, with the precise intention of stirring him to
return home:

> For you know what the mind is like in the breast of a woman.
> She wants to build up the household of the man who marries her,
> and of her former children, and of her beloved and wedded hus-
>   band,
> she has no remembrance, when he is dead, nor does she ask after
>   him.   (15.4–20)

Newton wants to compare the image of the neglected bed at home to
"Hephaistos' net that is said to resemble fine spider webs" (8.280), on
the grounds that the context in each case indicates a suspicion of
adultery.[45] But, in truth, the parallel is far from exact. The spider
webs in Ithaka merely signify that the wife may have abandoned her
husband's bed to make a marriage elsewhere; it is not an act of adulterous defilement. Moreover, the two references perform different,
quite contrary, functions that revolve around the two extremes of
excessive use and disuse, presence and absence. For Penelope's bed,
the spider webs are a *visible* sign of a wife's flight from the marital
bed, while in Hephaistos' case, the simile describes the *invisibility* of
the bonds he has designed to detain his spouse and to prevent her
(and her lover's escape). Fragility marks the literal gossamer threads
of the first; tensile strength the figurative properties of the second. If
Hephaistos' ruse is recalled once more on Ithaka, it is surely in the
other simile that describes Telemachos' uncommon punishment of

the unfaithful maidservants in stringing them up from a ship's cable,
which he fastened to the pillar of the house:

> and like thrushes, who spread their wings, or pigeons, who have
> flown into a snare set up for them in a thicket, trying
> to find a resting place, but the sleep given them was hateful;
> so their heads were all in a line, and each had her neck caught
> fast in a noose, so that their death would be most pitiful.
>
> (22.465–71)

We note the same sarcastic humor about bed and sleep as in
Hephaistos' ironic comments on the effects of his handiwork and the
same resort to entrapment in bonds as a fitting retribution for sexual
transgressions.

More portentous, however, are the extended echoes of Demodokos' song as the moment of *anagnōrisis* draws ever closer. The
first instance is Penelope's appearance before the Suitors in Book 18.
To prepare her entrance, Athena has attended to her physical en-
hancement while she was sleeping, renewing the beauty of her face
with an ambrosial salve, "such as fair-garlanded Kythereia uses,
whenever she joins the lovely dances of the Graces" (18.192–94). Both
the language and the context recall certain details of the bard's tale.
Only in these two passages is Aphrodite named as "fair-garlanded
Kythereia," and after her flight to Cyprus, the Graces were named as
the ones, who, to restore the goddess's beauty in the aftermath of her
misadventure, bathed and anointed her (8.364–66). Additionally, this
is the first time Penelope has explicitly exposed herself publicly to the
Suitors with a seductive aim in mind; as Newton rightly points out,
she arouses much the same response from them as did the spectacle of
Aphrodite among the other gods ("Their knees gave way, and the
hearts in them were bemused with passion, and each one prayed for
the privilege of lying beside her," 18.212–14; cf. 18.245–49).[46] It is
precisely after this scene, let us note, that Odysseus is most closely
identified with Hephaistos. He offers to tend the fires in the house
and is cruelly advised to take up lodgings instead in the smithy. The
old and ugly beggar likewise arouses laughter from the group, and it is
perhaps no accident that his chief tormentor is the ungrateful maidservant, whom we are told has been sleeping with one of the Suitors
(18.306–29).[47]

Finally, we can point to the significant recall of the Phaeacian
festivities in their pretended counterpart in Odysseus' house. In the
inverval between Penelope's refusal to recognize Odysseus and the
later *anagnōrisis*, Odysseus orders a celebration, replete with dancers

and bards, as a way of gaining time, he says, to hold off news of the Suitors' massacre. In this way, he says, "anyone who is outside, some one of the neighbors, or a person going along the street, who hears us, will think we are having a wedding" (23.130–40). For Newton, the general analogy between the two scenes holds, however they may differ in purpose.[48] But the marriage theme itself may be far more exact; although the song of Ares and Aphrodite is performed for a male audience only with male dancers miming all the parts,[49] the submerged idea of a wedding celebration as its motivating factor may not be far removed.

Marriage is uppermost in the minds of the Phaeacians. Nausikaa is of the right age to find a husband and, from her first meeting with Odysseus on the seashore, his possible role as her bridegroom is a complicating theme that runs uneasily throughout his sojourn on Scheria. Indeed, analyst critics had proposed an earlier version in which Odysseus was intended to wed Nausikaa, and folklorists have pointed to the widespread pattern of a handsome stranger meeting a young girl at a source of water and becoming her husband.[50] If this paradigm were operating silently behind Odysseus' reception at the court of Alkinoos, it might explain some of the ambiguities that critics have noted about the Phaeacians' brand of hospitality, particularly among the other would-be Suitors, who are hostile at first, yet end up showering him with gifts, once Odysseus has shown his mettle. In this context, as Steve Reece has lately suggested, the song of Ares and Aphrodite may not only safely articulate some of the erotic tension aroused by Odysseus' presence among the Phaeacian men, especially after his victory in the games, but also it might itself be an actual wedding song.[51] There is no certain evidence that such songs were performed during (or before) Greek wedding ceremonies. Nevertheless, ribald burlesques were no doubt a common feature of symposiast joking, and the idea of a prenuptial context for such rude "male talk" (as in other cultures) might well account for the bard's choice of this particular theme. A backhanded compliment for the bride, to be sure, and an obscene teasing of male virility, represented as a precise (and temporary) inversion of accepted social norms that are soon to be reaffirmed in the proper conduct of marriage.[52] A disguised wedding song in Book 8, a feigned wedding feast in Book 23: It is a tempting hypothesis that aligns the echoes of one in the other with still richer resonance for the reunion of Odysseus and Penelope in the allusive style of a (re)marriage.

The implicit reference to Hephaistos in the ruse of the bed, however, leads to yet another and even more vital point. Just before the recognition scene, Odysseus is bathed and dressed, and the goddess makes certain he will look his best:

> And over his head Athena suffused great beauty, to make him taller
> to behold and thicker, and on his head she arranged
> the curling locks that hung down like hyacinthine petals.
> And as when a master craftsman overlays gold on silver,
> and he is one who was taught by Hephaistos and Pallas Athena
> in art complete, and grace is on every work he finishes;
> so Athena gilded with grace his head and his shoulders.
>
> (23.159–62)

A surprising number of critics have been disturbed by the fact that this simile is repeated verbatim from an earlier episode, when Athena transformed Odysseus' appearance to present him before the eyes of Nausikaa (6.157–62), and some go so far as to insist that it is a late interpolation into the text.[53] It would be difficult to register the degree of my dissent from this opinion. In the first place, the simile is especially appropriate as a recall of an earlier would-be bride just at the moment when Odysseus and Penelope are to be reunited. Second is the explicit mention of Hephaistos that gives the cue to the further echoes of his role in the stratagem of the bed. But an additional value is to be gained from the description of Hephaistos' handiwork. It is one that will establish another set of relations that, I suggest, are designed to strengthen the sense of stable enclosure that the bed represents and thus offer further airtight proof of Odysseus' identity.

Odysseus is likened to an art object overlaid with gold and silver by the hands of one endowed with the gifts of both Athena and Hephaistos. The description of this craftsman might well apply to Odysseus himself, specifically in the case of the bed that he himself has made, which he decorates in precisely the same way by embellishing it with gold and silver (and ivory). In identifying person with object, body with artifact, and in tracing the shift from a passive to an active role as two essential steps to a process of transfiguration, a powerful link is created that suggests a parallel between the bed and its maker, between the site and object of ownership that matches the physical figure of the one who constructed it. Others have pointed out the ways in which the construction of the entire bedchamber recapitulates and condenses the essence of Odysseus himself: the secret of a secret self that now may be revealed, the interplay between inside and outside, by which the external can now bring to light the truth of that hidden part and give proof of a dissimulated identity.[54] And so it does, not only, as Starobinski observes, by replacing the assertion of "I am" with the active force of "I made it" but also through a set of semantic coincidences and transferrals, by which words of double meanings now coalesce into a powerful unity of reference. Let me explain.

The two key terms are *sēma* and *empedon*, each available for a *jeu de mots* at this critical moment. Penelope had first adverted to the "hidden signs that are only known to the two of us and no one else" (23.110). But it is left to Odysseus to join the two ideas of a *sēma* into one, when through the device of ring composition he first invokes its other, more literal, use as a distinguished mark (*mega sēma*) before he can claim at the end that this *sēma* of the bed is also a *sēma* of proof. And what, in fact, is the final verification, if not the query as to whether the bed is still *empedon* (23.203), that is, whether it remains still fixed in the earth? Only then is Penelope persuaded to acknowledge the bed as the *sēmata* she had required to ratify Odysseus' identity, and this, because she takes the sign as *empeda*, that is, as a solid and secure proof of who he is (23.205, 250; 24.346).[55] In other words, the *sēma* that is *empedon* (i.e., the bed rooted in the earth) emerges as a *sēma empedon* (a valid sign). In these two junctures—the maker with his object, the words with their literal and figurative meanings—the system of reference gains a deeper coherence and closes in upon itself as securely as the chamber that "Odysseus built around the tree trunk, finished it, with close-set stones, and roofed it well over, adding the compacted doors, and fitting them closely together (23.190–94).[56]

These are extraordinary measures, and rightly so, if we consider both the nature of the defensive system and what it aims to protect. If we return now to the beginning of this essay in which I quoted M. I. Finley on the habit in the heroic world "of translating every quality or state into some specific symbol, some concrete and material object," we might then instance the bed and its construction as a prooftext of this principle. But I believe there is more. The impulse to turn a social bond into a visible emblem and to represent the intimacy of inner feeling in external form has the power, in this case, not just to signify the stability of the marriage relationship but also to serve as the stabilizing factor itself of a quality, idea, or proposition that finally remains beyond the reach of all definitive proof. It is an attempt to master what is fundamentally an unmasterable situation.

First and foremost is the radical unknowability of the unexpressed secrets of a woman's desire. She might be pure of hands but not of heart, even if only for a brief moment, then or now. How is one to guarantee the constancy, the steadfastness, of that heart, especially under the present circumstances? The precondition, after all, that regulates the entire situation at Ithaka is the apparent freedom given to Penelope to *choose* the man for her husband whom her heart desires. If she is to choose "the best of the Achaeans," what would this title mean in designating the man she might desire? The contest of the bow, a traditional means for selecting a victorious suitor from among his rivals, might indicate that a heroic feat of physical prowess is to be the deciding factor. Yet because the poet structures his entire plot around Penelope's imagined state(s) of mind, we cannot exclude some cultural notion of feminine desire as an internalized emotion, hidden from view and maintained as a private and undivulged secret. If this is the case, how is that desire to be manifested, investigated, or controlled? Second, more substantively, is the nagging possibility of a real adulterous tryst that would simply have escaped the husband's notice. As a god, Hephaistos has the unusual advantage of Helios the Sun, the All-Seeing, as his reliable informer. He also has magical skills that can expose the errant couple and put them on potentially permanent display in the presence of eyewitnesses. This twofold scenario might be the wish fulfillment fantasy of more than one suspicious husband.

The case at Ithaka is perhaps an extreme example of the same problematic. Its more complex turns are predicated, first of all, on the figure of Penelope herself. The poem presents her in such a way as to assure us of her fidelity.[57] At the same time, it endows her actions with sufficient ambiguity to arouse the need for interpretation, often with diametrically different results, if we chart the range of opinions that swirl around the evaluation of three especially significant moments: her decision to appear before the Suitors, the dream of the geese, and the setting up of the contest of the bow. As Suzuki observes, "unlike Odysseus, Penelope is portrayed from without, and the poet, while according her subjectivity, does not seek to represent it; he sees her through the eyes of the male characters around her— Odysseus, Telemachos, and the Suitors, and he conveys their uncertainty about her."[58] Murnaghan goes further in outlining the dilemma. "Penelope's motives are difficult to assess," she remarks, "because the poet is generally uncommunicative about her thoughts, but not about Odysseus', leaving us to deduce her state of mind from outward gestures and speeches." She continues, "Because Penelope has been shown to be capable of duplicity, in particular through her trick with the shroud, it is not clear whether those speeches are to be taken at face value." Closely bound to these concerns is the asymmetrical quality of their knowledge. Hence, Penelope "is responding to the presence of the apparent stranger who is actually the returned Odysseus in disguise, so what seems to be a meeting of strangers is actually the reunion of husband and wife." Moreover, because Odysseus intends that she remain in this state of ignorance, his deception of her "is not the byproduct of the plot against the Suitors, but a major element in his strategy."[59]

Athena, after all, had bidden Odysseus not to declare himself to Penelope "until you test your wife even more." The first reason given is that a premature reunion might divert him from his obligation to punish the Suitors' infractions of social rules and give away his identity too soon. But underlying the goddess's advice is the unspoken possibility that she might yet betray him (13.190–93). This apparently clever narrative strategy, which maintains suspense about her fidelity until the very end, is, more culturally speaking, based on the profound mistrust of women as exemplified, above all, in the foil story of Klytaimestra but also intimated in the two tales told by Helen and Menelaos. As Murnaghan puts it, "the *Odyssey's* unusually sympathetic portrait of the exemplary wife is placed in a wider context of suspicion towards women from which even she cannot altogether escape. Through the presentation of Penelope as an exception to the general rule, the poem self-consciously depicts the formation and authorization of a tradition of misogyny even as it places the counterexample at the center of its story."[60] Furthermore, as often noted, every female figure in the poem, including Kalypso, Kirke, Arete, and even Nausikaa, contributes some element to the complex and composite portrait of Penelope. On the sinister side, Penelope most resembles Kirke. Does not she too have the charms to enchant men and turn them into swine, creatures who, like the Suitors, are perpetually at the mercy of their bellies? Like Kirke, she too might lure an unsuspecting man to her bed and, having persuaded him to lie in *philotēs* with her, take advantage of his nakedness and even unman him. Homeric epic categorically defines a woman's role in the household as divided equally between the two poles of loom and bed (e.g., *Iliad* 1.31). Are not these the same two elements that Penelope's guile puts into play—the ruse of her web in the first instance and the trick of the bed in the second? Who then could be utterly certain from the start that her gift for duplicity against the Suitors in the matter of the loom might not this time be turned against her husband, precisely with regard to the marital bed?

At the same time, the configuration of male sexual desire, delineated in this poem and elsewhere in Greek literature, itself creates the circumstances for the idea of such a betrayal. This psychological construct is evident in the timing of Penelope's appearance before the Suitors because it serves too as the occasion when Odysseus, for his part, catches his first glimpse of the wife he had left long ago. The motives given for Penelope's sudden desire to exhibit herself to them are very revealing. The fact that Athena and not she is the agent of this unexpected turn of affairs sustains a certain ambiguity in her choice of action. On the one hand, the goddess's intervention relieves Penelope of responsibility and might seem to guarantee the alienation of this desire from Penelope's "true" thoughts. Yet who can vouch for the troubled and complex sources of human desire? In the lover's discourse, the irresistible impulse is often attributed to divine agency as an outward projection. All the same, resort to this erotic psychology might also be a way of veiling (and hence expressing) what the person cannot recognize or acknowledge as internal to, or, at least, compatible with, the desiring self. Hence Penelope can laugh nervously at the idea that Athena put into her mind and express her wonderment that "my heart (*thumos*) desires, though before it did not, to show myself to the Suitors, although I still hate them" (18.163–65). And who can exclude the possibility of a merely convenient pretext, when she adds that she will use the same occasion to reproach her son for consorting with these insolent men (18.166–68)?

A further and essential point is the paradox that the disclosure of these motives only increases the uncertainties about her motives. The poet tells us that Athena conceived this plan "so that Penelope might all the more open up the desiring hearts (*thumos*) of the Suitors, and so that she might seem all the more precious in the eyes of her husband and son even than she had been before" (18.158–62). The tangible results of this encounter are the gifts she beguiles from the Suitors to add to Odysseus' household wealth, and in this way it might be said that she indeed proves more "precious" than before in Odysseus' eyes: He applauds her accomplishment and praises her too in that "she enchanted their spirits with blandishing words, while her own mind had other intentions" (18.281–83). He voices his approval of what he takes to be her deception of the Suitors, but he profits too from their voiced appreciation of her beauty, which Athena has just now restored with this express idea in mind (18.191). The twin ideas—to stir the hearts of the Suitors *and* to make herself more precious in the eyes of her husband—are framed in the proper order. They are not just an instance of parataxis but should also be construed in a relation of cause and effect. Odysseus may be permitted to test the behavior of this Aphroditean Penelope in front of the Suitors, a test, in his opinion, he is convinced she has passed. But he gains yet a further satisfaction. The Suitors' lovestruck reaction to her beautiful appearance renews the ardor of their desire for her and impels them to offer her still more bountiful gifts. Yet this response, witnessed by Odysseus, as he gazes on them gazing on her, validates *his* own desire in turn and renews it, in the flesh, we might say. Athena knows what she is doing.

This doubly voyeuristic scene is a classic instantiation of triangular or "mimetic" desire. This mechanism postulates the major spur to masculine desire as deriving not from some intrinsic quality of the beautiful object herself but rather as the result of a mimetic rivalry among men, whereby male subjects are led to desire the same woman precisely because she is the object of others' desire.[61] Hence the double bind of Penelope's position in the symbiotic interdependence of Odysseus and the Suitors: In order for her husband to desire her, she needs to prove her desirability to others, but by the same move, she also falls under the shadow of suspicion with respect to the status of her own desire. That same double bind requires that she continue her teasing of the Suitors, even to the extent of staging the contest of the bow, while at the same time ostensibly pining for Odysseus—a strategy whose underlying reasons she does not yet understand, or so we think. That same device of maintaining her ignorance also leads up to the kind of *anagnōrisis* the Greeks like best—the affective sympathy between persons and a like-minded affinity they reveal to one another as a precondition of mutual recognition, predicated in this instance on his identity and her fidelity, both of which will attain full acknowledgment in Penelope's ruse of the bed. If the *Odyssey* is justly admired for playing out this narrative strategy in its most extended and developed form, is it not because the erotic setting heightens the thrill of each obstacle to recognition, each detour and deferral on the way? Does not this ploy raise the stakes of the game by requiring men to try to chart the meandering and conflicting paths of what they imagine as a woman's desire?

In commenting on the pervasive appeal of recognition scenes in literature, Terence Cave probes some of its more troubling aspects. The "regime of anagnorisis invites us compellingly, seductively, violently to assent to its simulacrum of order," he argues, "but also to discover in the process that the means by which we define ourselves as individuals in relation to social and legal authority may be no less contrived and trivial than birthmark and casket."[62] A further point he makes is equally relevant, namely, that the power given to female characters in assenting to recognition of a male could also be construed as a "challenging of a male order, represented here by the desire to impose an anagnorisis which would leave the male firmly on top. Women [as men represent them] undo recognitions, or perform it in another way," he proposes, "disquietingly and always scandalously. . . . Only women know, in private, what is really going on. And they may not always care to say," especially when it comes to the "scandal of impossible or incomprehensible sexual knowledge."[63] The mystification continues. What male (even as astute a critic as Cave) is allowed to claim that he knows for sure what a woman thinks or feels?

Penelope's ruse of the bed might seem to follow his proposition. For the first time, she is permitted to take the upper hand. All finally rests in her choice to award or refuse acknowledgment of Odysseus' identity and to set the terms, those "secret signs" they both share, as a test of who he is. Yet if she reverses their roles to assume the role of testing the one who has tested her for so long, by the very nature of the stratagem she selects, she inevitably puts herself to the test as well. Her tears and her instant and spontaneous acceptance of the *sēma* may well offer satisfactory proof that Odysseus' fears are truly ungrounded. In this way, the reunion can take place through the "specially crafted object," which unlike the opposite case of Aphrodite, as Newton observes, proves "to be the touchstone of the wife's faithfulness."[64] But Penelope's ruse does not just attest to the fidelity she has maintained for so long in the past. It operates, too, in the present tense. In tricking Odysseus into revealing the secret of the bed, she not only proves herself to be his match in those very same qualities that characterize him (and therefore identifies her as a suitable wife for him, his "other half") but conversely, in the mode of her testing, she herself is also being tested again by what might prove a too swift capitulation to a potential impostor. This is, in fact, what she herself claims in defending her initial resistance:

> "Do not be angry with me nor be resentful, because
> I did not at first, when I saw you, embrace you as I do now.
> For always the *thumos* in my breast trembled
> lest some one of mortals would come my way and deceive me with
>   words."   (23.215–17)

Paradoxically, perhaps, the very trait of a *thumos* that was always *apistos*, of not trusting others, as the nurse charges, redeems her from Agamemnon's generic accusation that there is nothing "trustworthy" (*ouketi pista gynaixi*) in women" (11.456). At the same time, as Marylin Katz points out, the "coldness of Penelope's welcome upon Odysseus' homecoming provides the associative link with her negative exemplar [Klytaimestra] and this association, like the celebration of the fictional wedding and the trick of bed, configures *anagnōrismos* in the text as if a betrayal." Thus, she continues, "the transformation of duplicity into complementarity for Penelope is then configured in part around the duplicity that characterizes Odysseus, but incorporates also those aspects of *dolos, mētis,* and inflexibility associated with Klytaimestra and consequently with the alternative of Penelope's betrayal."[65]

Interestingly enough, Penelope knows nothing of Klytaimestra. Telemachos, in relating to his mother the tale of his own adventures, never mentions the name or the story of Agamemnon's wife (which he now knows in detail), and Odysseus, warned to keep Klytaimestra's example in mind when approaching his own wife, is not about to impart this dangerous information to Penelope. This serious gap in information is hardly an oversight. The only story of an errant wife in present time that Penelope is permitted to know (and this from Telemachos) is that of Helen, whose conduct she now curiously defends, just after explaining that her own reluctance to acknowledge her husband straight off was due to her fear of impostors because experience had taught her that "there are many who scheme for wicked advantage" (23.217).

> For neither would the daughter born to Zeus, Helen of Argos
> have lain in love with an outlander from another country (*emigē
>   philotēti kai eunēi*),
> if she had known that the warlike sons of the Achaians would bring
>   her
> home again to the beloved land of her fathers.
> It was a god who stirred her to do the shameful thing (*ergon aeikes*)
>   she
> did, and never before had she had in heart (*thumos*) this terrible
> folly (*atē*), out of which came suffering to us also.   (23.217–24)

A strange and disconcerting prelude to her final affirmation that Odysseus has passed her test:

> But now, since you have given me accurate proof (*sēmata ari-
>   phradea*) describing
> our bed, which no other mortal man beside has ever seen,
> but only you and I, and there is one serving woman. . . .
> So you persuade my heart (*thumos*), though it has been very stub-
>   born.   (23.225–27, 230)

Without resorting to the desperate expedient, as many critics have taken, of excising the previous embarrassing passage altogether, it must be admitted that Penelope's speech remains disturbing. Although it is true that the mention of Helen's departure recalls the reason why her husband left so many years ago, the way it is framed seems at best a kind of non sequitur—either a loose association following her claim of wicked schemers (seducers) or a conscious dissociation of herself from Helen's infidelity. At worst, in going so far as to excuse Helen's offense on two very different (and potentially incompatible) grounds (someone would bring her back, *atē* sent by the god made her do it), it might sound like an unconscious vindication of what we do not know (will never know) with regard to Penelope herself. In this seeming collusion between one woman and another under the guise of self-differentiation, is this a way of giving and taking back at the same time? And in the use of a divinely sent *atē* to explain what Penelope sees as contradicting the hitherto unblemished character of Helen, can she then exempt herself from the possibility of the same helpless capitulation in the face of desire? Above all, does Helen's undesired lapse fatally undermine the principles of steadfast mind and stubborn resolve that have guided Penelope's own actions and hence, in some way, undermine the fixed proof of the bed, which she immediately after reconfirms?

No resolution to every facet of this problem is fully satisfactory.[66] There are, however, some further interesting points to consider, ones that might provide a context by linking the passage to other episodes in the poem. Penelope's reference to the fact that the Achaeans brought Helen back might be one last allusion to the scene in Phaiakia. Following the love song of Ares and Aphrodite, we may remember, the bard tells another tale, this time at Odysseus' behest, of the starring role he played in the taking of Troy, a tale that ends with "Odysseus went, with godlike Menelaos, like Ares, to find Helen at the house of Deiphobos, and there endured the grimmest fighting that ever he had, but won it there too, with great-hearted Athena aiding" (8.517–19). If the previous song of Ares and Aphrodite had aligned Odysseus with Hephaistos, this one now leaves no doubt that Ares too is his model. If the story of the Wooden Horse looks forward, and even more directly, to future events on Ithaka, it also seems to align Helen and Penelope, whom Odysseus may reclaim for his own after his slaughter of the Suitors. Yet there is a crucial and obvious difference. Helen went away; Penelope did not. One left her husband's bed; the other remained where she was. Why then is it of such concern to Penelope that Helen would not have gone, had she known that the Achaeans would bring her back? Yet if Helen went away, we might add, so did Odysseus. Does Penelope's version hint at a reversal of genders and thus obliquely refer to Odysseus as well? This suggestion might perhaps seem oversubtle, but it just so happens that to clinch the moment of their final reunion, the text immediately resorts to the last instance of those "reverse sex similes" that are such an important and recurrent stylistic feature in the Odyssey.[67]

> He wept as he held his lovely wife, whose thoughts were virtuous
>   (*kedn' eiduian*).
> And as when the land appears welcome to men who are swimming,
> after Poseidon has smashed their strong-built ship on the open
> water, pounding it with the weight of wind and the heavy
> seas, and only a few escape the gray water landward
> by swimming, with a thick scurf of salt coated upon them,
> and gladly they set foot on the shore, escaping the evil;
> so welcome was her husband to her as she looked upon him.
>   (23.231–39)

Even as a specimen of a reverse simile, this one comes with a surprising twist; only at the last line are we informed that it applies to her, not to him, and to confuse matters further, Odysseus, not she, is the one who is moved to tears. Moreover, it is worth remarking that the content of the simile returns us directly to Odysseus' experience on the open seas in Book 5 that ended with his arrival, battered and bruised, on the shores of Scheria (5.394–95). Yet the theme of gender inversion recalls in turn the striking simile that described Odysseus' reaction to the bard's tale, when he wept like a woman "lying over the body of her dear husband, who fell fighting for her city and people," a woman who is shortly to be "led away into slavery, to have hard work and sorrow" (8.522–30). The effect of his weeping, we may recall, leads on directly to his self-revelation at the court of Alkinoos and the first full resumption of his true identity.

Odysseus goes to the house of Deiphobos to fetch Helen. He is compared to a woman who will shortly be led away to undergo hardship and grief. In this cross-referencing between Phaiakia and Ithaka, between experience and simile, between male and female, Penelope may be said to share in Odysseus' past in advance of his own recitation of his experiences that she is shortly to hear. And if Helen is the figure whose name elicits these interchanges, she is also the figure, as always, upon whom charges of infidelity can be conveniently displaced, even as her motives (and hence culpability) are always open to interpretation.[68] Penelope may be the first to launch this long literary and rhetorical tradition, but in context she raises these questions before returning to the all-too-visible *sēmata* of the bed and to accept Odysseus who, in identifying them, has "persuaded her *thumos*" of his identity.

In conclusion, this entire scene of recognition that revolves around the ruse of the bed continually loops back on itself, like the infinite turnings of a Möbius strip, as it plays off the entwined but also divergent issues of Odysseus' identity and Penelope's fidelity. It does so, as we have seen, through the device of an object that can be minutely described, located in space, and recalled to its functions and emblematic status through the opportunity given to Odysseus to reclaim it in the act of narrating how he first made it. This is an ekphrasis, after all, that describes a work of art. Its function is to transform representation into narration, and it stands in an intermediate space "between the outward force of perceived events and the inner ability to perceive them," so it may finally turn into a convincing sign-symbol of recognition.[69]

But there is one last paradox. The conditions of its representational function ensure its unrepresentability. No blueprint can be extracted from the details of the bed's manufacture, and in the long tradition from antiquity to the present day, no artist seems to have taken up the challenge to translate its presence into a visual reality that we may view with our own eyes. It is precisely the vivid and concrete reality of its material existence that ensures its efficacy as the double-sided sign it was meant to be, but, to retain its powers of persuasion, it must remain what it always was: a mental construct, an image in the mind's eye.[70]

Notes

Heartfelt thanks to Daniel Mendelsohn and Deirdre von Dornum for expert editing and invaluable counsel.

1. These cover a range of categories: cosmic phenomena, bodily marks, elements of a landscape, or some specimen of artisanal handiwork.
2. Finley, 1965, 122. See also Gernet, 1981, on "pre-monetary signs."
3. Griffin, 1980, 24.
4. Atchity, 1978, 1.
5. On the phenomenology of these objects, signs, and symbols and how they are viewed and received in Archaic poetry, see Prier, 1989.
6. For documentation and discussion of the relevant sources, see, most recently, Russo, Fernandez-Galliano, and Heubeck, 1992, at xxiii, 297.

7. For example, see Germain, 1954, 211; de Vries, 1956, 2.385; Eisler, 1910, 2.596–99; Dietz, 1971.

8. Translations throughout are, for the most part, by Lattimore, 1965.

9. On the two meanings of *sēma*, see Stanford, 1961, at 188–89; Russo, Fernandez-Galliano, and Heubeck, 1992, at 187–89: "Odysseus obviously means by *sēma* the special distinguishing mark, the unique feature involved in his construction of bed rather than the token of identity which P. seeks (cf. *sēmata*, 110; cf. also 202) for he is quite unaware that his response to his wife's orders to the maid (177–80) supplies the very *sēma* which Penelope presumably had in mind at 108–10." See also Besslich, 1966, 96; Eisenberger, 1973, 310, n. 21.

10. On *sēma* in connection with interpretation and the faculty of "mind" or *noos/noēsis*, see Nagy, 1983. On its place in Archaic thought, see Prier, 1976, 27: "The term for symbol in Greek is *sēma*. It may indicate any apparition of exceeding beauty or terror. It is always surrounded by an aura of the cosmic, supernatural, affective, or we should say, I think, 'metaphysical' or 'otherworldly.'" See the further development in Prier, 1989, especially 110, explaining the *sēmata* in Homer: "*Sēma* is more or less a synonym for *teras* (marvel, portent) and is intimately and often linked with the verb *phainesthai* (to appear for oneself and another . . .). It also stands with *phasthai* (to speak immediately for oneself and another), *piphauskomenos* (to make manifest for oneself and another, to tell of for oneself and another), and *teuchesthai* (to make or fashion for oneself and another)." In his description of the *mega sēma* of the bed, Odysseus uses *teuchesthai* at the outset, before proceeding to *describe* its actual making, and ends with *piphauskomai* in precisely the two meanings suggested by Prier.

11. See Newton, 1987, 17; Murnaghan, 1987, 116.

12. See, for example, Beye, 1966, 178 ("The live olive tree is still rooted in earth like their sexual knowledge of each other, personal and immutable"); Clarke, 1967, 78 ("the marriage of Odysseus and Penelope has a primal strength—it is secure, fixed in time and place, yet alive, natural, capable of further growth"); Thornton, 1970, 105 ("This is the 'sign' that Odysseus has for Penelope, a 'sign' which is also a beautiful symbol of the deep rootedness of their mutual loyalty"). On the "nature/culture" symbiosis of the bed, see Vidal-Naquet, 1986; Bonnafé, 1985; and Starobinski, 1975. On the reunion at "the dark of the moon" that brings the couple "into phase with the courtship of sun and moon," see Austin, 1975, 252. More generally, see Emlyn-Jones, 1984; Murnaghan, 1987, 140–41; and Katz, 1991, 177–82.

13. Suzuki, 1989. 76.

14. Katz, 1991, 181.

15. Scholiast at 23.288, ed. Dindorf, 1855.

16. This is what Telemachos expects her to do: "Why do you withdraw so from my father, and do not sit beside him and ask him questions and find out about him?" (23.98–99).

17. Germain, 1954, 212; Murnaghan, 1987, 141.

18. Menelaos, when told of the Suitors, had waxed indignant that, although being unwarlike (*analkides*), they should wish to lie in the bed of a strong-hearted man (*kraterophronos andros*) (4.331–34), but the lover's feat would give the lie to this contention.

19. As Vernant, 1980, 62–63, remarks, "It is as if the conjugal bed in which the king sleeps with the queen held powers which qualify the king's house to provide his kingdom with sovereigns who will make it bear fruit. To take the king's place at the heart of his house, in his bed, by becoming united with his wife, is to acquire a claim to reign after him over the land which his wife, in a way, symbolizes."

20. Suzuki, 1989, 88, borrowing from Lévi-Strauss's well-known formulation, 1967, 496: "Women, like words, are signs to be communicated and exchanged among men, but women too, as persons, are generators of signs. . . . In the matrimonial dialogue of men, woman is never purely what is spoken about; for if women in general represent a certain category of signs, destined to a certain kind of communication, each woman preserves a particular value arising from her talent, before and after marriage, for taking her part in a duet. In contrast to words, which have become wholly signs, woman has remained at once a sign and a value."

21. Cf. *Iliad* 3.441, 445; 6.25; 9.133 = 9.275 = 19.176; 14.207, 209, 295–96, 306, 314, 331, 360; 15.32; *Odyssey* 5.126; 15.420–21; 23.219.

22. Calame, 1992, 30–33, and see his entire analysis of epic scenes of lovemaking. For an excellent discussion of erotic terminology, see also Luca, 1981.

23. Hence the formula *lechos kai eunēn* (*Odyssey* 3.403; 7.347; 8.269; cf. 23.179), which comprises both the bed and its coverings.

24. Note that when Penelope takes Odysseus' description of the bed as the clear proof (*sēmata ariphradea*) she had demanded, she shifts from *lechos* to *eunē* (23.226), naming it for the first time as "ours" and using the more erotic term.

25. Another word is *akoitis*, which has a similar meaning, to *alochos* (as one who shares the same resting place, *koitos*), although corresponding more nearly to "spouse." Snell, 1987, s.v. *Akoitis* (or *parakoitis*) is always used alone, unlike *alochos*, which may be included in the larger social scene of children, parents, and household possessions. A man may be called a *parakoitēs*, but there is no such equivalent for *alochos*. The two words share some of the same adjectives, but we may observe their different nuances in *Iliad* 9.396–99, where Achilles, rejecting Agamemnon's offer of his daughter in marriage, states that he will take an *akoitis* for his own at home, "where his desire stirs him to wed a wife he has wooed (*gēmanta mnēstēn alochon*), a fitting bedmate (*eikuian akoitin*) to delight in the possessions the old man Peleus has acquired for him." Loraux, 1981, 32–34, correctly argues for the relation between *lechos* and *lochos* (of childbed), as signifying the connection between sex and reproduction in legitimating the status of the wife (*alochos*). See also Calame, 1992, 98–99.

26. This is especially the case in the tragic poets. Euripides' *Medea* is the richest example for the full range of lexical meanings.

27. As, for example, when Hera, to mollify Zeus' anger at his deception in their improvised bed, swears a holy oath on his head and on their *kouridion lechos* (*Iliad* 15.37).

28. Cf. Brilliant, Chapter 9, this volume.

29. On the positive valence of *tetlēoti thumōi* for Odysseus and its more ambivalent use for Penelope, see Emlyn-Jones, 1984, 13–14; Katz, 1991, 164–65.

30. Katz, 1991, 170–73, suggests that the innovation of the poem is the maintenance of an ideal of "exclusivity," so that for the first time courtship by suitors is considered a crime.

31. On these stories, see Schmiel, 1972; Dupont-Roc and Le Boulluec, 1976; Bergren, 1981; Zeitlin, 1981, 204–6; Goldhill, 1991, 62–64. On their relevance as two alternative paradigms for Penelope, see Andersen, 1977; Zeitlin, 1981; and Katz, 1991, esp. 77–80. Olson, 1990, is mostly derivative, but his claims that Menelaos' story is the "right" one and Helen's the "wrong" one, on the basis of his understanding of the "sexual dynamics" of the poem, seem to me ultimately naive and misguided.

32. *Moichagri[a]*, "a fine imposed on someone taken in adultery" is a *hapax*.

33. Burkert, 1960, 137, n. 16.

34. Translation of Lattimore modified.

35. One might justly compare their permanent state of attachment to Aristophanes' myth in Plato's *Symposium* (192c–e), where Hephaistos offers to reunite the two halves of the original spherical beings into their former love-locked existence.

36. The song in its context: on Ares and Aphrodite in Book 8: Bliss, 1968; Edinger, 1980; Braswell, 1982.

37. Cf. Athenaeus 5.192d–e.

38. On the Trojan songs of the bard, see especially the fine analysis of Pucci, 1987, 214–27. For the poet's "invention" of the unknown theme of the quarrel between Achilles and Odysseus, see Marg, 1956, 20–21; for its "traditionality," Nagy, 1979, 43.

39. For the definitive study of *mētis*, including craft, craftsmanship, and binding/unbinding, see Detienne and Vernant, 1978. On Hephaistos in particular, see in addition, Delcourt, 1957.

40. Edwards, 1985, argues for the *lochos* or ambush through *mētis* as defining the *kleos* of Odysseus. But *bia*, the quality relevant to both Achilles and Ares, is also fully deployed in the Iliadic style battle against the Suitors, as well be further mentioned in this chapter.

41. Newton, 1987.

42. See Braswell, 1982, 134; Newton, 1987, 13. Note, however, that in the funeral games in *Iliad* 23 (echoed in the games in Phaiakia), Odysseus actually won in the footrace (significantly, against Ajax: *Iliad* 23.740–83).

Demodokos' first song tells of a quarrel between Achilles and Odysseus, a first move, I suggest, to establish Odysseus' identity by posing his difference (dissent) from that other Homeric hero. Achilles, of course, is best known for his swiftness of foot, and if Odysseus wins the footrace in *Iliad* 23, it is because Achilles presides over the games but does not himself compete. Here Odysseus explicitly renounces the footrace, so as to emphasize instead his skill in archery, the trait for which he is best known (8.215–28).

43. Ibid.

44. Note too that when Odysseus first enters the house, he sits on the threshold, "leaning against a pillar of cypress wood which a carpenter had once smoothed and made straight by the rule" (17.340–41).

45. Newton, 1987, 18, n. 22.

46. Ibid., 16. This temptation scene might also recall Menelaos' story about Helen in her efforts to seduce the Greek chieftains at Troy (4.266–89). See Katz, 1991, 133.

47. Her behavior prompts Odysseus' threat to tell Telemachos, who, he claims, will savagely punish her (18.338–39), an exact preview of later events when, after the massacre of the Suitors, the father will bid his son to "cleanse" the house of its sexual "pollution" by the unfaithful maidservants.

48. Newton, 1987, 17, suggests the echo serves to distract the audience's attention from the darker side of Odysseus' revenge. Many critics have noted the "truth" in the pretended wedding feast as heralding the fact that the reunion of Odysseus and Penelope is to be a (re)marriage. See, for example, Besslich, 1966, 89; Segal, 1983, 44–45; Pucci, 1987, 91; Katz, 1991, 166–71.

49. Critics do not agree as to whether the dancers mime the song or dance independently. It is worth mentioning that later tradition knows just such a mime: "He danced the amours of Aphrodite and Ares, Helios tattling, Hephaistos laying his plot and trapping both of them with his entangling bonds, the gods who came in on them, portrayed individually, Aphrodite ashamed, Ares seeking cover and begging for mercy, and everything that belongs to this story, in such wise that Demetrius was delighted beyond measure with what was taking place and paid the highest possible tribute to the dancer; he raised his voice and shouted; I hear the story that you are acting, I do not just see it; you seem to me to be talking with your very hands" (Lucian, *de saltatione* 62–63).

50. Woodhouse, 1930, 54–65; see Reece, 1993, 104–21 for fuller discussion and bibliography. Cf. too Shapiro on Nausikaa, Chapter 8, this volume.

51. Reece, 1993, 115–16.

52. Olson, 1989b, claims that the song exposes the "hypocrisy" of the *Odyssey*'s "double standard" in order to debunk the absurdly high moral expectations of the poem that run counter to any notion of believable "reality" in the fallen world in which they (we?) all live. Peradotto, 1993, who views the song as an alternate and uncensored view of unlawful sexual desire

in a spirit of exuberant and life-giving comic license, better understands the properties of a literary text in its reference to some external "reality."

53. For discussion, see Russo, Fernandez-Galliano, and Heubeck, 1992, at xxiii, 157–62.

54. Above all, see Starobinski's remarkable essay on the "inside and the outside," 1975, and see further Katz's use of his work, 1991, 179–81.

55. *Sēmata* that are *empeda* are matched by the clarity and visibility (*ariphradēs*) of the *sēma* (11.126; 21.217; 23.73, 225, 273; 24.329).

56. From this point of view, we may also distinguish between the two craftsmen, Odysseus and Hephaistos. The latter, by means of his art, is uniquely the agent of transformation, but is not himself subject to physical changes. The ugly artist remains forever as he is, bound to his forge and deploying his skills of beautiful embellishment. Odysseus, by contrast, enjoys the benefits of both sides: An aesthetic persona (signifying his erotic status) merges with the artistry of what he has made. At the same time, embedded in the verb *piphauskomai* (related to the root for *phaos*) is an enduring relation between Hephaistos and Odysseus in the matter of fire and light. Aithon (the blazing one) is what Odysseus names himself in his lying tale to Penelope (19.183) when they sit by the fire at the hearth in their first intimate conversation, and in Book 23 the hearth again is prominent as the site of their two-phased reunion. In his arrival on Scheria, the transitional point of his journey from the fabulous world of his adventures to the realities of life on Ithaka, Odysseus is significantly linked to fire in the simile that compares his burrowing under a pile of heaped-up leaves in a dense thicket to a spark buried in the embers (5.490). Here too, as in Book 23, he plays true to form by making a bed in a place of private and hidden enclosure. See further Bonnafé, 1985, and on Odysseus and fire (light), see especially Bremer, 1976; and Flaumenhaft, 1982.

57. Aside from explicit statements (e.g., Odysseus' mother in the underworld in response to his query; 11.177–83), fidelity is figured by Penelope's immobility in the house and her continuous weeping—another sign that she has not forgotten her husband. Fidelity is less an affair of the heart than the mind (*noos*), and infidelity is as much equated with changing that *noos* or failing to remember as it is to engage in conscious and active deception. Hence, Penelope's epithet, *echephrōn* (keeping good sense) not only attests to her intelligence and perspicacity but also includes a capacity to remain steadfast in that *noos*, keeping her husband always in mind. *Sōphrōn* (and the noun, *sōphrosynē*), whose literal meaning is "to keep the mind safe," is unknown in Homeric diction but later becomes the standard word for chastity.

58. Suzuki, 1989, 91.

59. Murnaghan, 1986, 105.

60. Ibid., 107.

61. On the concept of mimetic or mediated desire (the male subject desires the object because the rival desires it), see Girard, 1977, 145.

62. Cave, 1988, 464.

63. Ibid., 494–95.

64. Newton, 1987.

65. Katz, 1991, 164.

66. For a recent and thoughtful discussion of the passage, see Murnaghan, 1987, 141–43, who concludes that "Penelope cannot believe that she might herself be an exception, a wife who in no sense betrays her husband even after so long a separation," while shrewdly comparing "Penelope's attention to the example of Helen" with Odysseus' "attention to the example of Agamemnon," both leading to hesitation in recognition/identification. Katz, 1991, 184–87, takes a more extreme position. Reviewing the multitude of other opinions on this passage, she reads this statement to mean that "Penelope both consolidates her own *kleos* by differentiating herself from Helen and undermines the fixity of its meaning at the same time. In this way she incorporates into the narrative as a self-conscious statement about herself the indeterminacy of meaning that has characterized her throughout the poem." However the text is interpreted, we should never lose sight of the fact that these are the poet's words and Penelope is his creation.

67. On reverse sex similes in the poem, see the classic essay of Foley, 1978.

68. See Suzuki, 1989, 90, who comments that the poet makes the Iliadic Helen a scapegoat for Penelope, "in order to exorcize anxiety-producing qualities from his own heroine."

69. Prier, 1989, 114.

70. This essay will also appear in my volume of essays, *Playing the Other: Gender and Society in Classical Greek Literature,* University of Chicago Press, 1995.

III

Representations of
Female Characters from
the *Odyssey* in Ancient Art

8

Coming of Age in Phaiakia:
The Meeting of Odysseus and Nausikaa

H. A. Shapiro

If, as A. J. Graham demonstrates elsewhere in this volume, Odysseus' far-flung travels reflect the large-scale colonization movement of the Greek Renaissance, then Scheria, the land of the Phaeacians, the setting of nearly one quarter of the poem, is surely the ultimate Greek colonist's fantasy of a faraway paradise. It has often been noted that one conspicuous fantasy element of Phaeacian society is a kind of gender reversal at the court. It is Arete, the queen, whom Odysseus is advised to supplicate on his entry into the palace (6.304–5); it is Arete upon whose favor Odysseus, the shipwrecked stranger, will depend for his success.[1] Nausikaa, the princess, is very much her mother's daughter: poised, self-assured, quick-witted. And just as Arete was the only child of a royal father who died young (7.63–67), so Nausikaa, as the only daughter and youngest child in a family of five sons (6.62–63), is the loved and cherished child of doting parents and an adoring people.

Yet amid the rich panorama of womanhood in the *Odyssey*,[2] Nausikaa is perhaps unique: neither a motherly figure, like Eurykleia or Antikleia (Odysseus' mother); a wife, like Penelope, Arete, or Helen; nor an experienced temptress, like Kirke or Kalypso; but rather a maiden on the brink of maturity and marriage.[3] This is, to be sure, a standard enough figure in Greek myth, but, curiously, Nausikaa is the only good example in the poem.[4] The whole episode is punctuated with so many hints at a possible (yet impossible) marriage of Odysseus to Nausikaa that one earlier critic supposed that a familiar folktale motif—handsome stranger arrives from overseas, wins the heart of the princess, and wins her hand in a test of valor—was in the poet's mind until he realized that it was utterly unsuited to the context of the *Odyssey* and the theme of the hero's return to his faithful wife.[5]

If Homer was the first great psychologist, then nowhere are his skills more evident than in the meeting and failed courtship of Nausikaa and Odysseus. The subtle portrait of an adolescent girl—shy and yet brave, proper yet eager, beautiful yet unaffected—is right on the mark. For Odysseus, the proud and wily hero now reduced to abject helplessness, this is the ultimate test of his skillful way with words, and he rises to the occasion in an extraordinary opening speech (6.149–85). The delicate situation and the shrewd character studies are so real, so universal, that every reader smiles in recognition. But how did the episode read to the Greeks themselves (or, more accurately, how did it play in performance by bard or rhapsode), say, to an Athenian audience of the Classical period? We have enough bits and pieces of evidence to form an impression, and it suggests that some reactions may be less "universal" than we would like to think.

The Nausikaa episode is extremely rare in ancient art, and I suspect this is in part because artists wisely recognized that the psychological nuances that are its chief interest were beyond their abilities to capture.[6] They found it more congenial to stick to animals and monsters when it came to the *Odyssey*. Yet there is one brief flicker of interest in Nausikaa, in the second and third quarters of the fifth century.[7] The scanty evidence comprises a rare conjunction of three elements that must all be somehow interconnected: a lost play by a great dramatist, a lost work by a great painter, and a few pale reflections of both in Athenian red-figure vase painting.

The play, by Sophokles, was entitled *Nausikaa* or *Plyntriai*, "The Washer Women," an allusion to the laundry that drew Nausikaa and her companions down to the river. Only one or two verses are preserved.[8] To modern readers raised on *Oedipus* and *Antigone*, the Nausikaa episode does not seem like the stuff of Sophoclean tragedy, yet modern editors insist it was not a satyr-play.[9] Nor do ancient reports that Sophokles himself played the title role and especially distinguished himself by his ball-playing skills help to dispel this odd feeling of incongruity.[10] Perhaps there is a good reason the play does not survive.

The lost painting, by Polygnotos, was not a large mural of the type for which he was most famous, but a small wooden *pinax* displayed in the Pinakotheke, or picture gallery, at the entrance to the Athenian Akropolis.[11] According to the ancient traveler Pausanias, "Polygnotos also painted Odysseus approaching the women washing clothes with Nausikaa at the river, just as Homer described it" (1.22.6). If this is to be read literally—that Odysseus was shown coming upon the girls while they were *in the act* of washing clothes—then Pausanias is in error, for this is not at all how Homer pictures the scene. Rather, the girls have earlier spread out the laundry to dry and are playing ball when their cries first awaken the sleeping Odysseus. Why this seemingly minor, yet conspicuous departure from the text? A look at the two preserved vases may offer some clues.

The earlier of the two is a neck-amphora in Munich, made about 440 B.C., that has given his name to Beazley's Nausicaa Painter (plates 24, 25).[12] Laundry is indeed much in evidence, as each of the five girls holds a damp garment and one is still wringing hers out. The scene thus matches the brief description of Polygnotos' painting and was quite possibly inspired by that famous, publicly displayed work. But this tampering with the sequence of events is hardly the only departure from the text; indeed, there are so many, and such flagrant ones, that one distraught German commentator at the beginning of the century speculated that the painter must have been a foreigner, a non-Greek emigré in Athens.[13] The branches that Odysseus has grabbed to cover his nakedness are not even close to where they should be. The same pose and branches also occur on a roughly contemporary kantharos that has been interpreted as an excerpt from the same scene, a single girl fleeing from the naked Odysseus (plate 26).[14] Worst of all, on the Munich amphora, one would be hard-pressed to say for sure which girl is the fair Nausikaa, so little is she differentiated from her companions. Yet Homer stresses how much taller and more graceful Nausikaa is than the other girls, in an elaborate simile comparing the princess to the goddess Artemis (6.101–9). If on our amphora Nausikaa is meant to be the girl nearest Odysseus, as seems likely, then why does she turn to flee instead of standing her ground, as the poet says (6.139)?[15] Needless to say, she does not stand head and shoulders above her friends, but is virtually indistinguishable from them in stature and dress.

All of this could be written off as hack work by an inept and mediocre artist—though certainly an Athenian one—but the unexpected presence of Athena may prompt us to think again. This is not a simple misunderstanding of the text or an inadvertent slip. Yet it cannot be taken literally, either, I believe. The painter may well have remembered Homer's comment that Nausikaa alone stood her ground because "Athena put courage into her heart and took fear from her body" (6.139–40),[16] though he recognized that she was not *physically* present at this moment. We have no way of knowing if Polygnotos' painting included the figure of Athena and should rather try to understand it as an innovation of the vase painter. It is his way of saying to us, "You remember how Athena instigated all this when she made Nausikaa throw the ball wide, into the water; how she gave Nausikaa the courage to stand her ground; how she will shortly spruce up the storm-tossed Odysseus for his entry into Phaiakia town; indeed how Athena is the hero's constant companion and protectress throughout his journey." This epiphany of the goddess is not necessarily visible to the others in the scene, only to us, and it is a technique with a venerable tradition in Greek art. Among many earlier instances that could be cited, to stay with the *Odyssey*, we may think of the well-known Polyphemos cup in Boston (plate 32), where Athena suddenly appears in Polyphemos' cave, to help Odysseus get the Kyklops drunk.[17]

Once we accept that a sculptor or painter might pursue his own agenda, in which fidelity to the text is not an especially high priority, then other apparent flaws make more sense too. The positioning of the branches—not one branch, as we would expect, but two—ensures that we will not overlook them: They are posed that way for *us*, not for Nausikaa.[18] Likewise, the laundry draped in the tree—instead of laid out on the rocks, as Homer would have it (6.93–95)—is much easier for us to recognize this way and allows the tree to do double duty. The painter could as easily have shown a ball game, but it is the laundry that most readily and unequivocally evokes this episode in our minds. *Plyntriai* is what Sophokles titled his play (although he evidently included a scene of the ball game as well), and it is *plyntriai*—laundresses—that the painter gives us. In other words, in every instance the artistic goal is narrative clarity and ease of recognition. The only breach of clarity is in the obscuring of Nausikaa's identity, and here one can only think that the painter was just not that interested in her. She is not the principal subject of this picture, but rather Odysseus.

For those still unhappy with the Nausicaa Painter's "deconstruction" of the Homeric episode, a second vase painting, about a decade later and now in the Boston Museum of Fine Arts, should offer some consolation (plate 27).[19] The action unfolds around the lid of a pyxis (a box for women's toiletries), with the tree serving as a natural caesura. Odysseus' branch is now more or less in the right place (it is rendered in dilute glaze and very hard to make out), and even more effective is his diffident, half-crouching pose. Nausikaa *does* stand her ground this time, and her cool detachment is heightened by the contrast with the frantic gestures of two fleeing companions (the third, still occupied with the laundry, is evidently unaware of the stranger's presence). The scene is altogether charming, though there is still much that a purist could quibble about. Athena is now less an invisible presence than an active participant in the action. She looks pointedly back at Odysseus and gestures with outstretched right hand in the direction of Nausikaa, lest the hero fall on his knees and start supplicating the wrong girl. Odysseus still wears the veil of Ino / Leukothea that had saved him from drowning off the coast of Scheria, but which he should have returned to the sea by now (5.459–60).[20] Although there is no doubt from their poses which girl is Nausikaa, her name is inscribed, as are the names of all her companions: Phylonoe, Leukippe, and Kleopatra. These are obviously not Homer's names because he leaves the companions anonymous, but are they Sophokles' names, or Polygnotos', or perhaps made up by someone else?[21] Could they even be the names of real people, friends of an Athenian girl who received this pyxis as a wedding gift?[22]

There is considerable variety in the costumes of the four girls, only one of which (on the girl still wringing out the laundry) looks at all appropriate for such a humble chore, much less for playing ball. Although it seems likely that the painter's main interest was in parading the latest fifth-century fashions, a verse that may belong to Sophokles' *Nausikaa* mentions the rather unusual *ependytes*, the very garment worn here by Nausikaa.[23] The long-sleeved patterned jacket, or *kandys,* worn by one of the fleeing girls, a garment of Persian origin, may likewise be a deliberately exotic touch used here to characterize the far-off and luxury-loving Phaeacians.[24]

One last detail of the scene should be pointed out: the pebbles, some in applied bits of clay, indicating the shore. Greek vase painting is notably lacking in landscape elements,[25] but these carefully remind us of the story's setting at the water's edge, which in Greek myth was always fraught with perils, especially for young women and maidens. We may think of Europa, carried off by the Zeus-bull as she gathered flowers with her friends by the shore; of Andromeda, chained to the rock and terrorized by a sea monster until rescued by Perseus; of Hesione, the Trojan princess also the victim of a sea monster until freed by Herakles; of Deianeira, Herakles' wife, ferried across a river by the centaur Nessos, who made advances in midstream; or of Amymone and Amphitrite, ravished by the sea god himself, Poseidon.

Homer himself was surely not unaware of the vulnerable position of these young, unescorted girls. Nausikaa's words of reassurance to her companions (6.199–200) imply that it was the possibility of an enemy attack that they were fleeing, rather than a sexual threat.[26] Yet elsewhere the poet does seem to acknowledge the sexual tension inherent in a tale of maidens alone, far from home, and without male escort, especially when he has them cast off their veils, the symbol of female modesty (6.100). Doing the laundry was one of the few activities that could place a girl in this situation and must have been recognized as particularly fraught with risk. Eumaios later recounts how a slave girl in his father's house, while doing the laundry, was seduced by a Phoenician merchant anchored at the shore (15.420–22).

It is little wonder, then, that recent critics have been quick to recognize an erotic undertone in this encounter of two strangers, one stark naked and the other as nearly undressed as a Greek woman might ever be in a public place, even if the poet is too discreet to make an explicit reference.[27] Indeed, the poet's delicacy in matters sexual is so extreme that it must have struck his ancient readers as almost naive. To take one famous instance, throughout the *Iliad* the poet never hints at a romantic interest in the heroic friendship of Achilles and Patroklos, while Classical Athenians, from Aeschylus to Plato, simply took their homoerotic relationship for granted.[28] Similarly, Helen's sexual charms are consistently treated with the utmost tact in Homer, compared, say, to the defiant seductress of Euripides in the *Trojan Women*.

The potential sexual threat to Nausikaa and her companions also resonates in Homer's description of their game as a kind of dance (6.101), led by the princess herself.[29] It was a well-known *topos* of Greek myth that young girls were a particularly irresistible target of rapists when playing with friends and performing in a dance—even in a sanctuary. Thus, while dancing in the sanctuary of Artemis Orthia in Sparta, Helen was abducted by Theseus (Plutarch, *Theseus* 31.2), and Poseidon was said to have first spied Amphitrite in a dance on the island of Naxos (Eustathios on *Odyssey* 3.91). Persephone was playing and gathering flowers with the daughters of Ocean when she was raped by the god Hades (Homeric *Hymn to Demeter* 4–5). And in the Homeric *Hymn to Aphrodite,* as part of her seduction of Anchises, the goddess poses as a mortal girl who had been abducted by Hermes while dancing and playing with other girls in honor of Artemis.[30] If Greek gods and heroes had no compunction about ravishing a girl dancing in honor of the virgin goddess Artemis, how much more tempting would the innocent Nausikaa look, as she danced with her friends by the deserted river bank?[31]

Certainly Ovid showed no trace of Homeric discretion when he parodied Odysseus' initial supplication of Nausikaa, inverting the sex roles and putting the words into the mouth of the lascivious water nymph Salmacis, addressed to the chaste Hermaphroditus (*Metamorphoses* 4.320–28). But how did the fifth-century Athenian audience react to the Nausikaa episode?

The combination of women, water, and danger fascinated the Greeks. All of the stories alluded to here, and more, were illustrated by Archaic and Classical vase painters, for whom rape was an especially congenial subject,[32] whether at the seashore or elsewhere, and some of the iconographical conventions they created are evident on our two Nausikaa vases. This is true, for example, of the two girls fleeing in fear and distress on the Boston vase, a type repeated in countless rape and abduction scenes. Generally the attacker, whether Poseidon, Zeus, Boreas, Theseus, or another, grabs his victim, while her female companions flee for help (plates 28, 29).[33]

Furthermore, Odysseus' half-crouching pose on the Boston pyxis (plate 27), even if motivated here by modesty, cannot have helped but remind Athenian viewers of the satyrs, perpetually aroused creatures, who steal upon their prey in a similar pose (plate 30).[34]

These iconographical parallels suggest that for the Classical Athenian there was no doubt as to the sexual nature of the threat to Nausikaa and her friends. We cannot know how much Sophokles might have made of this motif in his play. It is a good bet that it was well exploited by Philyllios, the poet of Old Comedy whose play on this episode is known only from the title.[35] The Nausikaa episode has recently been described as representing the "vielschichtigste" of all Odysseus' many relationships with women.[36] By paying particular attention to the vase paintings and what they imply about the jaded sensibility of Classical Athens, we may be inclined to reread the Nausikaa episode with a new appreciation of its many layers of meaning.

Notes

1. See Fenik, 1974, 5–7, who notes the difficulty that Arete does not seem to exercise the extraordinary power attributed to her, at least with regard to the fate of Odysseus. Cf. also Rose, 1969, 404-5. I have not been able to consult W. Mattes, *Odysseus bei den Phaiaken*, Würzburg, 1958.

2. The extraordinarily prominent role of female characters has often been noted. Most recently, Hölscher, 1989, 118, observed, "Das Epos lässt sich lesen wie der Roman eines Mannes in einer Fülle von Frauenbeziehungen."

3. For a recent treatment of Nausikaa as a "successful portrayal of puberty," see Austin, 1975, 200–202. See also Beye, 1966, 196.

4. Lattimore, 1969, 101, remarked that "Greek literature is not rich in vivacious ingenues."

5. Woodhouse, 1930, 60–64. This theory has not found favor with subsequent critics. For the fullest argument against it, see Lattimore, 1969. More sympathetic are Austin, 1975, 200; and Hölscher, 1989, 116–17.

6. The most complete surveys of the ancient representations are those of Touchefeu-Meynier, 1968, 203–8; Brommer, 1983, 95–97.

7. The only possible earlier depiction for which we have any evidence was on the early sixth-century Chest of Kypselos at Olympia, described by Pausanias at 5.19.9. The scene showed two girls riding in a mule-drawn cart, taken by the periegete to be Nausikaa and one of her companions. I do not understand the comment of Hainsworth, in Heubeck, West, and Hainsworth, 1988, at 6.141 (where Nausikaa alone stands her ground at the appearance of Odysseus): "This splendid moment inspired the artist of the Chest of Cypselus. . . ."

8. Pearson, 1963, 1:fr.781, 2:92; cf. n. 23 in this chapter.

9. Pearson, 1963, 2:92, notes, however, that plays with both titles, *Plyntriai* and *Nausikaa*, are recorded by playwrights of Old and Middle Comedy. Thus the material's comic potential was recognized early on.

10. See Athenaeus 20F for the story that Sophokles played the title role, and Pearson, 1963, 2:92. This provides a *terminus ante quem* for the play of 456.

11. On Polygnotos see Pollitt, 1990, 126–41, and 141 for the Nausikaa painting. Polygnotos' main activity is placed in the period ca. 475–450. The Pinakotheke, as the northwest wing of the Propylaea, was not completed until 432, but the painting must have been installed there from somewhere else.

12. Munich 2322; ARV^2 1107,2; $BAdd^2$ 329; *CVA* Munich 5 [Germany 20], plates 213, 214.

13. Hauser, 1905, 27.

14. London E156; ARV^2 1281; Touchefeu-Meynier, 1968, plate 31,1. Here the disheveled state of Odysseus' hair and beard are even more effectively rendered than on the Munich amphora.

15. The principal reason for identifying as Nausikaa the girl nearest Odysseus is that, for the viewer looking at the front side of the vase (plate 24), she forms a threesome with the other two protagonists, Odysseus and Athena. The three girls on the reverse are clearly subsidiary and completely preoccupied with the laundry; the girl at the handle is fleeing even more conspicuously than Nausikaa. See Simon, 1963, 59–60, who also observes that, in his confusion, the painter has placed a diadem, which should characterize Nausikaa alone, on both of the first two girls.

16. Hainsworth, in Heubeck, West, and Hainsworth, 1988, at 6.139–40,

remarks that this is "hardly more than a figure of speech, used because Nausicaa's bold behaviour calls for an explanation."

17. Boston 99.518; *ABV* 198; *BAdd*² 53. Another good example on a well-known vase is the cup tondo by Onesimos of ca. 500 B.C., showing the young Theseus received by Amphitrite at the bottom of the sea: Louvre G104; *ARV*² 318,1; *BAdd*² 214; *Euphronios: Der Maler*, 1991, 232. A large, imposing figure of Athena fills the middle of the scene, though surely neither Bacchylides, in his version of the story (*Ode* 17), nor any Greek audience would have imagined that Athena actually accompanied Theseus to Poseidon's watery realm. We might also add the numerous scenes in which Athena accompanies Theseus into the Labyrinth to fight the Minotaur; on these see my comments in Shapiro, 1991, 126–27.

18. One early commentator speculated that in Homer's original version the branch was meant as a token of supplication (as the branches indeed appear on the Munich amphora), but that a prudish rhapsode altered its purpose: Marx, 1887, 251. Cf. Hauser's discussion of the vase in Furtwängler and Reichhold, 1932, 101. For recent discussion of whether Homer intended the branch primarily as a sign of Odysseus' modesty or rather for his *own* protection, see Gutglueck, 1988.

19. Boston 04.18; *ARV*² 1177,48 (attributed to Aison); *BAdd*² 340; first published by Hauser, 1905. It was said to have been found in Athens.

20. For a possible parallel between Odysseus throwing away the veil of Ino / Leukothea and Nausikaa and her companions throwing off their veils to play ball (6.100), see Nagler, 1974, 47. The same word, *kredemnon,* is used for the veil in both instances.

21. Polygnotos was well known for giving names to the figures in his murals. At one point in his description of the Sack of Troy in the Lesche of the Cnidians at Delphi (10.26.2), Pausanias speculates that Polygnotos has invented some of the names given to figures in the painting.

22. Phylonoe and Kleopatra both occur on a slightly later cup signed by Xenotimos, showing the Birth of Helen: Boston 99.539; *ARV*² 1142,1; Caskey and Beazley, 1963, plate 99. Phylonoe is attested as the name of one of Helen's sisters (Apollodoros 3.10.6) and as such appears together with Helen on the hydria in the Kerameikos, inv. 2712; *ARV*² 1313,6; Schöne, 1990, 166–67 and plate 26, 1. Kleopatra occurs on a squat lekythos in the manner of the Meidias Painter: London E 697; *ARV*² 1324,45; Burn, 1987, plate 20a.

23. Pollux 7.45. See Miller, 1989, 313–14 on the line from Sophokles and Aison's pyxis.

24. On the *kandys*, see Knauer, 1985, 607–13.

25. See most recently Hurwit, 1991.

26. See Hainsworth, in Heubeck, West and, Hainsworth, 1988 at 6.199–200.

27. See, e.g., Beye, 1966, 196; Steinthal, 1991, 505. Albicker, 1991, suggests a deliberate double-entendre in the words *medea* at 6.129 (mind /

male genitals) and *mixesthai* at 6.136 (meet/have sexual intercourse with). The ambiguity of this verb in Nausikaa's speech at 6.288 has been noted by commentators: Cairns, 1990; but not at 6.136. I am grateful to Albicker for making available a copy of her paper.

28. See Dover, 1978, 197–99.

29. See Gross, 1976, 316.

30. The image of Artemis is ever-present during the Nausikaa episode, as both the poet (6.102) and Odysseus (6.151) liken the young princess to the goddess.

31. For the interpretation of Nausikaa as "the last and subtlest of Odysseus' temptations" see Lattimore, 1969, 101; and Steinthal, 1991, 508, on the Phaeacian episiode as Odysseus' rediscovery of his erotic self and, with it, a renewed determination to return to Penelope. Unlike in the other myths, the temptation for Odysseus is enhanced by the fact that Nausikaa at times, in her own reticent way, seems to be trying to seduce him; see Beye, 1966, 196.

32. The fullest corpus of images is Kaempf-Dimitriadou, 1979.

33. See the examples illustrated in Kaempf-Dimitriadou, 1979, plate 12 (Zeus and Aegina); plate 19 (Poseidon and Amphitrite); plate 29 (Boreas and Oreithyia). Note that on the vase illustrated in plate 19,1–3 (= Athens 1708, here plates 28, 29), one of the fleeing companions of Amphitrite holds a ball, suggesting that they had been playing a ball game when Poseidon burst on the scene.

34. Basel BS 407; *Para* 469; Beazley, 1967. Touchefeu-Meynier, 1968, 204, comments on the satyrlike appearance of Odysseus on the kantharos in London (plate 26).

35. See n. 9 in this chapter.

36. Hölscher, 1989, 118.

9

Kirke's Men: Swine and Sweethearts

Richard Brilliant

"Men are pigs and they like it that way."
Anna M. Warrock, *The New York Times*, Oct. 11, 1991

The animal nature of men and their surrender to the bestializing forces of unmediated desire have long been a *topos* of the moral critique of mankind, well before it was taken up by contemporary feminists. Whether or not this unflattering view is justified, the imagery of men as "pigs" has an arresting power due, no doubt in part, to the piggish behavior of pigs, gluttony and lust being their salient characteristics. Yet, like so many contemporary conventions of thought, deeply rooted in our culture, this imagery, too, seems to have an ancient source, located in the famous Kirke episode in Homer's *Odyssey* (10.135–574), when Odysseus' Companions were changed into pigs by Kirke's magic and remained in that deplorable state until they were redeemed as men by Odysseus with the help of Hermes and his magic. This complex episode has resonated over the centuries. It is well represented in works of Greek, Etruscan, and Roman art, often with significant differences in its iconography and application.[1] The Kirke episode was also picked up by Ovid in the *Metamorphoses* (Book 14), by Virgil in the story of Dido and Aeneas, by Petronius in the *Satyricon*, by the Renaissance playwrights Calderón and Corneille, by Hemingway in *The Sun Also Rises*, and by Joyce in the famous brothel scene in *Ulysses*. What is not so clear, however, in these various treatments of the Kirke episode is how much men—or women, for that matter—wish men to be pigs or act like them.

The Kirke narrative in Book 10 contains a number of distinct parts, leading to many levels of closure. The episode begins with the arrival of Odysseus and his Companions on Aiaia, Kirke's magical isle; then follows the Companions' disastrous encounter with Kirke, the "dread goddess who talks with mortals." On their own and without Odysseus' wise counsel, the Companions are first bewitched by the sight of Kirke's beautiful palace, by the sweet sound of her singing, and by her handsome weaving, all reminiscent of "home," and last by her gracious hospitality, when they drink the potion she offers, are stupefied, and, struck by her magic wand, are transformed into pigs. Eurylochos, the only Companion to escape, returns to the ship and informs Odysseus, who sets out to rescue his men, providentially finding Hermes along the way. Hermes tells Odysseus what he must do to resist Kirke's wiles and gives him the magical plant, moly, to help him ward off the goddess's magic. Following Hermes' instructions, Odysseus comes to the palace, drinks the potion Kirke gives him, but is not enchanted; when she strikes him with *her wand* he rushes at her violently with *his sword* (plates 31, 32, 34, 37). Terrified, Kirke submits, proposing that they make love in her beautiful bed. Odysseus forces her to swear that she will do no evil against him if he puts aside his weapon and agrees to her proposition (plates 35, 36, 40); she agrees, and they do. Postcoital sadness on Odysseus' part is due to his sorrow over his Companions' dire fate; moved by her lover's distress, Kirke changes them back into men, better looking than before. The entire company remains on Kirke's isle, lost in pleasurable pursuits for a year. Reminded of his destined return to Ithaka by his men, Odysseus asks Kirke for and receives from her the advice needed to get him into Hades, where he wishes to seek counsel from the soul of Teiresias, and then to extricate himself from it, an exit not usually available to mortal men (cf. plate 36). Before they leave Kirke's palace, one of the Companions, Elpenor, lost in drink, falls off the roof and dies, his shade passing into the underworld ahead of Odysseus. In Book 12.8–150 Odysseus and his Companions return to Aiaia from Hades, bury Elpenor, and learn from Kirke—as Odysseus had learned from Hermes—how to protect themselves from the dangerous Sirens (cf. plate 39) and from Skylla, the next stages in their journey home; and they set out. With this, the Kirke narrative in the *Odyssey* comes to an end, but not its ramifications, its metaphorical connection with the general themes of "The Return."

The Return is many things, but prominent among them is the notion of change, as Odysseus, wily warrior and victor at Troy, is forced to become a suppliant, a stranger in strange lands beset by powerful females—Kirke, Kalypso, the Sirens, Skylla—before he can return to his former life as king of Ithaka, husband of Penelope, and father of Telemachos. In a sense, Odysseus is a man without the right woman, subjected to the perils imposed by his experience of other females—Nausikaa, perhaps, the only exception. Kirke signifies the great danger of exotic vice, the lure of the illicit erotic, and the adverse consequences of an encounter with it, as represented in the confrontation between the boar-headed man and the nude Kirke on an Archaic clay altar from Sicily (plate 31).[2] The Companion's surrender to an alluring woman has diminished his natural state of manhood, transforming his countenance. For such a person, to succumb to an enchanting woman is to be victimized by his own sensuality as much as by hers (*voluptas*). Although Odysseus resists Kirke's magic, he too succumbs to her physical charms and indulges in their enjoyment for a full year, admittedly less than the nearly eight years he later devotes to Kalypso. Petronius made much of this sexual interlude in the *Satyricon* (127, 129, 130, 134); he characterized Encolpius as a comic version of Odysseus, persecuted over land and sea by the wrath of Priapus (rather than Poseidon) and obsessed with his beautiful but fickle girlfriend, Kirke, a giver of pleasure.[3]

Odysseus' reluctance to take the food and drink offered by Kirke after they had sex conforms to a traditional folktale pattern, indicating that it is all right to have sex with a witch but never to dine with her.[4] Indeed, taking sustenance from a witch is very dangerous, perhaps because long before the development of contemporary anthropological theory it was understood that supping together rather than sleeping together implied the deeper, more equal relationship. Kirke's very act of proffering the magic potion to her intended victims (plates 31, 32, 38) symbolizes both the risk to the recipient and the breach in the rules of hospitality, when a stranger is betrayed by his host(ess).

The very discovery, deep in the woods, of a magical palace and a beautiful mistress is the stuff of dreams and of the heroic sagas.[5] The year with Kirke passes like a dream until the hero's better nature reasserts itself. That better nature has no savage aspect, unlike the bestial transformation imposed on the Companions (plate 32) or in the aggressive charge of the sword-brandishing Odysseus at his first meeting with Kirke (plate 34). Of course, Odysseus' sword is the male counterpart to Kirke's magical wand, and both weapons are put aside when they revert to civil behavior (plate 35). For both Odysseus and

Kirke, the aggressive gesture, typical of the masculine role, has been displaced by the prospective intimacy; like Ares and Aphrodite, the weapons have been relinquished and the hostility laid aside in expectation of the sensual experience of love they are about to share.[6] Thus, Odysseus, who may be swinish but never a swine, and Kirke, who actualizes the swinishness in men, become sweethearts, for a while.

Changes in behavior may be subtle, but Homer also explores the change from wakefulness to sleep, from resistance to submission, and from humanity to animality effected by drinking something one should not. Kirke's magic potion, aided and abetted by the powers in her magic wand, transforms men into animals, or at least seems to do so. The many artistic representations of this transformation tend to retain some aspect of the human appearance of the subject, making more monstrous the hybrid being that results, while retaining sufficiently visible clues for the iconographic topic (plates 31, 32, 34, 36, 38). Ovid, *Metamorphoses* (14.276–415), makes much of the process of transformation in both directions, and seems to be more interested in the changes taking place than in the narrative in which they occur.

The attitude of the Painter of the Boston Polyphemos is very different. His mid-sixth-century cup depicts on one side the transformation of the Companions into monsters by Kirke with Odysseus coming up behind (plate 32) and on the other the analogous effort of Odysseus and his Companions to get Polyphemos, the one-eyed monster, drunk and helpless (plate 33).[7] It is important to emphasize the relationship between drinking and its perils as an example of the moral imperative in mythological representations, especially when found decorating a winecup. However, the careful delineation of these monstrous beings is also important because Circean iconography was not restricted to the representation of swinish men but offered other hybridized creatures with the heads of rams and asses (plates 32, 34, 36), animals similarly associated with lustful behavior. But, then, Kirke and her female relatives are closely associated with hybrid monsters in Greek mythology, bespeaking a profound awareness of their ability to create, even propagate, monsters that transgress the boundaries between humans and animals much in the way that the gods transgress the boundaries between themselves and humankind.[8]

The hybrid monster exemplifies the very fact of the transgression of boundaries, of a transition not yet accomplished, still frozen in place, and, as such, even more to be feared because of its palpable deformation of the natural categories of being. Whether such creatures are born monstrous, as was the Minotaur, or subsequently made that way through magic, they retain the power to shock us, to shake our sense of what is right in the world. Kirke herself was mistress of the beasts (*potnia thērōn*). She was, also, an extraordinarily proficient metamorphoser in a clan of witches: sister to that Pasiphae of Crete who with Daidalos' aid mated with the bull and produced the Minotaur, and aunt to Medea, sorceress and slayer of her own children.[9] All of these powerful women behaved unconventionally, if conventions can ever apply to divine or semidivine beings, and all did so in a manner contravening the patterns of normal relationships with men, Kirke with Odysseus, Pasiphae with Minos, Medea with Jason.

Kirke held Odysseus in the darkness of time wasted, much like the nymph Kalypso, if not for as long.[10] Hermes aided Odysseus in his dealings with Kirke and Kalypso and, in the end, made it possible for him to escape their sexual hold. Hermes, the conveyor of souls to the underworld, brought Odysseus forth from his bondage to women, yet Kirke herself, daughter of the Sun (Helios), lighted his way to Hades and back, perhaps because as one with the power to change bodies and souls, she could bring him safely through the boundary between life and death. As Gregory Nagy has pointed out, Odysseus wandered in the far West until he came upon Aiaia (10.135); from there he went to the underworld, traveling beyond the sea as far as the cosmic river, Okeanos (11.21–22), and, on his return, Odysseus found Aiaia in the East, the abode of Eos and the sunrise of Helios (12.1–4).[11] This perilous journey was made possible with the aid of a benevolent witch, Kirke, whose own transformation goes no less to the root of her nature than that of the Companions, the shape of whose existence she had altered forever. There can be little doubt that the representation of Odysseus, Kirke, and the monstrously deformed Companions on Etruscan cinerary urns (plate 36) reflects the Etruscans' understanding of the perils of the journey to Hades, undertaken by Odysseus, who, after all, came back.[12]

However complete the Kirke episode may be, however rich its implications, and however vivid its imagery, one must never forget that the episode is embedded as a story within other stories, all culminating in the epic account of Odysseus' Return. Telling the Kirke story is not only the function of the *Odyssey,* it is also the act of Odysseus himself at the court of Alkinoos, the Phaeacian king, to whom the hero related the tale of his adventures. A late-third-century B.C. mold-made relief bowl ("Megarian type") illustrates this storytelling episode in dramatic terms, set within the stagelike architecture of Alkinoos' palace; the *dramatis personae* appear in the scene— Kirke, several monstrously deformed Companions, and an onrushing

Odysseus—as if the story is so vivid in the telling that Alkinoos can visualize it, perhaps even empathize with the plight of the Companions as he crouches, nude, skinny, and old before "Kirke" (plate 37).[13] This bowl resembles several other similar Hellenistic terra-cotta bowls that illustrate scenes from the epic poems and Greek plays, possibly derived from illustrated texts now lost. Like the cup by the Painter of the Boston Polyphemos (plates 32, 33) it was used in wine-drinking parties; in both, inscriptions identify the characters, and one can imagine the holder-beholder entering into the spirit of the scene depicted, if only vicariously.

As represented on the relief bowl, Alkinoos seems to be both observer and participant, the polysemic mode of the composition reflecting the similar actions of the poem's audience and of the multi-valent construction of the *Odyssey*. This layering effect or the inter-weaving of narrative strands enhances the intertextuality of the Kirke episode, replete with the resonance of prior events and the adumbration of events to come, already known. Perhaps the most pertinent connection should be made between the Kirke episode as a proleptic interlude and Odysseus' conclusive homecoming to his own house and to his wife, Penelope. Horace understood the connection very well:[14]

> On the other hand, Homer gives us a useful example
> Of virtue and wisdom at work in noble Ulysses:
> "The tamer of Troy, whose piercing glance traveled into the hearts
> Of man, as he entered into their cities. Borne to the end
> Of the world to discover the homeward path overseas for his friends,
> He tossed on his troubles, UNSINKABLE, a true man of parts."
> You know about Circe's drink, and the siren voices:
> Had Ulysses let himself go and drunk what he wanted,
> He'd have lost his true shape and from then on lived like a nitwit
> At the mercy of a sleazy mistress, lived like a hog
> Settling down cosily in the mud, lived like a dog.
> In comparison with him, the rest of us look rather weak:
> As they put it in Greek, we simply don't COUNT. We CONSUME.
> We're Penelope's suitors, cloudbrains; we're like the young men
> At Alcinous' court who spend more time than they should
> On appearance, who pride themselves on sleeping until noon
> And lulling their cares by strumming on languid guitars.
> *Epistles* I.2 *To Lollius Maximus* (22 B.C.) 17–31

Similarities between exotic Kirke and domestic Penelope, artfully conceived by Homer, have been acknowledged by many authors from Horace to James Joyce.[15] Singers and weavers both, Kirke and Penel-

ope ensnared men, distracting them by their beauty;[16] they un-
manned these intrusive males, the Companions and Suitors, rendering them helpless by the exercise of their feminine arts, at least until
the advent of Odysseus. Indeed, the *Odyssey* exploits the swine motif
in the concluding books of the poem: the Suitors are depicted like
swine (17); Eurykleia, Odysseus' nurse, washes his dirty feet, dis-
covers the scar of an old boar's tusk wound, and from it recognizes her
master in disguise (19.386–502); Eumaios, Odysseus' faithful swineherd, helps his master rid his house of human swine. Pig husbandry
may have been an important part of the Homeric agrarian economy,
but swine did not belong in a noble house, and neither did the
Suitors.

Iconographically, the strongest connection between Kirke and
Penelope was established through their persona as weavers.[17] Several
black-figure Cabiran skyphoi, made in Boeotia in the late fifth century, represent Kirke's loom as her characteristic attribute (plate 38).
These drinking cups appear to define the attraction and peril of drinking by repeating the cup's very shape in the skyphos offered to Odysseus by Kirke in the painting. However, the iconographic program
has a more serious purpose, using the Kirke imagery as a means of
signifying the use of drugged potions in the celebration of the Cabiran
cult in its sanctuary near Thebes, thereby advocating the desirability
of imbibing consciousness-altering drugs in the service of the gods.[18]

Still, the crouching figure of the boar-headed Companion, set
beside the loom (plate 38), insistently affirms the power of Kirke, the
divine magician, to effect the conversion of forms and essences, a
theme that will have a significant place in Neo-Platonic thought and
imagery in Late Antiquity.[19] Kirke, surrounded by animals in her lair,
rules over a kind of earthly paradise, however fragile, the "home" that
lies away from one's own home. Perhaps, the poignancy of the abject,
crouching figure of the deformed Companion, waiting for rescue by
Odysseus, anticipates this Late Antique eschatological conception but
in more mundane, narrative terms. Surely, Odysseus and the Companions want to return to their homes. The ongoing nature of their
travels and the manifested connection between one episode and another are strongly implicated in the painting of a Corinthian aryballos
from the second quarter of the sixth century in Boston, representing
Odysseus and the Sirens *and* Kirke's house (plate 39).[20]

Here, Kirke's palace seems to look much more like a loom (cf.
plate 38) than any palace (cf. plate 40), as if the image of the loom
signaled metonymously her residence and her characteristic activity

within it. And yet, Kirke herself appears, sitting behind the Sirens on a rock, as if she were continuing her protection of Odysseus, strapped to the mast of his vessel and listening to the destructive allure of the Sirens' song but incapable of responding to it. As if to enforce the connection between Kirke and the Sirens, between the weaver-singer and the feathered singers, the ship's beak has the form of a boar's head pointing directly toward Kirke and her palace. Complementing this effort to assimilate the two episodes, a falconlike bird hovers over the prow of Odysseus' ship, making a visual pun on Kirke's name[21] and, thus, functions as an emblematic signal of the extension of her protective magic over the horizon. In this Archaic vase, Kirke appears both as a witch in the company of witches, the Sirens, and as a tutelary deity. The opposing aspects of her ambivalent character, developed in the Homeric narrative, are harmoniously resolved in furthering Odysseus' Return.

Reflecting on the Circean iconography as a whole, Kirke and Odysseus relate to each other not so much by the intensity of their erotic connection as by the subtle variation in holding or sharing power. The so-called Rondanini *Tabula Odysseaca* in Warsaw (plate 40) visualizes these power relationships, so familiar to a Roman audience, in a narrative sequence of well-defined vignettes.[22] The sequence begins *in medias res* at the lower left in the encounter between Odysseus and Hermes, continues in the right middle with Odysseus forcing Kirke into submission, and culminates in their *joint* liberation of the still-monstrous Companions from their rather elegant pen. Because beasts do not belong in houses, much less palaces— although Kirke's is an exception—the emergence of the Companions into the open anticipates their emergence into a human state of being, a reverse metamorphosis made possible by the altered behavior of Kirke and Odysseus toward each other.

Sweethearts they become and produce a son, Telegonos, according to the *Telegony*, a poem written by Eugammon of Cyrene in the sixth century B.C. This post-Homeric poem tells a strange tale of convoluted family relationships, set neatly in a symmetrical frame: Telegonos unwittingly kills his father, Odysseus, on Ithaka, and transports his body together with his widow, Penelope, and their son, Telemachos, back to Kirke's isle; once there, Telemachos marries Kirke and Telegonos marries Penelope, and thus Odysseus' sons, his wife, and his mistress live together forever. With this tale, the Heroic Age comes to an end.[23]

Surely it is simpler to know Kirke as the sometime witch and contender for Odysseus' affections than to think of her as simultaneously Penelope's daughter-in-law and mother-in-law, a combination much more to be dreaded.

Notes

1. See *LIMC* VI, s.v. "Kirke," (F. Canciani); s.v. "Circe," (M. Le Glay), 48–60; Buitron and Cohen, 1992, 78–80.

2. Musée du Louvre CA 5956; Devambez, 1973, 1–23.

3. Arrowsmith, 1959, 186; Blickman, 1988, 7–16. Note that Encolpius means "lap" or "crotch."

4. Dyck, 1981, 196–98.

5. Carpenter, 1962, 18, 20.

6. Connor, 1988, 41–53, esp. 44–49; see also Segal, 1968, 419–42.

7. See Snodgrass, 1982, 5–12; Davies, 1986, 182–83; Raeck, 1984, 1–25, esp. 17–25; Schefold, 1978, 264–67.

8. A principal theme of R. Calasso's 1993 mythographic novel, *The Marriage of Cadmus and Harmony.*

9. See Germain, 1954, 249–52, 258–60; Kerenyi, 1944, esp. 65–90 (Kirke), 91–116 (Medea).

10. See Kaiser, 1964, 197–213.

11. Nagy, 1979, 206.

12. Van der Meer, 1977–78, 57–131, esp. 64; cf. Laviosa, 1964, no. 15, "Ulysses at Circe's Court."

13. Brommer, 1972, 105–17, figs. 3–5; see Weitzmann, 1959, 40–41 on the derivation of such scenes from illuminated manuscripts.

14. Translated by S. Palmer Bovie (University of Chicago Press) 1959, 170, 171.

15. E.g., Horace, *Odes* I.17.17–20; see Gilbert, 1952, 313–48, 385–405; Beye, 1966, 175, 178–79.

16. *Non deest forma quae sollicitet oculos*, Seneca, *Letter* 88.7, in the context of using Odysseus' travails as a metaphor for the demands of an honorable life.

17. The weaver who weaves cloth and magic is a familiar *topos*; see Nagler, 1977, 77–85; Snyder, 1980–81, 193–96; Foley, 1978, 17–26. One should also remember that Ariadne, who by her disloyal use of thread brought death to her brother, the Minotaur, was Kirke's niece; on Arachne, the weaver, see also D'Ambra, 1993, 104–8, "Women's Work."

18. British Museum 93.3–3.1; *LIMC* VI, s.v. "Odysseus," (O. Touchefeu-Meynier), 960–61 and plates 631, 632; Hill, 1941, 120, 121, fig. 3; Walters, 1892–93, 77–87, plate 4.

19. See Moret, 1991, 227–66, figs. 11–13; Turcan, 1979, 161–74.

20. Schefold, 1966, 96, fig. 46; Bulle, 1900, 31–37; Fairbanks, 1928, 67, no. 467.

21. After Darcy, 1985, 185–91, on *kirkos* as a bird of prey, a falcon, or a place at the limits.

22. Sarduska, 1964, 61–64, plate 12; Schefold and Jung, 1989, 347, fig. 309. On the representation of Kirke's palace in Roman art, including the painting of the Odyssey Frieze from the Esquiline, see Tamm, 1968, 181–86.

23. Evelyn-White, 1967, xxxiii.

10

Les Femmes Fatales: Skylla and the Sirens in Greek Art

Jenifer Neils

Homer's *Odyssey* contains many femmes fatales, irresistible women who attempt to detain Odysseus on his homeward journey. The "lovely haired" goddesses Kirke and Kalypso are the most obvious temptresses, and the bulk of the hero's ten-year odyssey is spent in their thrall. In a more subtle way, even young, innocent Nausikaa, "like the immortal goddesses in form and size" (6.16), plots, through her parents' offer of marriage, to keep him forever on her isle. But surely the most *fatal* of all the females in the *Odyssey* are the creatures that Odysseus and his men encounter in Book 12: the Sirens, Skylla, and Charybdis. The Sirens are enchanting songstresses who dwell in a meadow and lure sailors to their deaths on the beach below. Charybdis Odysseus bypasses on his first voyage but reencounters at the end of the book. She sucks in ships and spews them out blenderized into small pieces. According to later sources, Skylla was once a beautiful woman but was transformed by the jealousy of either Amphitrite (Scholiast on Lykophron, *Alexandra* 45 and 650) or Kirke (Ovid, *Metamorphoses* 14, 1–73) into a multiheaded hybrid. She lives in a seaside cave and grabs whatever passes, fish or man, to appease her carnivorous appetite. Although the hero needs the help of the gods, Hermes and Athena, to escape the clutches of Kirke and Kalypso, he is left to his own devices in dealing with these life-threatening female monsters. Through his own skill and craftiness, the ever-resourceful Odysseus manages to survive these perils of the sea, just as earlier he outwitted Polyphemos and the Lastrygonians.

Over the years, historians of both art and myth have sought the origins of these creatures.[1] Unlike the *Iliad*, which is based on quasi-historical legend, much of the *Odyssey*—in particular, these monsters—is clearly the stuff of folklore, and they appear in other sea-faring sagas, like the *Argonautika*.[2] Although not described in great detail by Homer, each can be interpreted as a personification of a hazard commonly experienced at sea. Charybdis is most obviously a whirlpool, a phenomenon that can be found throughout the Mediterranean in tidal channels. It has been suggested that the Sirens, whose only characteristic, according to Homer, is their irresistible music, represent the seductive nature of calm waters. Indeed, as the ship of Odysseus approaches the Sirens' isle, "then at once the wind stopped and there was a windless calm and a god put the waves to sleep" (12.168–69). In the case of Skylla, Kirke provides Odysseus with a more detailed physical description:

> She has a voice as loud as a new-born puppy's,
> but she herself is an evil monster. No one would enjoy
> the sight of her, not even if a god should encounter her.
> She has twelve feet, all hanging in the air,
> and six necks, very long ones, and on each
> is a terrifying head, with three rows of teeth in it
> crowded close together, filled with dark death.   (12.86–92)

She seems to combine various aspects of the more frightening denizens of the deep: Her voice is like that of a barking seal, her multiple appendages suggest an octopus or squid, and the triple set of teeth recalls the dogfish, a variety of small shark. As a cannibalistic cave dweller, she reminds the reader of Polyphemos, and just as he dispatched six of Odysseus' dear comrades, so does she, albeit more quickly. Once the hero has made it past this monstrosity, he indulges in a rare commentary:

> That was the most pitiful thing I saw with my eyes
> in all the hardships I suffered crossing the sea's pathways.
>   (12.258–59)

This "pitiful thing" is most fully realized visually in the art of the Hellenistic period in such masterpieces as the fragmentary marble sculptural group found in Tiberius' grotto at Sperlonga or the colossal tomb monument found at Bargylia in Caria.[3] The monumental Sperlonga group included Odysseus, his ship, and an oar-wielding Skylla, yanking the helmsman by his hair, while her dog protomes snatched Odysseus' companions. Originally, with her six canine heads and grotto setting, this Skylla closely evoked Homer's description, as she surely was intended to. Also in the Hellenistic period one finds magnificent representations of the monster alone—that is, not in a specific narrative context—as on the emblema of the second century B.C. now in the Metropolitan Museum of Art (plate 41).[4] Made in gilt silver repoussé, it shows a frontal Skylla hurling a boulder poised overhead in her upraised hands. Three dog protomes, each a different breed, emerge from under her finlike skirt to feed on sea life. Like her counterpart in Sperlonga, she displays a very feminine nude torso and luxuriously long hair. This tradition of Skylla as half erotic and half monstrous continues to flourish in Roman art.

Given the relative detail with which Homer describes this monster as well as Odysseus' own statement about the horror of his adventure, one is surprised that this masterpiece of *terribilità* is not depicted in earlier Greek art, where hybrid monsters are so popular. Archaic artists had no trouble with Gorgons, which are not described at all by Homer other than a mention of their terrible noise.[5] The Hydra of Lerna with her multiple heads also presented no problem for Greek artists; in fact, Herakles and the Hydra is the first Greek myth that we have definitively represented.[6] Likewise, Odysseus' other two adventures, with the Sirens and Charybdis, do not occur with the frequency of, for instance, the Polyphemos adventure (plate 7). Granted, that episode is accorded 450 lines, and it falls into that category of deed well loved by Archaic artists, in which the hero conquers a monster, rather than simply surviving its torments.

One could argue that Polyphemos is easy to depict, simply a man enlarged, and all early artists neatly avoided the challenge of dealing with a single eye by presenting the giant in strict profile.[7] As for the multiheaded Hydra, a Near Eastern model was near at hand, and easily adapted for Herakles' labor.[8] Although some scholars, such as Buschor, have suggested the Egyptian soul bird, the Ba-bird, as a prototype for the Siren,[9] even more readily available was another model, namely, the bronze attachments that appear along the rim of metal cauldrons dedicated at Greek sanctuaries as early as the eighth century B.C.[10] These usually male, human-headed bird protomes no doubt served as the inspiration for the earliest extant depictions of Sirens, who, as seen on Protocorinthian vases, are bearded.[11] It takes more than fifty years for them to become female, and even longer before they appear in a scene with Odysseus. As for Skylla, Hanfmann suggested a possible iconographic prototype on a tenth-century B.C.

gold bowl from Hasanlu, although the figure is usually taken to be a mountain god with three dogs, and at any rate is not a common character in the art of the Near East.[12]

Having pointed out the paucity of images and some far-fetched prototypes, let us now look at the scant evidence for these adventures in art. Not surprisingly, given the artistic challenge of representing a swirling pool of water, Charybdis occurs not at all,[13] although Odysseus' escape may be represented on a sixth-century B.C. black-figure skyphos from Sicily (plate 42).[14] Here we see a nude, bearded male stretched out on the back of a large turtle. The tree at the right gives the clue for interpreting this scene: To judge by the shape of its leaves, it is a fig tree. In the *Odyssey* (12.430–44), on the hero's second encounter with the whirlpool, he clings to a fig tree, until the vortex spits out the timbers of his ship. This vase painting may represent a variant in which he travels to safety on the back of a sea turtle and thus may serve to identify the similar image on a metope from the Heraion at Foce del Sele.[15] It is interesting to note that all these images of Odysseus on a turtle appear in the West, suggesting the existence of an alternate legend that depicts the inhabitants of the sea as friendlier to the hero. Such an interpretation makes geographical sense, as the whirlpool of Charybdis was traditionally located in the Strait of Messina.

Also from the West, where we increasingly find some of the earliest representations of Greek myth, is a vase fragment from the late-eighth to early-seventh century that could possibly be our earliest representation of a Siren because it preserves part of a frontal winged female (plate 43).[16] It comes from Pithekoussai, the source also of "Nestor's" cup discussed by Graham,[17] and not far from the Sirens' traditional residence south of Naples as recorded by Strabo (*The Geography* C 22; 1.2.12).[18] Although tentatively identified as a sphinx, with her outline face, long hair, and splayed wings, she resembles an orientalizing Siren on a fragment of a vase from Praisos.[19]

Odysseus' encounter with the Sirens appears first on two small perfume flasks produced in Corinth in the first half of the sixth century B.C. The earlier of the two, now in Basel (plates 44, 45),[20] shows a much abbreviated depiction; in fact, the identification is not without question. The front of the vase shows Herakles and his henchman Iolaos slaying the Hydra of Lerna, flanked by Athena and two chariots. Tucked under the handle at the back is a separate scene, set on a dark sea. A boar-prowed warship, in full sail and equipped with three oarsmen and a tillerman, moves to the right. Standing before the mast is a larger male figure, arms and legs astride, who looks back, pre-

sumably at the large bird, which holds a snake in its talons. Is this
Odysseus, bound "hand and foot" to the mast; if so, where are the
Sirens, sitting in their meadow? Before discussing the Siren on this
vase, it is worth considering a recently published Attic white-ground
oinochoe from the late sixth century B.C. in Berlin (plate 46).[21] This
vase undoubtedly depicts the Siren adventure, for three of these
creatures sit on the cliff at the right, and we can even detect the wax in
the oarmen's ears. What makes this representation relevant for the
Corinthian perfume flask is the position of Odysseus' arms. Inexplica-
bly he has two sets, one lashed to the mast, the other gesticulating in
both directions. I believe that in both cases the artist is attempting to
show what Odysseus says in Homer: "I ordered my companions to
free me" (12.193); he goes on to say "by nodding with my brows," but
this is more difficult to render artistically.[22] As we shall see presently,
moreover, a later artist comes up with a better solution.

The only Siren in sight on the Basel aryballos appears way over on
the other side behind Athena, and it seems to have nothing to do with
the ship scene. In fact, the first female Siren in Greek art occurs in
exactly the same position on a lost early Corinthian aryballos from
Aigina.[23] This bird-lady has the problematic name of "Wous" or
"Eous"; despite continuing ingenious attempts to decipher it, this
name has still, in the words of Payne, "defied explanation."[24] Because
on both vases this female-headed bird is more closely related to
Athena and chariots than to the *Odyssey*, as are other Sirens in later
Athenian art, we must leave her in peace, and move on to look at the
second Corinthian aryballos.

This well-known vase in Boston (plate 39)[25] is not without its own
problems of interpretation, but the main scene is not one of them. In
fact, of all the extant representations of Odysseus and the Sirens, it
comes closest to the text of the poem. Not only is Odysseus now
bound "hand and foot" but also the sails are stowed and two Sirens are
on the cliff at the right. (Homer twice uses the dual, otherwise the
plural, in reference to the Sirens.) We can contrast this vase with the
only extant Athenian red-figure version of this episode, the well-
known name vase of the Siren Painter (plate 47).[26] Here the sails are
furled, rather than "put away in the hollow ship" (12.171), and there is
a triad of Sirens. What these vases have in common is the individuality
of the open-mouthed Sirens—note how their plumage is carefully
differentiated—and the accent on a plunging figure. The red-figure
Siren diving seaward, eyes closed, is usually related to the legend,
recorded much later (Lycophron, *Alexandra* 712–15), that if a ship
passed safely the Sirens must commit suicide. (Because, a generation

earlier, the *Argo* had already escaped by the ruse of Orpheus drowning them out with his lyre playing, the Siren population should already have been diminished.)

The reverse of this fascinating red-figure vase has close ties with the obverse (plate 48). Here are three winged figures, Erotes, flying over the sea, their number paralleling that of the Sirens on the other side. Their leader, holding a decorated fillet, is labeled Himeros (Desire), which clearly relates to the one labeled Siren, Himeropa.[27] If the Erotes are out cruising for boys, as seems likely, given the love gifts in their hands (fillet, wreath, hare), then perhaps the vase painter is subtly referring to the erotic potential of Sirens, who are sometimes depicted raping sleeping men.[28] Erotes and Sirens appear together in other contexts, notably that of reveling, as seen on a Laconian cup, where they bring garlands to the reclining banqueters.[29]

To return to our theme, diving birds and singing Sirens seem to represent the earlier tradition, whereas all other Attic vase paintings show a different version in which the Sirens are instrumentalists and no other birds are present, a tradition that extended into South Italian and Roman art. Of necessity, these Sirens are equipped with arms. As Haspels so aptly noted over half a century ago: "This is the general rule: sirens have arms only when they need them."[30] (An early exception to this rule occurs on a Melian neck-amphora, but as Beazley pointed out: "They are talking to each other, and being Greek, need hands for the purpose."[31]) These musical Sirens frequently appear on late-sixth-century white-ground vases, where they seem to be entertaining anonymous humans, as on a lekythos in the British Museum,[32] or animals, as seen on another lekythos in Bari,[33] or simply dolpins, as on an oinochoe in London[34]

The music-loving dolphins reappear on one of the two late-sixth-century depictions of Odysseus and the Sirens. This white-ground lekythos in Athens (plates 49, 50)[35] deletes the ship, leaving only Odysseus, wearing his familiar petasos, tied to the mast. One Siren plays the double pipes, the other a lyre. These same instruments appear on the black-figure oinochoe in the Callimanopulos collection (plates 2, 3).[36] Lovely, enticing, and jewel-bedecked, they await the ship that is propelled forward by the thrust of its oars as well as by the wind in its billowing sail. Here for the first time the Sirens are labeled as such, Odysseus is named, and the viewer is even treated to his very words, "LUSE" or "loose me."

While the armless Siren leads a flourishing existence in the decorative arts, as a terra-cotta perfume container, as a bronze mirror support, or as an attachment plate for metal vase handles,[37] the music-making armed variety comes to be associated with the under-world, a usage consistent with their appearance on white-ground vases, which were destined for the grave. She is not a soul-bird as some would like,[38] but one whose ethereal music connotes another world. As such the Siren becomes a common motif on fourth-century marble funerary monuments; rather than death-dealing, she mourns the dead with gesture and music.[39] Corroborating this change of char-acter is the subtle change in appearance; she becomes less birdlike and more human, until finally she is simply a woman with bird legs, as on the unique terra-cotta funerary group of a life-sized lyre player and two Sirens, which probably came from a subterranean Greek tomb in South Italy (plate 51).[40] The wingless Sirens stand on rocks listening to the male musician seated on a klismos with footstool. He has been identified as Orpheus, but the setting does not suggest the scene in the *Argonautika* (4.891–911) when he quieted the Sirens with his music. Rather we may be seeing the deceased, once a talented musi-cian, whose passing is mourned even by the Sirens. In the Etruscan sphere the transformation is complete; a number of urns from Volterra (plate 52),[41] in fact, depict the Sirens like Muses, that is, fully draped women seated on rocks playing musical instruments. They no longer seem to be a threat to Odysseus, but rather appear to be serenading him on his homeward journey.

Turning now to Skylla, her artistic development takes the oppo-site tack. When she first appears in the early fifth century, whether in terra-cotta relief work or on coins, she is shown not as a rapacious monster, but as a somewhat demure (often even draped) denizen of the sea. Given her presence on the coins of South Italy and Sicily,[42] she seems to be closely associated with this part of the Mediterranean. This location is confirmed by a fragment of the Archaic poet Ste-sichoros (fr. 44) who places Skylla in Sicily.

In the art of Magna Graecia she is depicted as fairly benign and can even have a helpful nature, as when she escorts Europa over the sea (plate 53) or carries Thetis on her back when the Nereid brings new arms to her son Achilles.[43] From the waist up, she is a lovely bejeweled woman, with a lower body in the form of a fishtail and two dog protomes at the waist. Like other sea creatures, she is equipped with a trident or steering oar. Literary sources tell us that a late-fifth-to early-fourth-century painter, Androklydes of Kyzikos, painted a Skylla with most delicate and lifelike fish around her. As we have seen, even in the third-century repoussé relief in New York (plate 41), Skylla is not shown attacking humans. This aspect is played down until the Hellenistic period.

How does one account for this dearth in Greek art of representations of such vivid episodes from our earliest epic? The *Odyssey* was composed in an era of exploration and colonization following a long and difficult dark age. The terrors of such sea journeys are clearly reflected in the rudimentary vase paintings executed during the floruit of Homer.[44] In fact, the very earliest figural composition, on a Middle Geometric skyphos of around 850 B.C., shows a battle at sea.[45] Such scenes are common on late-eighth-century Attic kraters that stood atop male burials in the Dipylon cemetery. One scene, on the neck of an oinochoe, may even depict the final shipwreck of Odysseus at the end of Book 12 in which he loses all his men.[46] The most vivid sea disaster is shown on a vase again found at Pithekoussai, and of local manufacture.[47] Oddly enough, these naval disasters end with the Geometric period. Thereafter, the Greeks sail along the seas as confidently as the Phaeacians. Perhaps the Greeks' changing response to their maritime environment affected artists' output by making mishaps at sea less popular with their patrons. As the Greeks grew more confident in their seafaring abilities, their concern for the fatal aspects of these sea creatures declined, only to be revived in the Hellenistic period, when detailed narrative depictions of the *Odyssey* became popular.

In literature we know the femme fatale by her actions, but in the artistic sphere the clues are more subtle. The main trait that provides an immediate visual distinction between the good female characters of the *Odyssey* from the evil is degree of dress. The women and female monsters who would prevent the long-sought homecoming of Odysseus are routinely shown nude or bare-breasted. The Sirens are uncivilized and hence unclothed. Skylla's upper body can be draped, but when she is fighting Odysseus, her upper torso is bare. Most interesting are the depictions of Kirke, who is never described thus in the *Odyssey* but appears nude in the earliest Greek representations (see plates 31, 32).[48] Given the rarity of full female nudity in pre-Classical Greek art, it would have been fairly shocking to see any woman shown in this manner.[49] Conversely, the best of women, namely, Penelope, is always fully draped and characteristically seated, to show that she is securely at home. The unwed princess Nausikaa, as Shapiro has shown,[50] falls somewhere in between because she too would like to keep the hero at her side. Hence she is only partiallly dressed, appearing before the hero unveiled and barefoot. These are the artistic signs that reveal the nature of female characters in the *Odyssey* and demonstrate the subtle ways in which ancient artists depicted these dramatic encounters of male and female.

Notes

I wish to record my thanks to Beth Cohen for inviting me to participate in the symposium at Bard College and for her many helpful suggestions throughout the preparation of this chapter.

1. On these female monsters in Greek art, see Touchefeu-Meynier, 1968, 145–90 (Sirens) and 275–80 (Charybdis); and Buitron and Cohen, 1992, 108–35 (Sirens) and 136–53 (Skylla). On Sirens in particular, see Candida, 1970–71, 212–53, figs. 1–17; Gropengiesser, 1977, 582–610; Puglia Doria, 1987, 65–98; Hofstetter, 1990. On Skylla and Charybdis, see Waser, 1894.
2. See Page, 1973.
3. Sperlonga: Pollitt, 1986, 122–25; Andreae, 1982. Bargylia: Waywell, 1990, 386–88.
4. New York 1981.11.22. See Bothmer, 1984, 55, no. 95.
5. See Riccioni, 1960, 127–206; and Karagiorga, 1970.
6. See Fittschen, 1969, 147, 213–21.
7. On Polyphemos, see Buitron and Cohen, 1992, 31–37.
8. See Bisi, 1964–65, 21–42; plates 1–7.
9. Buschor, 1944.
10. See Hermann, 1966, 27–113, plates 1–2, 4–41.
11. Hofstetter, 1990, 35–40.
12. Hanfmann, 1987, 259–60.
13. It has been said that the wavy lines with stars above the head of Skylla on an Apulian bell-krater fragment in the J. Paul Getty Museum (86.AE.417) may represent the swirling waters of Charybdis, and the feathers next to it, the tail of a Siren, but the piece is too fragmentary to make a definitive identification. See Buitron and Cohen, 1992, 137, fig. 33.
14. Touchefeu-Meynier, 1968, 276, no. 506, plate 39, 2. See also Zancani Montuoro, 1959, 221–29.
15. Schefold, 1978, 268–69, fig. 361. See also Van Keuren, 1989, 139–46, plate 40b, where the figure is identified as Tantalos.
16. Buchner, 1970–71, 67; Ridgway, 1992, 94, fig. 26.
17. See Graham, Chapter 1, this volume.
18. On the location of the Sirens' cliff, see Edlund, 1987, 45–47.
19. See Kunze, 1932, 124–41; Levi, 1945, 280–93.
20. Basel BS 425. See Amyx, 1988, 180–81, plate 67:2a–b. Amyx (644) states that the identification of this scene as Odysseus and the Sirens "does not seem right." The vase is illustrated in Buitron and Cohen, 1992, 109, fig. 30.
21. Formerly Mainz, collection of F. Brommer. See Brommer, 1983, 85, plates 33b and 34.
22. See *LIMC* VI, s.v. "Odysseus," (O. Touchefeu-Meynier), 962, no. 152, on the gesture.
23. Once at Breslau; see Payne, 1931, 287, no. 481.

24. Payne, 1931, 161, no. 4; Kanowski, 1973, 73–74; Brown, 1975, 137–39.

25. Boston, Museum of Fine Arts 01.8100. See Payne, 1931, no. 1282.

26. London, British Museum E 440. *ARV*[2] 289,1; Buitron and Cohen, 1992, 130–31, no. 42, illustration on p. 120.

27. Shapiro, 1993b, 112–13.

28. See, e.g., the Hellenistic or Roman relief in Johns, 1982, 106, fig. 87.

29. Pipili, 1987, 71–72, 118, nos. 194 and 198.

30. Haspels, 1936, 158, n. 2. Sirens need arms for purposes other than making music, as, for instance, the Siren on a volute-krater by Polion in Ferrara (*ARV*[2] 1171,1) who holds a fan behind the enthroned Hera.

31. Quoted in Haspels, 1936, 159, n. 2. For the Melian neck-amphora from Rheneia, see Kunze, 1932, plate 31.

32. London, British Museum B 651: Haspels, 1936, 256, no. 48.

33. Bari 2732; see Haspels, 1936, 158, plate 48, 2.

34. London, British Museum B 510; *ABV* 429; Hofstetter, 1990, plate 14, 2.

35. Athens, National Museum 1130; *ABV* 476; Hofstetter, 1990, A 90.

36. See Buitron and Cohen, 1992, 127–28, no. 38; Hofstetter, 1990, A 139.

37. On these decorative functions, see Buitron and Cohen, 1992, nos. 34, 35, 36, 40, and 41.

38. As, e.g., Vermeule, 1979, 75–76.

39. See Woysch-Méautis, 1982, 91–99, 137–40; Buitron and Cohen, 1992, 132–33, no. 44, illustration on 122.

40. Malibu, J. Paul Getty Museum 76.AD.11; see Hofstetter, 1990, 260–61, W 24, plate 36.

41. Candida, 1971; Brilliant, 1984, 47–48, plate 15.

42. See Holloway, 1978, 56–57; Buitron and Cohen, 1992, no. 47; and Buitron-Oliver and Cohen, Chapter 3, this volume.

43. On Skylla escorting Europa, see Jentoft-Nilsen, 1983, 139–48, figs. 1–8.

44. See Graham, Chapter 1, this volume.

45. Eleusis, Archaeological Museum 741: Coldstream, 1968, 26.

46. Munich 8698. See Schefold, 1966, 27, plate 8.

47. Buchner, 1953–54; Brunnsaker, 1962; Ridgway, 1988.

48. See *LIMC* VI, s.v. "Kirke," nos. 4, 13, 14, and 19; and Buitron-Oliver and Cohen, Chapter 3, this volume.

49. For a recent discussion of female nudity in Greek vase painting, see Cohen, 1993.

50. See Shapiro, Chapter 8, this volume.

11

The Intimate Act of Footwashing: *Odyssey* 19

Christine Mitchell Havelock

Sophokles wrote a play, *Niptra*, which no longer survives, about Odysseus' return home, and it has been conjectured that theatrical performances of this drama may be the source for the depictions of Eurykleia washing the feet of Odysseus in Classical art.[1]

This chapter, however, considers the possibility that the ancient Greek artist might have been inspired by oral performance, that is, by the singing or recitation of Homer's *Odyssey*. The epics of Homer were of central importance in Greek civilization, constituting one of the primary sources in Classical times for the education of the young and for the entertainment of all. For the most part they were spoken aloud and thus heard rather than read, for literacy was limited to a small percentage of the population.[2] We recall how Demodokos, accompanying himself on the lyre, sang to an eager audience in the *Odyssey* (8.44–520). Trained rhapsodes were reciting the Homeric epics by perhaps the mid-sixth century and continued to do so through the fourth and probably later.[3] An artist would at some time surely have been present in the audience. In that case his experience of the poem would have been entirely aural, and his emotional reaction therefore would have been one of intense identification. While listening to the spell-binding rhapsode, visual images would have been imagined and activated in his mind,[4] and probably committed to memory. Let us understand, then, that the Greek artist was a listener, rather than a reader.[5]

Even if the artist was present at a theatrical performance, hearing would again have been of primary importance. Because the body movements of the actors were restricted and their masks froze facial expression, excitement, tension, emotion, and action were conveyed chiefly by the words themselves and by the human voice. Understanding and enjoyment came via the ear far more than the eye.[6] Therefore, it seems to me that the painter or sculptor need not have relied on a visual model. If the drama dealt with a Homeric theme already familiar through recitation, the words spoken from the stage would still be new, yet resonant of Homer as remembered. Thus they would have heightened significance and impact.

In short, we should not assume that the artist was illustrating or imitating an episode he had either seen in the theater or read, but rather one he had primarily heard. In this chapter I will show that there may be another way of considering the relationship between word and image, and this will shed a new light on certain works of art.[7] An important part of my final conclusion will be concerned with Greek as opposed to Roman perceptions of social class.

In Book 19 of the *Odyssey*, Homer describes the washing of Odysseus' feet by an aged servant, the nurse Eurykleia. This occurs soon after the hero, disguised as an old beggar, returns home to Ithaka after his long wanderings abroad. It is one of the most critical and dramatic episodes of the poem.

In his youth, Odysseus had been wounded while hunting on Mount Parnassos. Because Eurykleia had regularly cared for his person and thus knew his body intimately, while she bathes the "stranger" in Book 19, she notices the telltale scar and suddenly realizes that he is her master, Odysseus. The sudden memory of the scar also alerts Odysseus.[8] No sooner does he agree to the footwashing than he knows he has made a mistake; the nurse must be silenced. Indeed, he is so deeply disturbed that he reaches for her throat and threatens to kill her if she betrays him (19.482–90).[9]

As a young girl, Eurykleia had been bought to be a slave-concubine by Odysseus' father, Laertes, but she soon became a close and trusted member of the family, serving it generation after generation. She was obedient, ubiquitous, sometimes feisty, but always loving toward all of them. She is not, however, a tragic figure or Classical heroine on the scale of a Helen or a Penelope. Although neither complicated nor especially individualized, Eurykleia is an exceedingly important dramatic instrument in the poem. Her discovery of the wound threatens to thwart the hero's well-laid plans and consequently places him in mortal danger.[10]

We may now turn to the footwashing episode as it was interpreted by two Greek sculptors and one vase painter. This will yield insights into the artists' reactions both to the narrative and to Eurykleia's role as a slave or nurse in different historical periods. Let us be guided by a purely visual analysis while bearing in mind that the artist must have been relying on memory rather than consulting a written text of the poem. Finally, a third relief of the same subject executed early in the Imperial Roman period will be contrasted with the two Greek reliefs.

The earliest surviving example of the theme in Greek art, ca. 460 B.C., occurs on a fragmentary terra-cotta plaque from Melos, now in the Metropolitan Museum in New York (plate 54). [11] The missing head of Eurykleia can be supplied by another relief taken from the same mold that came from Corinth and is now in Athens (plate 55). [12]

At the left, Odysseus, wearing his familiar conical hat (pilos), is seated on a stool facing right. He looks lordly and youthful; he is bearded and his lean body is nude except for a mantle over his back. His head is slightly lowered, indicating his interest in the woman before him. He holds out his left leg so that his foot is raised above the basin on the ground. Eurykleia is kneeling in front of him, and she rather tenderly grasps his extended foot: "This [scar] the old woman took with the flat of her hands/ [and recognized as she felt it]" (19.467–68). It is difficult to decide her age. Her features are indistinctly revealed in the Athenian relief fragment (plate 55), but she does not seem particularly old or wizened. Her body is full and round; one shoulder is actually bare. She looks down as if concentrating entirely on the footwashing. In this relief the essential act of footbathing is perfectly clear. The scene is dramatically dominated by the two figures of Odysseus and Eurykleia, even though they do not occupy the majority of the relief ground. United by a parenthetical composition, their interaction and mutual involvement are immediately understood. Inevitably, their concentration compels the spectator to recall that the footwashing episode is crucial to the hero's ultimate fate.

One may recognize the same event with equal ease in the depiction by the Penelope Painter on the Attic red-figure skyphos in Chiusi (plate 56). [13] Dated shortly after 440 B.C., it is almost contemporary with the Melian relief. One side of the vase shows Penelope seated in mourning before her loom while Telemachos gazes at her (plate 17). [14] The other side represents the footwashing with even greater clarity and concentration than the Melian relief. On the vase Odysseus is once again at the left. Contrary to the *Odyssey*, he is standing rather than sitting; he supports himself with a staff and carries the equipment appropriate to a beggar: a knapsack attached to a stick, a drinking cup, a basket, and a goatskin bag. Although bearded, he is still young and lean. He also wears his pilos. He thrusts his left leg far into the center of the visual field. Eurykleia again kneels next to a shallow basin as she holds his foot. This time her right hand moves up his silhouetted lower leg as if searching for the scar. Indeed, perhaps she has just felt it, for she raises her head toward her master. Surprisingly, in the field directly above Eurykleia is inscribed the word *Antiphata*, a name not known in literary tradition. This discrepancy has been explained as a slip of memory, a confusion with the hero's mother Antikleia, or perhaps the influence of theater.[15] A bearded Eumaios, Odysseus' faithful swineherd, identified by the inscription above him, stands behind Eurykleia; he appears to be looking at Odysseus and offering him food of some kind, perhaps a loaf of bread. In the *Odyssey* Eumaios is let into the secret of Odysseus' identity during a completely separate and very moving episode that occurs well after the footwashing. Brommer suggested that the vase shows both Eurykleia and Eumaios recognizing their master.[16] If the swineherd is indeed recognizing his master here, it is an event of minor importance, for his presence is not acknowledged by Odysseus and therefore does not dilute the tense exchange between Odysseus and the old nurse. Eumaios furnishes the necessary formal balance, and his master pays him no attention.

Returning to the terra-cotta relief from Melos (plate 54), the Ionic columns along the background locate the drama in Odysseus' palace. Two figures who seem completely unaware of the main action also stand in the background. Their heads and eyes shown in profile appear to be directed beyond the pair in front. The handsome youth at the left, who leans on a spear, is usually identified as Telemachos; the draped woman standing next to him, who raises one hand to her face in a gesture of melancholy or contemplation, can only be Penelope. Yet, according to Homer's account, Telemachos was not present during the footwashing but in another part of the palace fast asleep. Penelope also knew nothing about the nurse's discovery; although she was in the same room at the time, her attention had been deliberately diverted by Athena.[17] Furthermore, according to Homer, she was sitting down rather than standing (19.55–59). I will come back later to the question of discrepancies between text and image. For the moment we could agree that the mood of the relief as a whole is one of almost ceremonial calm. This very quietness suggests that something ominous and important is happening.

The footwashing scene was represented about a century later, ca.

350–300 B.C., by another Greek artist on a white marble relief, perhaps a votive, found in Thessaly in 1899, but now also in Athens (plate 57).[18] The scene, framed by pilasters bearing an architrave crowned by a pediment, suggests, once again, a domestic interior. The two principal figures occupy approximately three quarters of the field. Odysseus is seated in the exact center; he wears the pilos, a tunic, and a cloak. His left leg is extended, and the nurse, instead of holding his foot, seems to be dropping it in surprise. Rather than kneeling on the ground as in the earlier scenes, she stands, leaning forward over the basin. Simultaneously, Odysseus reaches for her face as if to stop her from speaking. Thus a specific moment is explicitly represented here—the moment of revelation. The two main figures are strongly activated. As they lean toward one another, the arched backs of Odysseus and Eurykleia, together with the sweeping movement of his cloak and of their arms crossing the space between them, create an emphatic feeling of intense and breathless alarm. In this case also, the old nurse Eurykleia has a strong young body.

At the right stands Penelope, working at her upright loom. Rendered in very low relief, the loom stretches across much of the background, and one of its posts descends in a severe vertical between Odysseus and the nurse. This line increases the tension between them. Penelope holds a shuttle in her right hand and perhaps the thread in her left. As we have seen, Homer states (19.476–79) that she is emotionally detached from the footwashing. By now Penelope certainly should no longer be weaving. In this relief, however, she is neither a mournful recluse nor a retiring observer, but a real player in the drama.[19] Dressed in a bulky himation, she is an impressive, even a monumental figure. Even though her back is turned, she virtually towers over the other two, dominating them while she continues her work at the loom as the virtuous mistress of the household.[20] Yet her head is slightly turned to the left as if she senses some problem nearby. Unfortunately, the faces of all three figures are destroyed. Although Odysseus is clearly looking steadfastly at his nurse, I agree with Robert that Eurykleia seems to be looking at Penelope, whom she wishes to alert about the identity of the stranger.[21] In her more upright stance, the nurse in this relief simultaneously confronts both master and mistress, and her deep emotional ties to each, which are thus fully revealed, are in accord with her functional standing within the household at Ithaka.

My last example is a Roman terra-cotta relief plaque (plate 58), one of a series that formed a frieze decorating the wall of a house, probably at Tusculum. Now in the National Museum of the

Terme in Rome, it is usually dated to the first half of the first century A.D.[22]

On the one hand, the curtain draped across the background once again locates the event in a domestic setting, its rather pretentious heaviness and swing also add a dramatic, theatrical touch. On the other hand, the action and the rendering of the figures are now handled with a new realism and specificity. Compared with the two Greek reliefs, we must slow down, so to speak, in the way we read and interpret the action. The act of footwashing is made inescapably clear, as before, by the closed composition that physically unites Odysseus and Eurykleia. But here there are distracting details and veristic additions that actually mute the dramatic impact of the footwashing scene. Eurykleia, for the first time, is portrayed as a truly old woman—with a bent and bony torso, thin hair, and a flabby face. Here she has already recognized her master because, in a quite revolting fashion, he prevents her from speaking by putting his hand right over her mouth and nose. The basin of water at her feet is upended in accordance with Homer's account (19.468–70), and Odysseus' beggarly disguise seems more believable because of his crooked staff and thinning hair. A further notable detail is the fleece-covered stool, which Homer says was ordered by Penelope:

> She spoke, and added a word to her housekeeper, Eurynome:
> Eurynome, bring a stool with fleeces on it,
> so my guest may hear me and say what he has to say
> sitting down; I want to question him thoroughly. (19.96–99)

Consistent with the Homeric narrative as well is the fact that Penelope herself is not included in the scene on this terra-cotta plaque. In the epic poem, the dog Argos recognized his master long before the footwashing episode and immediately thereafter died flea-ridden and neglected (17.290–327), but in this relief Argos is conspicuous in the foreground curled up in front of the stool.

Here, too, while Odysseus' body is turned toward Eurykleia as he tries to cope with her verbosity, his head is twisted completely away from her to look at an old stooped man directly behind him. This causes an awkward and inorganic turn in the hero's posture, which must arise from the artist's overriding concern to portray an exchange between the two men. The old man is bearded, and he wears a long gown and a furry cloak; he appears to be holding a cup in his right hand. Most probably he is Eumaios, and he and Odysseus stare at each other. Thus we must also be witnessing the moment when Eumaios becomes aware that the scar has been exposed, and when he too knows the secret of the stranger's identity. Unlike Eurykleia's accidental and fraught discovery, in the poem Odysseus reveals the scar to Eumaios at a time of his own choosing. He pulls off his rags, and the swineherd weeps when he sees the familiar old wound. In sum, then, in this Roman representation a single discrete episode from Book 19 (386–94), the footwashing, is followed by a later discrete episode from Book 21 (221–25), Eumaios' recognition. Thus here Odysseus' disguise is broken twice over. Rather than permitting us to savor fully the obviously charged interaction between Odysseus and the nurse, the sculptor forces us to move our eyes to the left and empathize with a second interaction, that between Odysseus and Eumaios. The dog, whose head is turned out toward the spectator, is a further distracting element in the composition.

The following is what I believe may be deduced from this brief analysis of three sculptures in relief and one vase painting. First of all, general discrepancies between the text of the *Odyssey* and the visual representations exist in the Greek relief from Melos (plates 54, 55), the vase by the Penelope Painter (plate 56), and the marble relief from Thessaly (plate 57). Telemachos, we recall, had no business being in the recognition scene on the Melos relief; neither did Penelope. In that work, Penelope and Telemachos are neither conversing, nor looking at one another, nor even looking at the main event—the footwashing. Nevertheless, we read them as a pair, as mother and son, who belong together and are similar in pose, height, and direction of gaze. Standing quietly side by side, the two do not belong to a discrete episode that can be identified in the *Odyssey* or, I would suppose, in any other ancient text. Why then did the sculptor include them? Perhaps they are there mainly to fill the space of the background but also because both Penelope and Telemachos are part of the fabric of the poem and because they are unforgettably involved with the fate of Odysseus. The sculptor achieves his expressive goal by designing his relief so that the footbathing act is dominant and central; then regardless of narrative logic, of time before or after, or of fidelity to text, he adds two other persons crucial to the story as a whole.

The footwashing episode, during which Odysseus reacts so strongly to his nurse, is also vividly recalled by the Penelope Painter on the Attic skyphos in Chiusi (plate 56). Without worrying whether Odysseus' standing pose was correct or incorrect according to the text, or whether Eumaios rightly belonged in the scene, he stresses the true kernel of the episode, the personal encounter between master and nurse. The figure of Eumaios balances the scene in a formal way, yet he too is part of the fabric of the poem.

In the relief from Thessaly (plate 57), the footwashing event is again a major focus of interest, but here Penelope is neither relegated to the background nor excluded from the dramatic action. Contrary to the *Odyssey*, the three persons are represented together in a single pregnant moment. They are all absorbed by the potential implications of the footwashing. The sculptor may not be true to the text of Homer, but I would contend that he is true to Homer's dramatic purpose. Penelope is to learn of the stranger's identity much later, and at that time she is not weaving. But the sculptor is indifferent to chronological consistency in the ordering of events. As Auerbach has stated, Homer "knows no background. What he narrates is for the time being the only present, and fills both the stage and reader's mind completely."[23] The artist seated in the audience must also have been filled with this sense of present action. Although I have stated that this scene depicts a certain moment in the story of the footwashing, one might nevertheless wonder if such chronological dissection reflects modern rather than ancient Greek concepts of time.[24] The sculptor of the Thessalian relief did not, in my view, reshape the poem or conflate more than one episode into a single scene. He more likely is creating a dramatic composition inspired by sound and memory that is formally independent of any written text. One notices the unique composition of each of the three Greek works of art under discussion. Although the footwashing is the principal event in all, there really is no repetition in mood, composition, or conception, as if the artist of each was not constrained by any precedent or visual model. His aural recollections, insofar as they may be perceived in the work of art, seem fresh and new.[25]

Harris has posited that the literacy rate was very low (between five and ten percent) among the elite in fifth-century Athens, and hardly more in the Hellenistic period.[26] Thus it would appear unlikely that either of the two Greek sculptors was holding the Homeric text in one hand and clay or a chisel in the other. Nor does the presence of inscriptions on the Chiusi vase signify that the Penelope Painter was reading the *Odyssey*. The fact that Eurykleia is labeled *Antiphata* suggests that the inscription had a value of its own, as decoration perhaps, quite apart from meaning.[27] "We easily overestimate literacy from the prevalence of inscriptions and inscribed objects in antiquity (there are telling modern parallels that should warn us), and underestimate the importance of oral tradition and of images themselves as means of communication."[28]

In the Roman relief (plate 58), by contrast, the impact of the primary motif, the footwashing, is compromised. Thus I believe that the Roman artist—or his patron—had read rather than heard the *Odyssey*.[29] Clearly, the narrative in this relief has a fidelity to the text itself and a temporal component that are absent in the earlier Greek reliefs. The Roman plaque reflects a chain of events developing over time that is consistent with the sequence of events in the Homeric text. In the epic poem, the disguised Odysseus' true identity is first perceived by the dog Argos, then by Telemachos, followed by Eurykleia, Eumaios, Penelope, and Laertes. In composing the relief, the artist has selected, along with Argos, only the two recognition scenes that involve the servant class, and they are meant to be viewed in the order in which they occur in the poem. The centralized and parenthetical pair, Odysseus and Eurykleia, dominates and controls the composition. Odysseus awkwardly twists his head toward Eumaios even as he suppresses Eurykleia, as if the two servants are being given almost equal but successive time. The isolated form of the dead dog in the foreground suggests an event long over. Apparently, although the three episodes are conflated, each is to be seen as distinct. Furthermore, the realistic details included in the relief (for example, the fleece covering the stool) suggest to me that the sculptor was able to consult the text as a kind of reference book for such specific information.[30] He was illustrating the *Odyssey*, not reliving it.[31]

Finally, we may consider Eurykleia's status as nurse-slave in these works of art. Her pose and place in the compositions of the two Greek reliefs and of the vase painting seem to be consistent with both Homeric and Classical Greek social attitudes and customs.[32] Even though she may kneel and serve—as in the Melian relief and the Chiusi vase (plates 54, 55, 56)—she is neverthelesss incorporated into the family circle.[33] The servants at Ithaka—above all, Eurykleia and Eumaios—play an important role in the successful outcome of Odysseus' Return. They are dependent upon their master, but they also genuinely love and protect him. At the very start of the epic, the nurse is entrusted with major family secrets; she witholds knowledge of Telemachos' departure for Pylos and Sparta from his own mother (2.349–76), and she is forbidden to speak of Odysseus' Return to Ithaka with his own wife. She is shown with all three family members in the Melos relief. But she owes her very life to Odysseus, and should she betray him the punishment would be severe. In the relief from Thessaly, Eurykleia is comparable in scale and dignity to Penelope and Odysseus. There Odysseus reaches out his hand toward her more in entreaty than in anger (plate 57).

Eurykleia's function and status in the *Odyssey* are inextricably bound to her old age. She is now beyond sex and erotic innuendo. She is sharply differentiated from the other domestic maids, particularly Melantho, who are young and ill-serve their mistress and master by sleeping with Penelope's Suitors. Their devious behavior is contrasted with Eurykleia's consistent trustworthiness. Their foolishness and traitorous acts are contrasted with her seriousness and absolute loyalty. She is virtually a grandmother to Telemachos. Odysseus allows her to wash his feet because she is old. Yet in the Greek works of art discussed here, Eurykleia's age is not stressed. Indeed, one may notice a divergence between Eurykleia's actual (or poetic) old age and her portrayal in the art of the fifth and fourth centuries B.C.

There is just a hint of her age on the Chiusi skyphos: Her hair is tinted white (plate 56). Pfisterer-Haas mentions a slight sagging of the chin and a small fold under the eye but rightly remarks that the features are summarily handled and in poor condition.[34] The general impression remains that the nurse's face is full and fleshy, and her figure vigorous and pliant. This generally youthful characterization seems to be quite deliberate on the part of the artist. In other words, her vigorous appearance is not a result of artistic incompetence because very old age and its negative connotations were skillfully rendered by another Greek vase painter at about the same time.[35] Odysseus carries the gear suitable to a vagabond, but then the Penelope Painter, either unaware of or ignoring the lines of the poem, has depicted him as a robust, youthful man. Eumaios, too, is shown with black hair and beard and a nude, athletic torso, as if he were anything but old. The action of footwashing appears to have been the most important thing the painter wanted to express. Apparently for him as a listener it was the footwashing, more than the age of the participants, that propelled the narrative. Because their ages are not strongly contrasted, the intimate relation between Eurykleia and Odysseus is reinforced; in fact, the generally youthful appearance of all three protagonists on the Chiusi vase implies a certain equality among them. That this remains true into the fourth century can be seen on a pelike from Rhodes in Kerch Style.[36] Odysseus looks like a revered king. He is seated wearing his pilos and a voluminous himation that covers everything but his feet, which are next to the bowl held by a kneeling young Eurykleia. The two look at one another, and Odysseus gently gestures to her to be still. Behind them, Eumaios stands alongside three women, and all of these background figures are outsiders who do not play a role in the central drama.

Eurykleia's profile on the terra-cotta relief fragment in Athens (plate 55) is sketchily rendered as well as poorly preserved and therefore difficult to interpret. According to Jacobsthal, her hooked nose may indicate advancing age. It seems rather to be a kind of mannerism that also is detectable in the profiles of youthful characters on other Melian reliefs.[37] In sum, neither her figure nor her face conveys an impression of advanced age. In light of the earlier Greek examples (plates 54, 55, 56), it seems unlikely that Eurykleia's head in the Thessalian marble relief of the late fourth century (plate 57) should be restored as either strongly individualized or elderly.

In the mid-fourth century, terra-cotta figurines of old nurses who were stock characters in Middle and New Comedy begin to appear. Continuing through the entire Hellenistic period, they become increasingly caricature-like and grotesque. Only in very late Hellenism and in the first century A.D. do they become naturalistic studies of old age. These nurses, who each carry a baby, are themselves bundled in voluminous drapery, and their lowered heads are sometimes almost buried between their shoulders. A masklike face, a bulbous nose, and heavy, drooping flesh are characteristic (plate 59).[38] It would have been incongruous to place such a grotesque head on the energetic and pliant form of Eurykleia in the Greek relief from Thessaly (plate 57). Odysseus' old nurse, the first to recognize the telltale scar, was anything but a comic figure in the epic. In contemporary marble sculpture, an older woman is clearly portrayed in an Athenian grave relief of the late fourth century. However, even in funerary art the appearance of an elderly female is very rare.[39] In this instance she acts as a foil to the youthful deceased.[40] Thus, in Greek art, Eurykleia's precise age is less important than her servile role within the household and the affection with which she is regarded by all its members. Therefore, in the footwashing episode she need not be portrayed wrinkled or decrepit.

In the Roman relief (plate 58), by contrast, the interdependency and emotional interrelationships between master and servant evident in the Greek examples are no longer present.[41] Eurykleia's painfully stooped posture, brittle body, and wrinkled face stress her old age, subservience, and otherness. She has lost all dignity, a quality so remarkably retained in the Greek examples. This painstaking description of old age is characteristic of Roman art, and it also occurs in the depiction of Eurykleia on a contemporary, Early Imperial, terra-cotta plaque (plate 60) showing the seated mourning Penelope amid maidservants.[42] In the Roman footwashing relief, Odysseus jams his hand over Eurykleia's mouth, as if she were known to be hopelessly garrulous. Her ugliness almost seems to explain and justify his harsh gesture. Perhaps we may see here a parallel to the brutal scorn cast upon the physical decline of old women, which is expressed in excruciating detail in the contemporary writings of Martial and Horace.[43]

In conclusion, by surveying the many representations from the *Odyssey* in ancient art, we learn that the footwashing during which the nurse makes her startling discovery of Odysseus' scar was never a favorite subject in the visual arts.[44] The preferred episodes are Odysseus' violent dispatch of the giant Polyphemos, his resistance to the seductive song of the Sirens, and the magic potion of Kirke. Penelope, the loving wife, also was portrayed far more often. The footwashing episode certainly revealed Odysseus' scar, and on a deeper level, it also exposed his weakness and vulnerability. This might explain these negative statistics. Rather than underscoring Odysseus' heroic and almost divine prowess, it unmasked his vulnerability and humanity. That this revelation should be carried out by a very old woman of the servant class makes the episode all the more poignant. For these reasons I am inclined to think the subject of the footwashing was not highly popular in Classical antiquity, which preferred its men to be remembered as triumphant heroes.

Notes

In loving memory of Eric A. Havelock. I am indebted to two former Vassar College colleagues, Eve D'Ambra and Steven Ostrow, for helpful comments on an earlier version, and to Beth Cohen for many valuable suggestions for the final version.

1. On the *Niptra:* Robert, 1900, 337–38; Sutton, 1984, 88–90. It has often been suggested that theatrical performances of dramas are depicted in vase paintings because the stage is shown, but the painted scene is normally a conflation of several episodes. See Trendall and Webster, 1971, 2–11. But cf. Boardman, 1989, 222, on the improbability of stage plays as a source. Also see Taplin, 1993, chapters 1 and 3.

2. See Harris, 1989, chapter 4.

3. Cf. Herington, 1985, 50; Shapiro, 1992, 72–75.

4. See Bakker, 1993, 18–19.

5. I am assuming that the artist would react to oral performances like other members of the Greek audience. Audience reaction is best analyzed by Havelock, 1963, chapters 1 and 2.

6. Cf. Arnott, 1988, 1480–82; Taplin, 1993, 6–11, 21–29.

7. For Archaic Greek artists Cook, 1983, 1–6, is skeptical as to how widely they used epic poetry for their subjects, believing folktales to have been the most prevalent source. Moreover, Cook seems to take for granted that artists relied on a written text. The validity of my approach, at least for

the art of the sixth century B.C., is firmly suggested by Boardman, 1991b, 82: "Most people did not learn their myth-history from books."

8. The remembrance of the scar, which occurs again with Eumaios, is another indication of the importance of memory as a theme in the *Odyssey*, a point underlined by Foley, Chapter 6, and by Schein, Chapter 2, both in this volume. In an oral society, the memory of the bard who is reciting, as well as the faculty of remembering on the part of the audience itself, was surely keener than in a literate society. See Ong, 1982, 57–69; and Harris, 1989, 30–33.

9. See the exceptionally interesting analysis by Auerbach, 1953, chapter 1. He compares the Homeric narrative style and its "delight in physical existence" with the Old Testament narrative of the sacrifice of Isaac, which does not attempt to "bewitch the senses." This may permit us to further understand the intense identification with the action felt by the Greek audience at an oral performance, as proposed by Havelock, 1963, chapters 1 and 2.

10. On the importance of Eurykleia's discovery of the scar for the poem as a whole, see Murnaghan, 1987, 21–39.

11. New York, Metropolitan Museum, Fletcher Fund, 1925, 25.78.26; Richter, 1926, 80; Robert, 1900, 325–38; Jacobsthal, 1931, 71; Touchefeu-Meynier, 1968, 249.

12. Athens, National Archaeological Museum, no. 9753; Jacobsthal, 1931, 71–74; Touchefeu-Meynier, 1968, 249.

13. Chiusi, National Etruscan Museum, 1831; ARV^2 1300,2; Touchefeu-Meynier, 1968, 248–49; Stanford and Luce, 1974, 149.

14. See Buitron and Cohen, Chapter 3, this volume.

15. Cf. Touchefeu-Meynier, 1968, 249.

16. Brommer, 1983, 100.

17. For Athena's controlling role, see Murnaghan, Chapter 4, this volume.

18. Athens, National Archaeological Museum no. 1914; Robert, 1900, 325–28; Müller, 1913, 82–83; Goetze, 1938, 248; Hausmann, 1960, 53–54; Biesantz, 1965, 143–44.

19. Moebius, 1934, 59, speculates that such classical three-figure reliefs may have been influenced by a choregic drama group located near the find-place (Gomphoi) in Thessaly. I am skeptical about this.

20. For the meaning of weaving as a female task: Keuls, 1983; and Brilliant, Chapter 9, this volume.

21. Robert, 1900, 326.

22. Rome, National Archaeological Museum of the Terme inv. 62 751; Helbig, 1969, 72–73; Touchefeu-Meynier, 1968, 253; Stanford and Luce, 1974, fig. 37; Richardson, 1982, 30–31. On these so-called Campana reliefs, see Rohden and Winnefeld, 1911, 252–53; Tortorella, 1981.

23. Auerbach, 1953, 4–5.

24. On the subject of time in an oral society, it is worthwhile quoting

two authorities: Havelock, 1963, 182–83: "If the saga has to be composed of doings and happenings, it is equally true that these can occur in a series in which separate doings are so to speak self-contained, each of them in time registering an impact upon the audience, who identify with them successively without attempting to organize them reflectively in groups. . . . Thus the memorized record consists of a vast plurality of acts and events, not integrated into chained groups of cause and effect, but rather linked associatively in endless series." Ong, 1982, 97: "Before writing was deeply interiorized by print, people did not feel themselves situated every moment of their lives in abstract computed time of any sort."

25. A poorly preserved fourth-century amphora shows the footwashing with Eumaios (or Telemachos) and Penelope in the background: *LIMC* IV, s.v. "Eurykleia," (O. Touchefeu), 101. In mood, but not in composition, it is rather similar to the Thessalian relief.

26. Harris, 1989, 114, 146.

27. Also unusual on the Chiusi vase is the non-Attic spelling of Odysseus' inscribed name (Cf. *LIMC* I, s.v. "Antiphata," (O. Touchefeu-Meynier), 860).

28. Boardman, 1991, 82. Inscriptions on vases are occasionally inexact or entirely nonsense, which suggests that the potters and / or painters themselves did not read and write or did not attach importance to accuracy or meaning. For some of the difficulties and issues, also see Boardman, 1974, 11–12; Havelock, 1982, 187–205; Hurwit, 1990, 180–97; on nonsense inscriptions, see Immerwahr, 1990, 44–45.

29. The text of the *Odyssey* was translated into Latin by Livius Andronicus in the third century B.C.

30. Recently scholars of the Medieval period have investigated the question of orality and literacy in relation to manuscript illumination. Baüml, 1980, 237–64, esp. 262, for example, has noticed that vernacular literacy in the thirteenth century developed at the same time as naturalism in Gothic art. This may parallel the increasing illusionism of later Hellenistic and late Republican art and the growth of literacy during the same period. Camille, 1985, 33: "There is also the very important fact that many of the written elements in medieval pictures are, because of their size, location or position, unreadable. It is as if the very presence of language served to authenticate the image."

31. The episodes of the famous *Odyssey* frieze follow the same order as the poem itself, suggesting that the artist of the original painting—perhaps a Greek of the Hellenistic period—was also consulting a text. Cf. Blanckenhagen, 1963, 100–114, plates 44–53.

32. However, Wiedemann, 1987, 14–19, states that Homer's treatment of the slaves in the household of Odysseus may reflect an ideal situation more than contemporary attitudes and customs.

33. Giess, 1962, 46–47, discusses the widespread eastern custom in ancient times of washing the feet of a stranger when he entered a home; she

argues that this was an act of respect in the case of Eurykleia and Odysseus, one not demeaning to the nurse who thereby brings the guest into the family circle. This is very different from the symbolic and humbling nature of Christ washing the feet of Peter, which contrasts and therefore separates God and man.

34. Pfisterer-Haas, 1989, 20.

35. See the decrepit old Thracian nurse Geropso on an Attic red-figure vase (ca. 470 B.C.) from Cervetri, now in Schwerin, by the Pistoxenos Painter, *ARV*² 862,30. White-haired, toothless, and bent over, she is altogether a caricature of an old hag and contrasts with the boyish Herakles beside her; cf. Pfisterer-Haas, 1989, 113, fig. 8.

36. *LIMC* IV, s.v. "Eurykleia," 101, plate 51, no. 5, Rhodes, Archaeological Museum 14.174.

37. Jacobsthal, 1931, 73. He disagrees with Robert, 1900, 335, that the head is "strikingly young." It seems to me that for technical reasons—the use of molds on this relatively small scale—it is risky to draw conclusions about noses on Melian reliefs; for instance, note the similarity between Eurykleia's "old" nose and the profile of the young dancer in Jacobsthal, plate 21, no. 37, or of Penelope on plate 51.

38. For further examples in Pfisterer-Haas, 1989, figs. 36–64.

39. Other examples in marble are controversial in date and hence difficult to use as *comparanda:* the two older attendant women in the corners of the west pediment of the Temple of Zeus at Olympia are often dated from the fourth to first century B.C.; cf. Ashmole and Yalouris, 1967, 22, figs. 67–68; Ridgway, 1970, 18–19; Pfisterer-Haas, 1989, 25. An alleged copy of a portrait from the Athenian Acropolis of Lysimache, a priestess of Athena for sixty-four years, in the British Museum. The original has been dated from the late fifth century to as late as the first century B.C. Cf. Pfisterer-Haas, 1989, 101; Ridgway, 1981, 232. However, none of these female figures is an active participant in a mythological narrative, as is Eurykleia. Representations of old women appear more often in the media of vase painting and terra-cotta than in stone before the Hellenistic period.

40. See Pfisterer-Haas, 1989, 116, catalogue number II 28, figs. 34, 35.

41. There is evidence to suggest that a slave was not considered part of the Roman family. See Dixon, 1992, 154–55. For the nurse, especially in Roman art: Kampen, 1981, *passim.*

42. See also Stanford and Luce, 1974, fig. 35. Whether the old woman at the right is Eurykleia or Eurynome has been questioned. See *LIMC* IV, s.v. "Euryname II," (O. Touchefeu), 108.

43. Cf. Bertman, 1989, 157–71, who compares the attitude toward old age in Greek versus Latin poetry.

44. See Buitron and Cohen, 1992, 24–174.

References

Adkins, A.W.H. 1975. *Merit and Responsibility*. Reprint (1960). Chicago.

Albicker, S. L. 1991. "Ambiguity and Sexual Innuendo in *Odyssey* 6." Paper delivered to the Classical Association of the Atlantic States, New York, September 28.

Alexiou, M. 1974. *The Ritual Lament in Greek Tradition*. Cambridge.

Allen, T. W., ed. 1917. *Homeri Opera*, III and IV. Oxford.

Amory, A. 1963. "The Reunion of Odysseus and Penelope." In Taylor, 1963, 100–121.

Amyx, D. A. 1988. *Corinthian Vase-Painting of the Archaic Period*. Berkeley.

Andersen, Ø. 1977. "Odysseus and the Wooden Horse." *Symbolae Osloenses* 52, 5–18.

Anderson, W. S. 1958. "Calypso and Elysium." *CJ* 54, 2–11. (Reprinted in Taylor, 1963, 73–86.)

Andreae, B. 1982. *Odysseus: Archäologie des europaischen Menschenbildes*. Frankfurt.

Andreae, B. 1983. *L'Immagine de Ulisse*, trans. G. Bejor. Turin.

Arnold-Biucchi, C. 1990. *The Randazzo Hoard 1980 Sicilian Chronology Early Fifth Century B.C.*, ANS Numismatic Studies, 18. New York.

Arnott, P. 1988. "Drama." In *Civilization of the Ancient Mediterranean*, ed. M. Grant and R. Kitzinger, III, 1477–87. New York.

Arrowsmith, W. 1959. *Petronius, The Satyricon*. Ann Arbor.

Arthur, M. 1983. "The Dream of a World without Women: Poetics and the Circles of Order in the *Theogony* Proemium." *Arethusa* 16, 97–116.

Ashmole, B. and N. Yalouris. 1967. *Olympia: The Sculptures of the Temple of Zeus*. London.

Atchity, K. J. 1978. *Homer's Iliad: The Shield of Memory*. Carbondale and Edwardsville, Ill.

Atchity, K. J. and E.J.W. Barber. 1987. "Greek Princes and Aegean Princesses: The Role of Women in the Homeric Poems." In *Critical Essays on Homer,* ed. K. Atchity, R. Hogart, and D. Price, 15–36. Boston.

Athanassakis, A. N., trans. 1976. *The Homeric Hymns.* Baltimore and London.

Auerbach, E. 1953. *Mimesis: The Representation of Reality in Western Literature,* trans. W. Trask. Princeton.

Austin, N. 1975. *Archery at the Dark of the Moon.* Berkeley.

Bakker, E. J. 1993. "Discourse and Performance: Involvement, Visualization and 'Presence' in Homeric Poetry." *ClAnt* 12, 1–29.

Barber, E.J.W. 1992. "The Peplos of Athena." In Neils, 1992, 103–17.

Barron, J. P. and P. E. Easterling. 1985a. "Archilochus." In Easterling and Knox, 1985, 117–28.

Barron, J. P. and P. E. Easterling. 1985b. "Hesiod." In Easterling and Knox, 1985, 92–105.

Bassi, K. 1994. "Male Nudity and Disguise in the Discourse of Greek Histrionics." *Helios* 21.

Bäuml, F. H. 1980. "Varieties and Consequences of Medieval Literacy and Illiteracy." *Speculum* 55, 237–64.

Beazley, J. D. 1967. "An Oenochoe in Basel." *AntK* 10, 142–43.

Bell, T. 1991. "The Two Bodies of Odysseus." Paper presented at the 1991 annual meeting of the American Philological Association, Chicago, December 28, 1991.

Beloch, K. J. 1924. *Griechische Geschichte,* 2d ed. I.1. Berlin and Leipzig.

Bennett, C. E., trans. 1978. *Horace, the Odes and Epodes.* Loeb Classical Library. Cambridge, Mass., and London.

Berard, C., et al. 1989. *A City of Images: Iconography and Society in Ancient Greece.* Princeton.

Bergren, A. 1981. "Helen's 'Good Drug': *Odyssey* IV 1–305." In *Contemporary Literary Hermeneutics and Interpretation of Classical Texts,* ed. S. Kresic, 201–14. Ottawa.

Bergren, A. 1983. "Language and the Female in Early Greek Thought." *Arethusa* 16, 69–95.

Bertman, S. 1989. "The Ashes and the Flame: Passion and Aging in Classical Poetry." In *Old Age in Greek and Latin Literature,* ed. T. M. Falkner and J. de Luce, 157–71. Albany.

Besslich, S. 1966. *Schweigen-Verschweigen-Übergehen. Die Darstellung des Unausgesprochenen in der Odyssee.* Heidelberg.

Beye, C. R. 1966. *The Iliad, the Odyssey, and the Epic Tradition.* New York.

Biesantz, H. 1965. *Die Thessalischen Grabreliefs.* Mainz.

Bisi. A. M. 1964–65. "L'Idra: antecedenti figurativi orientali di un mito greco." In *Mélanges de Carthage,* 21–42. Paris.

Blanckenhagen, P. von. 1963. "The Odyssey Frieze." *RM* 70, 100–114.

Blatter, R. 1975. "Fruhe Kirkenbilder." *AntK* 18, 76–78.

Blickman, D. 1988. "The Romance of Encolpius and Circe." *AeR* 33.1–2, 7–16.

Bliss, F. R. 1968. "Homer and the Critics: The Structural Unity of *Odyssey* 8." *Bucknell Review* 16.3, 53–73.

Boardman, J. 1974. *Athenian Black Figure Vases*. London.

Boardman, J. 1981. "No no Nausicaa." *JWalt* 39, 38.

Boardman, J. 1989. *Athenian Red Figure Vases: The Classical Period*. London.

Boardman, J. 1991a. "Cypriot, Phoenician and Greek Seals and Amulets." In *La Nécropole d'Amathonte tombes 110–385*. Études Chypriotes 13, ed. V. Karageorghis, O. Picard, and C. Tytgat. Nicosia.

Boardman, J. 1991b. "The Sixth-Century Potters and Painters of Athens and Their Public." In *Looking at Greek Vases*, ed. T. Rasmussen and N. Spivey, 74–102. Cambridge and New York.

Bonnafé, A. 1985. "L'olivier dans l'Odyssee et le fourré du Parnasse: reprises de termes et reprises de thèmes." *Quaderni di Storia* 21, 101–36.

Bothmer, D. von. 1984. *A Greek and Roman Treasury*. New York.

Bourriau, J. 1988. *Pharoahs and Mortals: Egyptian Art in the Middle Kingdom*. Cambridge.

Braswell, K. 1982. "The Song of Ares and Aphrodite: Theme and Relevance to *Odyssey* 8." *Hermes* 110, 129–37.

Braun, T.F.R.G. 1982. "The Greeks in Egypt." *CAH* III².3, 32–56.

Bremer, D. 1976. *Licht und Dunkel in der frühgriechischen Dichtung*. Archiv für Begriffsgeschichte. Supplementheft 1. Bonn.

Bremmer, J. M. 1986. "A Homeric Goat Island." *CQ* 36, 256–57.

Brillante, C. 1983. "Episodi iliadici nell'arte figurata e conoscenza dell'*Iliade* nella Grecia arcaica." *RhM* 126, 97–125.

Brilliant, R. 1984. *Visual Narratives, Storytelling in Etruscan and Roman Art*. Ithaca.

Brommer, F. 1972. "Das Kirke-Abenteuer auf Reliefbechern." *AA* 87, 105–17.

Brommer, F. 1980. "Theseus and Nausicaa." *JWalt* 38, 109–12.

Brommer, F. 1983. *Odysseus: Die Taten und Leiden des Helden in Antiker Kunst und Literatur*. Darmstadt.

Brown, E. L. 1975. "Io's Name on a Corinthian Aryballos." *AJA* 79, 137–39.

Brunnsaker, S. 1962. "The Pithecusan Shipwreck" *Opuscula Romana* 4, 165–242.

Buchner, G. 1953–54. "Figürlich bemalte spätgeometrische Vasen aus Pithekussai und Kyme." *RM* 60–61, 37–55.

Buchner, G. 1970–71. "Recent Work at Pithekoussai (Ischia), 1965–1971." *Archaeological Reports*, 63–67.

Buitron, D. and B. Cohen. 1992. *The Odyssey and Ancient Art: An Epic in Word and Image*, exh. cat., Edith C. Blum Art Institute, Bard College. Annandale-on-Hudson.

Buitron-Oliver, D. 1991a. "A Cup for a Hero." Occasional Papers on Antiquities 7, *Greek Vases in the J. Paul Getty Museum* 5, 65–74.

Buitron-Oliver, D., ed. 1991b. *New Perspectives in Early Greek Art.* Washington.

Bulle, H. 1900. "Odysseus und die Sirenen." In *Strena Helbigiana*, 31–37. Leipzig.

Burkert, W. 1960. "Das Lied von Ares und Aphrodite zum Verhältnis von *Odyssee* und *Ilias.*" *RhM* 103, 130–44.

Burkert, W. 1976. "Das hunderttorige Theben und die Datierung der Ilias." *WS* 89, 5–21.

Burkert, W. 1985. *Greek Religion,* trans. J. Raffan. Cambridge, Mass.

Burn, L. 1987. *The Meidias Painter.* Oxford.

Buschor, E. 1944. *Die Musen des Jenseits.* Munich.

Butler, S. 1967. *The Authoress of the Odyssey.* Reprint (1897). Chicago.

Cairns, D. L. 1990. "Mixing with Men and Nausicaa's Nemesis." *CQ* 40, 263–66.

Calame, C. 1992. *I Greci e l'eros: symboli, pratiche e luoghi.* Rome and Bari.

Calasso, R. 1993. *The Marriage of Cadmus and Harmony,* trans. T. Parks. New York.

Camille, M. 1985. "Seeing and Reading: Some Visual Implications of Medieval Literacy and Illiteracy." *Art History* 8, 26–49.

Campbell, D. A., ed. and trans. 1988. *Greek Lyric,* II. Loeb Classical Library. Cambridge, Mass., and London.

Candida, B. 1970–71. "Tradizione figurativa nel mito di Ulisse e le Sirene." *Studi classici e orientali,* 19–20, 212–53.

Candida, B. 1971. "Ulisse e le Sirene. Contributo alla definizione di quattro officine volterrane." *Rendiconti dell'Accademia Nazionale dei Lincei* 8.26, 199–235.

Carpenter, R. 1962. *Folk Tales, Fiction and Saga in the Homeric Epics* (Sather Classical Lecture, 1948). Berkeley.

Caskey, J. L. and J. D. Beazley. 1963. *Attic Vase Paintings in the Museum of Fine Arts, Boston III.* Oxford.

Castriota, D. 1992. *Myth, Ethos, and Actuality: Official Art in Fifth-Century B.C. Athens.* Madison.

Cave, T. 1988. *Recognitions: A Study in Poetics.* Oxford.

Chamberlain, C. 1984. "The Meaning of *Prohairesis* in Aristotle's *Ethics.*" *TAPA* 114, 147–57.

Christie's, cat. 1988. *The Collection of the Late Henning Throne-Holst.* 8 June. London.

Clarke, H. W. 1967. *The Art of the Odyssey.* Englewood Cliffs.

Clay, J. S. 1983. *The Wrath of Athena: Gods and Men in the Odyssey.* Princeton.

Cohen, B. 1983. "Paragone: Sculpture versus Painting: Kaineus and the Kleophrades Painter." In Moon, 1983, 171–92.

Cohen, B. 1993. "The Anatomy of Kassandra's Rape: Female Nudity Comes of Age in Greek Art." *Source* 12.2, 37–46.

Coldstream, J. N. 1968. *Greek Geometric Pottery.* London.

Coldstream, J. N. 1977. *Geometric Greece.* London.

Coldstream, J. N. 1982. "Greeks and Phoenicians in the Aegean." In *Phönizier im Westen*, ed. H. G. Niemeyer, 261–75. Mainz.

Coldstream, J. N. 1993. "Mixed Marriages at the Frontiers of the Early Greek World." *OJA* 12, 89–107.

Compernolle, R. van. 1983. "Femmes indigènes et colonisateurs." In *Modes de contacts et processus de transformation dans les sociétés anciennes (Collection de l'École française de Rome)*, 1033–49. Pisa and Rome.

Connor, P. J. 1988. "The Cup and the Sword." *AA*, 41–53.

Cook, R. M. 1983. "Art and Epic in Archaic Greece." *BABesch* 58, 1–10.

Crane, G. 1988. *Calypso: Backgrounds and Conventions of the Odyssey.* Beiträge zur klassischen Philologie, 191. Frankfurt am Main.

Culican, W. 1991. "Phoenicia and Phoenician Colonization." *CAH* III².2, 461–546.

Dalby, A. 1992. "Greeks Abroad: Social Organization and Food among the Ten Thousand." *JHS* 112, 16–30.

D'Ambra, E. 1993. *Private Lives, Imperial Virtues: The Frieze of the Forum Transitorium in Rome.* Princeton.

Darcy, L. 1985. "The Name of Circe and the Portolans of Archaic Greece." *EtCl* 53.2, 185–91.

Davies, M. 1986. "A Convention of Metamorphosis in Greek Art." *JHS* 106, 182–83.

Davies, M. 1991. *Poetarum Melicorum Graecorum Fragmenta.* Oxford.

Delcourt, M. 1957. *Héphaistos ou la légende du magicien.* Bibliothèque de la Faculté de Philosophie et Lettres de l'Université de Liège 146. Paris.

Detienne, M. and J.-P. Vernant. 1978. *Cunning Intelligence in Greek Culture and Society*, trans. J. Lloyd. Atlantic Highlands, N.J.

Devambez, P. 1973. "Une 'arula' sicilienne au Louvre." *Monuments et Mémoires Fondation Eugène Piot* 58, 1–23.

Dietz, G. 1971. "Dass Bett des Odysseus." *Symbolon* 7, 9–32.

Dimock, G. E. 1956. "The Name of Odysseus." *The Hudson Review* 9, 52–70. (Reprinted in Taylor, 1963, 54–72.)

Dindorf, W. 1962. *Scholia Graeca in Homeri Odysseam ex codicibus acuta et emendata.* Reprint (1855). Amsterdam.

Dixon, S. 1992. *The Roman Family.* Baltimore and London.

Doherty, L. E. 1990. "Joyce's Penelope and Homer's: Feminist Reconsiderations." *Classical and Modern Literature* 10, 343–49.

Doherty, L. E. 1991. "The Internal and Implied Audiences of Odyssey 11." *Arethusa* 24, 145–76.

Doherty, L. E. 1992. "Gender and Internal Audiences in the *Odyssey*." *AJP* 113, 161–77.

Dover, K. 1978. *Greek Homosexuality.* New York.

Dupont-Roc, R. and A. Le Boulluec. 1976. "Le charme du récit (Odyssée IV,

219–289)." In *Écriture et théorie poétiques: Lectures d'Homère, Eschyle, Platon, Aristote*, ed. J. Lallot and A. Le Boulluec, 30–39. Paris.

Dyck, A. R. 1981. "The Witch's Bed but Not Her Breakfast." *RhM* 124, 196–98.

Easterling, P. E. and B.M.W. Knox. 1985. *The Cambridge History of Classical Literature*, Vol. I, *Greek Literature*. Cambridge.

Edinger, H. G. 1980. "The Lay of Demodocus in Context." *The Humanitarian Association Review* 31, 45–52.

Edlund, I.E.M. 1987. "The Sacred Geography of Southern Italy in Lycophron's *Alexandra*." *Opuscula Romana* 16:2, 45–47.

Edwards, A. T. 1985. *Achilles in the Odyssey: Ideologies of Heroism in the Homeric Epic*. Beiträge zur klassischen Philologie 171. Königstein.

Eisenberger, H. 1973. *Studien zur Odyssee*. Wiesbaden.

Eisler, R. 1910. *Weltmantel und Himmelszelt*. 2 vols. Munich.

Emlyn-Jones, C. 1984. "The Reunion of Penelope and Odysseus." *Greece and Rome* 31, 1–18.

Euphronios: Der Maler. 1991. Exh. cat., Antikenmuseum Berlin, Staatliche Museen Preussischer Kulturbesitz. Milan.

Evelyn-White, H. G. 1967. "Introduction." In *Hesiod, The Homeric Hymns and Homerica*, trans. H. G. Evelyn-White, ix–xlii. Loeb Classical Library. Cambridge, Mass., and London.

Fairbanks, A. 1928. *Catalogue of Greek and Etruscan Vases*. Boston.

Fellmann, B. 1972. *Die Antikendarstellungen des Polyphemabenteuers*. Munich.

Felson-Rubin, N. 1987. "Penelope's Perspective: Character from Plot." In *Homer: Beyond Oral Poetry*, ed. J. M. Bremer, I.F.J. de Jong, and J. Kalff, 61–83. Amsterdam. (Reprinted, revised, and expanded in Schein, 1995.)

Felson-Rubin, N. 1993. *Regarding Penelope: From Character to Poetics*. Princeton.

Fenik, B. 1974. *Studies in the Odyssey*. Hermes Einzelschrift 30. Wiesbaden.

Finley, M. I. 1955. "Marriage, Sale and Gift in the Homeric World." *Revue internationale des droits de l'antiquité*, ser. 3, no. 2, 167–94.

Finley, M. I. 1965. *The World of Odysseus*, 2d ed. New York.

Fittschen, K. 1969. *Untersuchungen zum Beginn der Sagendarstellungen bei den Greichen*. Berlin.

Flaumenhaft, M. J. 1982. "The Undercover Hero: Odysseus from Dark to Daylight." *Interpretation* 10, 9–41.

Foley, H. P. 1978. "'Reverse Similes' and Sex Roles in the *Odyssey*." *Arethusa* 11, 7–26. (Reprinted in *Women in the Ancient World: The Arethusa Papers*. 1984. Ed. J. Peradotto and J. P. Sullivan, 59–78. Albany. Also reprinted in *Homer's The Odyssey*. 1988. Ed. H. Bloom, 87–101. New York.)

Foley, H. P., ed. 1981. *Reflections of Women in Antiquity*. New York and London.

Foley, H. P. 1992. "*Anodos* Dramas: Euripides' *Alcetis* and *Helen*." In *Innovations of Antiquity*, ed. R. Hexter and D. Selden, 133–60. New York and London.

Foley, H. P., ed. and trans. 1994. *The Homeric Hymn to Demeter*. Princeton.

Ford, A. 1992. *Homer: The Poetry of the Past*. Ithaca and New York.

Fraenkel, H. 1975. *Early Greek Poetry and Philosophy*, trans. M. Hadas and J. Willis. Oxford.

Francis, E. D. 1990. *Image and Idea in Fifth-Century Greece*. London and New York.

Franke, P. R. and M. Hirmer. 1972. *Die griechische Münze*. Munich.

Frankfort, H. 1954. *The Art and Architecture of the Ancient Orient*. Harmondsworth.

Frazer, J. G., trans. 1979. *Apollodorus: The Library*. Loeb Classical Library. Cambridge, Mass., and London.

Friis Johansen, K. 1967. *The Iliad in Greek Art*. Copenhagen.

Froning, H. 1988. "Anfänge der kontinuierenden Bilderzählung in der griechischen Kunst." *JdI* 103, 169–99.

Furtwängler, A. and K. Reichhold. 1932. *Griechische Vasenmalerei III*. Munich.

Garland, R. 1990. *The Greek Way of Life*. Ithaca.

Gaskin, R. 1990. "Do Homeric Heroes Make Real Decisions?" *CQ* 40. 1–15.

Gauer, W. 1990. "Penelope, Hellas und der Perserkönig." *JdI* 105, 31–65.

Germain, G. 1954. *Genèse de l'Odyssée*. Paris.

Gernet, L. 1981. "The Mythical Idea of Value in Greece." In *The Anthropology of Ancient Greece*, trans. J. Hamilton and B. Nagy, 73–111. Baltimore.

Giess, H. 1962. *Die Darstellung der Fusswaschung Christi in die Kunstwerken des 4–12 Jahrhunderts*. Rome.

Gilbert, S. 1952. *James Joyce's Ulysses*, 2d ed. New York.

Gilligan, C. 1982. *In a Different Voice*. Cambridge, Mass.

Girard, R. 1977. *Violence and the Sacred*, trans. P. Gregory. Baltimore.

Goetze, H. 1938. "Die attischen Dreifigurenreliefs." *RM* 53, 189–280.

Goldhill, S. 1991. *The Poet's Voice: Essays on Poetics and Greek Literature*. Cambridge.

Graham, A. J. 1978. "The Foundation of Thasos." *BSA* 73, 61–98.

Graham, A. J. 1982. "The Colonial Expansion of Greece." *CAH* III².3, 83–162.

Graham, A. J. 1984. "Religion, Women and Greek Colonization." In *Religione e città nel mondo antico. Atti. Centro ricerche e documentazione sull'antichità classica* XI (1980–81), 293–314. Rome.

Greifenhagen, A. 1982. "Odysseus in Malibu." *Pantheon* 40, 211–17.

Gresseth, G. 1970. "The Homeric Sirens." *TAPA* 101, 203–18.

Griffin, J. 1980. *Homer on Life and Death.* Oxford.

Griffith, M. 1985. "What Does Aeneas Look Like?" *CP* 80, 309–19.

Gropengiesser, H. 1977. "Sänger und Sirenen." *AA* 582–610.

Gross, N. P. 1976. "Nausicaa: A Feminine Threat." *CW* 69, 311–17.

Güntert, H. 1919. *Kalypso: Bedeutungsgeschichtliche Untersuchungen auf dem Gebiet der Indogermanischen Sprachen.* Halle.

Gutglueck, J. 1988. "A Detestable Encounter in *Odyssey* VI." *CJ* 83, 97–102.

Hanfmann, G.M.A. 1987. "The Scylla of Corvey." *Dumbarton Oaks Papers* 41, 259–60.

Hansen, P. E. 1976. "Pithecusan Humour: The Inerpretation of 'Nestor's Cup' Reconsidered." *Glotta* 54, 25–43.

Hansen, P. E. 1983. *Carmina Epigraphica Graeca.* Berlin and New York.

Hansen, P. E. 1989. *Carmina Epigraphica Graeca 2.* Berlin and New York.

Harris, W. V. 1989. *Ancient Literacy.* Cambridge.

Harsh, P. W. 1950. "Penelope and Odysseus in *Odyssey* XIX." *AJP* 71, 1–21.

Haspels, C.H.E. 1936. *Attic Black-Figured Lekythoi.* Paris.

Hauser, F. 1905. "Nausikaa." *ÖJh* 8, 18–41.

Hausmann, U. 1960. *Griechische Weihreliefs.* Berlin.

Havelock, E. A. 1963. *Preface to Plato.* Cambridge.

Havelock, E. A. 1982. *The Literate Revolution in Greece and Its Cultural Consequences.* Princeton.

Helbig, W. 1969. *Führer durch die öffentlichen Sammlungen klassischer Altertümer in Rom,* 4th ed. Vol. III, *Die staatlichen Sammlungen.* Tubingen.

Herington, J. 1985. *Poetry into Drama: Early Tragedy and the Greek Poetic Tradition.* Berkeley.

Hermann, H.-V. 1966. *Die Kessel der orientalisierenden Zeit, Olympische Forschungen VI.* Berlin.

Heubeck, A. and A. Hoekstra. 1989. *A Commentary on Homer's Odyssey,* Vol. II, *Books IX–XVI.* Oxford.

Heubeck, A., S. West, and J. B. Hainsworth. 1988. *A Commentary on Homer's Odyssey,* Vol. I, *Books I–VIII.* Oxford.

Higgins, R. 1967. *Greek Terracottas.* London.

Hill, D. K. 1941. "Odysseus' Companions on Circe's Isle." *JWalt* 4, 119–22.

Hiller, S. 1976. "Der Becher des Nestor." *AntW* 7, 22–32.

Hofstetter, E. 1990. *Sirenen im archaischen und klassischen Griechenland.* Würzburg.

Holloway, R. R. 1978. *Art and Coinage in Magna Graecia.* Bellinzona.

Hölscher, U. 1939. *Untersuchungen zur Form der Odyssee. Hermes* Einzelschrift 6. Berlin.

Hölscher, U. 1989. *Die Odyssee: Epos zwischen Märchen und Roman.* Munich.

Hurwit, J. M. 1990. "The Words in the Image, Orality, Literacy, and Early Greek Art." *Word and Image* 6, 180–97.

Hurwit, J. M. 1991. "The Representation of Nature in Early Greek Art." In Buitron-Oliver, 1991b, 33–62.

Immerwahr, H. R. 1990. *Attic Script: A Survey*. Oxford.

Jacobsthal, P. 1931. *Die Melischen Reliefs*. Berlin.

James, T.G.H. 1991. "Egypt: The Twenty Fifth and Twenty Sixth Dynasties." *CAH* III².2, 677–747.

Janko, R. 1982. *Homer, Hesiod and the Hymns*. Cambridge.

Janko, R. 1992. *The Iliad: A Commentary IV*. Cambridge.

Jentoft-Nilsen, M. 1983. "A Krater by Asteas." *Occasional Papers on Antiquities 1, Greek Vases in the J. Paul Getty Museum* 1, 139–48.

Johns, C. 1982. *Sex or Symbol: Erotic Images of Greece and Rome*. Austin.

Just, R. 1991. *Women in Athenian Law and Life*. New York and London.

Kaempf-Dimitriadou, S. 1979. *Die Liebe der Götter in der attischen Kunst des 5. Jhts. v. Chr.* AntK-BH 11. Basel.

Kahn, L. 1980. "Ulysse, ou la ruse et la mort." *Critique* 36, 116–34.

Kahn, L. 1982. "La Mort à visage de femme." In *La Mort, les morts dans les sociétés anciennes*, ed. G. Gnoli and J.-P. Vernant. Cambridge and Paris.

Kaiser, E. 1964. "Odysee-Szenen als Topoi II. Der Zauber Kirkes und Kalypsos." *MusHelv* 21.4, 197–213.

Kakdridis, J. 1971. "The Recognition of Odysseus." In *Homer Revisited*, 151–63. Publications of the New Society of Letters at Lund 64. Lund.

Kampen, N. B. 1981. *Image and Status: Roman Working Women in Ostia*. Berlin.

Kanowski, M. G. 1973. "The Siren's Name on a Corinthian Aryballos." *AJA* 77, 73–74.

Karagiorga, T. G. 1970. *Gorgeie Kephale*. Athens.

Katz, M. A. 1991. *Penelope's Renown: Meaning and Indeterminacy in the Odyssey*. Princeton.

Kebric, R. B. 1983. *The Paintings in the Cnidian Lesche at Delphi and Their Historical Context. Mnemosyne*, suppl. 80. Leiden.

Kerenyi, K. 1944. *Tochter der Sonne: Betrachtungen über griechische Gottheiten*. Zurich.

Keuls, E. 1983. "Attic Vase-Painting and the Home Textile Industry." In Moon, 1983, 209–30.

Kirk, G. S. 1968. "War and the Warrior in the Homeric Poems." In *Problèmes de la guerre en Grèce ancienne*, ed. J.-P. Vernant, 69–117. Paris.

Kopcke, G. 1990. "Handel." In *ArchHom* M.

Knauer, E. R. 1985. "Ex Oriente Vestimenta—Trachgeschischliche Beobachtungen zu Ärmelmantel und Ärmeljacke." *Aufstieg und Niedergang der roemischen Welt*, Part II: *Principate*, 12.3, ed. H. Temporini and W. Haase, 578–741. Berlin and New York.

Kraay, C. M. 1976. *Archaic and Classical Greek Coins*. Berkeley and Los Angeles.

Krauskopf, I. 1974. *Der Thebanische Sagenkreis und andere Griechische Sagen in der Etruskischen Kunst.* Mainz.

Kunze, E. 1932. "Sirenen." *AM* 57, 124–41.

Lacey, W. K. 1966. "Homeric HEDNA and Penelope's KYRIOS." *JHS* 86, 55–68.

Latacz, J. 1977. *Kampfparänese, Kampfdarstellung und Kampfwirklichkeit in der Ilias, bei Kallinos und Tyrtaios.* Zetemata 66. Munich.

Latacz, J., ed. 1991. *Zweihundert Jahre Homer-Forschung: Ruckblick und Ausblick,.* Colloquium Rauricum, Vol. 2. Stuttgart and Leipzig.

Lattimore, R., trans. 1965. *The Odyssey of Homer.* New York.

Lattimore, R. 1969. "Nausikaa's Suitors." In *Classical Studies Presented to Ben Edwin Perry*, 88–102. *Illinois Studies in Language and Literature*, special issue 58. Urbana.

Laviosa, C. 1964. *Scultura Tardo-Etrusca di Volterra.* Florence.

Leduc, C. 1992. "Marriage in Ancient Greece." In *A History of Women in the West I: From Ancient Goddeses to Christian Saints*, ed. P. Schmitt Pantel, 233–95. Cambridge, Mass.

Leimbach, R. 1980. Review of Latacz, 1977. *Gnomon* 52, 418–25.

Levi, D. 1945. "Gleanings from Crete." *AJA* 49, 270–329.

Lévi-Strauss, C. 1967. *The Elementary Structures of Kinship*, trans. J. H. Bell, J. R. von Sturmer, and R. Needham. Boston.

Ling, R. 1991. *Roman Painting.* Cambridge.

Loraux, N. 1981. "Le lit, la guerre." *L'homme* 20, 37–67.

Lorimer, H. L. 1950. *Homer and the Monuments.* London.

Lowenstam, S. 1981. *The Death of Patroklos: A Study of Typology.* Königstein.

Lowenstam, S. 1992. "The Uses of Vase-Depictions in Homeric Studies." *TAPA* 122, 165–98.

Luca, R. 1981. "Il lessico d'amore nei poemi omerici." *Studi italiani di filologia classica* 53, 170–98.

Maas, M. and J. M. Snyder. 1989. *Stringed Instruments of Ancient Greece.* New Haven and London.

Marg, W. 1956. "Das erste Lied des Demodokos." In *Navicula Chilonensis: Festschrift für Felix Jacoby*, 16–29. Leiden.

Markoe, G. 1985. *Phoenician Bronze and Silver Bowls from Cyprus and the Mediterranean.* Berkeley.

Marquardt, P. 1985. "Penelope *Polutropos.*" *AJP* 106, 32–48.

Marx, F. 1887. "Ueber die Nausikaaepisode." *RhM* 42, 251–61.

Meiggs, R. and D. Lewis. 1988. *Greek Historical Inscriptions*, rev. ed. Oxford.

Meister, K. 1984. "Agathocles." In *CAH* VII².1, 384–411.

Miller, M. C. 1989. "The *Ependytes* in Classical Athens." *Hesperia* 58, 313–29.

Moebius, H. 1934. "Diotima." *JdI* 49, 45–60.

Moon, W. G., ed. 1983. *Ancient Greek Art and Iconography.* Madison.

Moret, J.-M. 1991. "Circé Tisseuse sur les vases du Cabirion." *RA* 1991.2, 227–66.

Morris, I. 1986. "The Use and Abuse of Homer." *ClAnt* 5.1, 81–138.

Mossé, C. 1981. "La femme dans la société homérique." *Klio* 63, 149–57.

Motte, A. 1973. *Prairies et jardins de la Grèce antique.* (*Mémoires de la classe de lettres de L'Académie royale de Belgique,* 2 série, 66.) Brussels.

Müller, F. 1913. *Die Antiken Odysee-Illustrationen in Ihrer Kunsthistorischen Entwicklung.* Berlin.

Murnaghan, S. 1986. "Penelope's Agnoia: Knowledge, Power, and Gender in the *Odyssey.*" *Helios* 13, 103–15.

Murnaghan, S. 1987. *Disguise and Recognition in the Odyssey.* Princeton.

Murnaghan, S. 1992. "Maternity and Mortality in Homeric Poetry." *ClAnt* 11, 242–64.

Murnaghan, S. 1994. "Reading Penelope." In *Epic and Epoch: Essays on the Interpretation and History of a Genre,* ed. S. Oberhelman, V. Kelly and R. Golshan, 76–96. Lubbock.

Murray, O. 1980. *Early Greece.* Brighton.

Nagler, M. N. 1974. *Spontaneity and Tradition: A Study of the Oral Art of Homer.* Berkeley.

Nagler, M. N. 1977. "Dread Goddess Endowed with Speech." *ArchNews,* 6, 77–85.

Nagler, M. N. 1995. "Dread Goddess Revisited." In Schein, 1995.

Nagy, G. 1979. *The Best of the Achaeans: Concepts of the Hero in Archaic Greek Poetry.* Baltimore and London.

Nagy, G. 1983. "*Sema* and *Noesis:* Some Illustrations." *Arethusa* 16, 35–55.

Nagy, G. 1992. "Homeric Questions." *TAPA* 122, 17–60.

Neils, J. 1992. *Goddess and Polis: The Panathenaic Festival in Ancient Athens,* exh. cat., Hood Museum of Art, Dartmouth College. Hanover, N.H., and Princeton.

Neumann, G. 1965. *Gesten und Gebarden in der griechischen Kunst.* Berlin.

Newton, R. 1987. "Odysseus and Hephaestus in the *Odyssey.*" *CJ* 83, 12–20.

Niemeyer, H. G. 1984. "Die Phönizier und die Mittelmeerwelt im Zeitalter Homers." *JRGZM* 31, 1–94.

Nussbaum, M. C. 1986. *The Fragility of Goodness.* Cambridge.

Oakley, J. H. 1990. *The Phiale Painter.* Mainz.

Oakley, J. H. and R. H. Sinos. 1993. *The Wedding in Ancient Athens.* Madison.

Olson, S. D. 1989a. "The Stories of Helen and Menelaus (*Odyssey* 4.240–89) and the Return of Odysseus." *AJP* 110, 387–94.

Olson, S. D. 1989b. ":*Odyssey* 8: Guile, Force, and the Subversive Poetics of Desire." *Arethusa* 22, 135–45.

Olson, S. D. 1990. "The Stories of Agamemnon in Homer's *Odyssey.*" *TAPA* 120, 57–72.

Ong, W. J. 1982. *Orality and Literacy.* London and New York.

Otto, W. F. 1954. *The Homeric Gods: The Spiritual Significance of Greek Religion*, trans. M. Hadas. New York.

Page, D. 1973. *Folktales in Homer's Odyssey*. Cambrige, Mass.

Palmer Bovie, S., trans. 1959. *Satires and Epistles of Horace*. Chicago.

Paquette, D. 1984. *L'Instrument de musique dans la céramique de la Grèce antique*. Paris.

Pasquier, A. 1992. "Le Massacre des Prétendants: une nouvelle image de lá céramique campanienne par le pientre d'Ixion." *Revue du Louvre* 5/6, December, 13–39.

Payne, H. 1931. *Necrocorinthia*. Oxford.

Pearson, A. C., ed. 1963. *The Fragments of Sophocles*. Reprint (1917). Amsterdam.

Pedrick, V. 1988. "The Hospitality of Noble Women in the Odyssey." *Helios* 15, 85–101.

Peradotto, J. 1993. "The Social Control of Sexuality: Odyssean Dialogics." *Arethusa* 26, 173–82.

Pfisterer-Haas, S. 1989. *Darstellungen alter Frauen in der grieschischen Kunst*. Frankfurt.

Pipili, M. 1987. *Laconian Iconography of the Sixth Century B.C.* Oxford.

Pollard, J. 1965. *Seers, Shrines and Sirens*. South Brunswick, N.J.

Pollitt, J. J. 1972. *Art and Experience in Classical Greece*. Cambridge.

Pollitt, J. J. 1986. *Art in the Hellenistic Age*. Cambridge.

Pollitt, J. J. 1990. *The Art of Ancient Greece: Sources and Documents*, 2d ed. Cambridge.

Porter, E. J. 1991. *Women and Moral Identity*. North Sydney, Australia.

Porter, H. N. 1962. "Introduction." In *The Odyssey of Homer*, trans. G. H. Palmer, ed. and rev. H. N. Porter, 1–20. New York.

Powell, B. B. 1977. *Composition by Theme in the Odyssey*. Meisenheim am Glan.

Powell, B. B. 1992. "Writing, Oral Poetry and the Invention of the Narrative Style in Greek Art." In Buitron and Cohen, 1992, 180–85.

Prier, R. A. 1976. *Archaic Logic: Symbol and Structure in Heraclitus, Parmenides, and Empedocles*. The Hague and Paris.

Prier, R. A. 1989. *Thauma Idesthai: The Phenomenology of Sight and Appearance in Archaic Greek*. Tallahassee.

Pritchett, W. K. 1985. *The Greek State at War IV*. Berkeley.

Pryce, F. N. 1928. *Catalogue of Sculpture in the British Museum*. I.1, *Prehellenic and Early Greek*. London.

Pucci, P. 1977. *Hesiod and the Language of Poetry*. Baltimore and London.

Pucci, P. 1979. "The Song of the Sirens." *Arethusa* 12, 121–32. (Reprinted in Schein, 1995.)

Pucci, P. 1987. *Odysseus Polutropos: Intertextual Readings in the Odyssey and the Iliad*. Ithaca.

Puglia Doria, L. B. 1987. "Le Sirene: Il Canto, la Morte, la Polis." In *Annali: Sezione de archeologia e storia antica*, 65–98. Naples.

Raaflaub, K. A. 1991. "Homer und die Geschichte des 8. Jh.s v. Chr." In Latacz, 1991, 206–56.

Raeck, W. 1984. "Zur Erzählweise archaischer und klassischer Mythenbilder." *JdI* 99, 1–25.

Redfield, J. 1973. "The Making of the Odyssey." In *Parnassus Revisited*, ed. A. C. Yu, 141–54. Chicago.

Reece, S. 1993. *The Stranger's Welcome: Oral Theory and the Aesthetics of the Homeric Hospitality Scene.* Ann Arbor.

Riccioni, G. 1960. "Origine e sviluppo del Gorgoneion e del mito della Gorgone Medusa nell'arte greca." *Rivista del Istituto* 9, 127–206.

Richardson, E. H. 1982. "A Mirror in the Duke University Classical Collection." *RM* 89, 27–34.

Richter, G.M.A. 1926. "New Accessions in the Classical Department." *Bulletin of the Metropolitan Museum of Art* 21, 80–82.

Ridgway, B. S. 1970. *The Severe Style in Greek Sculpture.* Princeton.

Ridgway, B. S. 1981. *Fifth Century Styles in Greek Sculpture.* Princeton.

Ridgway, D. 1988. "The Pithekoussai Shipwreck." In *Studies in Honour of T.B.L. Webster*, ed. J. H. Betts, J. T. Hooker, and J. R. Green, II, 97–107. Bristol.

Ridgway, D. 1992. *The First Western Greeks.* Cambridge.

Rieu, E. V., trans. 1946. *The Odyssey.* Penguin Classics edn. Harmondsworth.

Robert, C. 1892. *Die Nekyia des Polyglot.* Hallisches Winckelmannsprogram 16. Halle.

Robert, C. 1900. "Die Fusswaschung des Odysseus auf zwei Reliefs des Fünften Jahrhunderts." *AM* 25, 325–38.

Robertson, M. 1975. *A History of Greek Art.* 2 vols. Cambridge.

Robinson, E.F.G. 1971. *A Catalogue, of the Calouste Gulbenkian Collection of Greek Coins*, Part 1, *Italy, Sicily, Carthage.* Lisbon.

Rohden, H. von and H. Winnefeld. 1911. *Die architektonische römische Tonreliefs der Kaiserzeit* IV, 1. Berlin and Stuttgart.

Rose, G. P. 1969. "The Unfriendly Phaeacians." *TAPA* 100, 387–406.

Rougé, J. 1970. "La colonisation grecque et les femmes." *Cahiers d'histoire* 15, 307–17.

Russo, J. 1968. "Homer against His Tradition." *Arion* 7.2, 275–95.

Russo, J. 1982. "Interview and Aftermath: Dream, Fantasy, and Intuition in *Odyssey* 19 and 20." *AJP* 103, 4–18.

Russo, J., M. Fernandez-Galliano, and A. Heubeck. 1992. *A Commentary on Homer's Odyssey*, Vol. III, *Books XVII–XXIV*. Oxford.

Rutter, N. K. 1979. *Campanian Coinages 475–380 B.C.* Edinburgh.

Sadurska, A. 1964. *Les Tables Iliaques.* Warsaw.

Schaefer, H. 1960. "Eigenart und Wesenszüge der griechischen Kolonisation." *Heidelberger Jahrbücher* 4, 77–93.

Schaps, D. M. 1979. *Economic Rights of Women in Ancient Greece.* Edinburgh.

Schefold, K. 1966. *Myth and Legend in Early Greek Art*, trans. A. Hicks. New York.

Schefold, K. 1978. *Gotter- und Heldensagen der Griechen in der spätarchaischen Kunst*. Munich.

Schefold, K. 1991. "Die Bedeutung der Kunstgeschichte für die Datierung der frügriechischen Epik." In Latacz, 1991, 513–26.

Schefold, K. and F. Jung. 1988. *Die Urkönige, Perseus, Bellerophon, Herakles und Theseus in der klassischen und hellenistischen Kunst*. Munich.

Schefold, K. and F. Jung. 1989. *Die Sagen von der Argonauten, von Theben und Troia in der klassischen und hellenistischen Kunst*. Munich.

Schein, S. L., ed. 1995. *Reading the Odyssey: Selected Interpretive Essays*. Princeton.

Schmiel, R. 1972. "Telemachus in Sparta." *TAPA* 103, 463–72.

Schöne, A. 1990. "Die Hydria des Meidias-Malers im Kerameikos. Zur Ikonographie der Bildfriese." *AM* 105, 163–78.

Segal, C. P. 1968. "Circean Temptations in Homer, Vergil, Ovid." *TAPA* 99, 419–42.

Segal, C. P. 1983. "*Kleos* and its Ironies in the *Odyssey*." *AntCl* 52, 22–47. (Reprinted in Schein, 1995.)

Seneca. 1962. *Ad Lucilium Epistulae Morales* II, ed. and trans. R. M. Gumnere. Loeb Classical Library. Cambridge and London.

Shapiro, H. A. 1989. *Art and Cult under the Tyrants in Athens*. Mainz.

Shapiro, H. A. 1991. "Theseus: Aspects of the Hero in Archaic Greece." In Buitron-Oliver, 1991b, 123–39.

Shapiro, H. A. 1992. "*Mousikoi Agones:* Music and Poetry at the Panathenaia." In Neils, 1992, 53–75.

Shapiro, H. A. 1993a. "Hipparchos and the Rhapsodes." In *Cultural Poetics in Archaic Greece: Cult, Performance, Politics*, ed. C. Dougherty and L. Kurke, 92–107. Cambridge.

Shapiro, H. A. 1993b. *Personifications in Greek Art*. Zurich.

Sharples, R. W. 1983. "'But Why Has My Spirit Spoken Me Thus?': Homeric Decision-Making." *Greece and Rome* 30, 1–7.

Shaw, J. W. 1989. "Phoenicians in Southern Crete." *AJA* 93, 165–83.

Simon, E. 1963. "Polygnotan Painting and the Niobid Painter." *AJA* 67, 43–62.

Slatkin, L. 1991. *The Power of Thetis: Allusion and Interpretation in the Iliad*. Berkeley and Los Angeles.

Snell, B. 1960. *The Discovery of Mind*. New York and Evanston.

Snell, B., ed. 1987. *Lexikon des frühgriechische Epos*, fasc. 12, Göttingen.

Snodgrass, A. M. 1982. *Narration and Allusion in Archaic Greek Art*. The Eleventh J. L. Myres Memorial Lecture. London.

Snyder, J. M. 1980–81. "The Web of Song: Weaving Imagery in Homer and the Lyric Poets." *CJ* 76.3, 193–96.

Sotheby's, cat. 1990. *The Nelson Bunker Hunt Collection. The William Herbert Hunt Collection*. June 19. New York.

Stanford, W. B., ed. 1961. *The Odyssey of Homer*, 2d ed., 2 vols. London and New York.

Stanford, W. B. and J. V. Luce. 1974. *The Quest for Ulysses*. London.

Stansbury-O'Donnell, M. D. 1990. "Polygnotos' Nekyia: A Reconstruction and Analysis." *AJA* 94, 213–35.

Starobinski, J. 1975. "Inside and Outside." *Hudson Review* 28, 333–51.

Stehle, E. Forthcoming. *Performance and Gender in Ancient Greece: Nondramatic Poetry in Its Setting*. Princeton.

Steinthal, H. 1991. "Frauen um Odysseus." *Gymnasium* 98, 497–516.

Sutton, D. F. 1984. *The Lost Sophocles*. Lanham, Md.

Suzuki, M. 1989. *Metamorphoses of Helen: Authority, Difference, and the Epic*. Ithaca and London.

Svenbro, J. 1976. *La Parole et le marbre*. Lund.

Tamm, B. 1968. "Aula regia." *Stockholm Studies in Classical Archaeology, Opuscula V*, 181–86.

Taplin, O. 1993. *Comic Angels and Other Approaches to Greek Drama through Vase-Paintings*. Oxford.

Taylor, C. H. Jr., ed. 1963. *Essays on the Odyssey*. Bloomington.

Thalmann, W. G. 1984. *Conventions of Form and Thought in Early Greek Epic Poetry*. Baltimore and London.

Thornton, A. 1970. *People and Themes in Homer's Odyssey*. London and Dunedin.

Tortorella, S. 1981. "Le lastre Campana, problemi di produzione e di iconografia." In *L'Art décoratif à Rome à la fin de la République et au début du Principat*, 61–80. Rome.

Touchefeu-Meynier, O. 1968. *Thèmes Odysséens dans l'art antique*. Paris.

Trendall, A. D. 1987. *The Red-figured Vases of Paestum*. Rome.

Trendall, A. D. 1989. *Red-figured Vases of South Italy and Sicily: A Handbook*. London.

Trendall, A. D. and T.B.L. Webster. 1971. *Illustrations of Greek Drama*. London and New York.

Tudeer, L. O. Th. 1913. *Die Tetradrachmenprägung von Syrakus*. Berlin.

Turcan, R. 1979. "Ulysse et les pretendus pretendants." *JAC* 22, 161–74.

Tyrrell, W. B., and F. S. Brown. 1991. *Athenian Myths and Institutions*. Oxford and New York.

Tzavella-Evjen, H. 1983. "Homeric Medicine." In *The Greek Renaissance of the Eighth Century B.C.: Tradition and Innovation*, ed. R. Hägg, 185–88. Stockholm.

Van der Meer, L. B. 1977–78. "Etruscan Urns from Volterra. Studies on Mythological Representations." *BABesch* 52-53, 57–131.

Van Keuren, F. D. 1989. *The Frieze from the Hera I Temple at Foce del Sele*. Rome.

Vermeule, E. 1979. *Aspects of Death in Early Greek Art and Poetry.* Berkeley, Los Angeles, and London.

Vernant, J.-P. 1980. *Myth and Society in Ancient Greece,* trans. J. Lloyd, Atlantic Highlands, N.J.

Vernant, J.-P. 1982. "Le Refus d'Ulysse." *Le Temps de la réflexion* 3, 13–18. (Reprinted, trans. by V. Farenga, in Schein, 1995.)

Vidál-Naquet, P. 1986. *The Black Hunter: Forms of Thought and Forms of Society in the Greek World,* trans. A. Szegedy-Maszak. Baltimore.

Voigt, C. 1933. *Überlegung und Entscheidung.* Berlin.

Vries, J. D. de. 1956. *Algermanische Religionsgeschichte,* 2 vols. Berlin.

Walters, H. B. 1892–93. "Odysseus and Kirke on a Boeotian Vase." *JHS* 13, 77–87.

Waser, O. 1894. *Skylla und Charybdis in der Literatur und Kunst der Griechen und Romer.* Zurich.

Waywell, G. B. 1990. "The Skylla Monument from Bargylia: Its Sculptural Remains." In *Akten des XIII. Internationalen Kongresses für klassische Archäologie, Berlin, 1988,* 386–88. Mainz.

Wees, H. van. 1988. "Kings in Combat: Battles and Heroes in the *Iliad.*" *CQ* 38, 1–24.

Wees, H. van. 1992. *Status Warriors, War, Violence and Society in Homer and History.* Amsterdam.

Weicker, G. 1902. *Der Seelenvogel in der alten Literatur und Kunst.* Leipzig.

Weitzmann, K. 1959. *Ancient Book Illumination.* Cambridge, Mass.

Weitzmann, K. 1970. *Illustrations in Roll and Codex: A Study of the Origin and Method of Text Illustration.* Princeton.

West, M. L. 1985. *The Hesiodic Catalogue of Women.* Oxford.

West, M. L. 1992. *Ancient Greek Music.* Oxford.

West, S. 1988. "The Transcription of the Text." In Heubeck, West and Hainsworth, 1988, 33–48.

Wickert-Micknat, G. 1982. "Die Frau." In *ArchHom* R.

Wickert-Micknat, G. 1983. *Unfreiheit im Zeitalter der homerischen Epen.* Wiesbaden.

Wiedemann, T.E.J. 1987. *Slavery: Greece and Rome.* New Surveys in the Classics 19. Oxford.

Williams, B. 1993. *Shame and Necessity.* Berkeley.

Winkler, J. J. 1990. *Constraints of Desire: The Anthropology of Sex and Gender in Ancient Greece.* New York.

Winter, I. 1990. Review of Markoe, 1985. *Gnomon* 62, 236–41.

Wohl, V. J. 1993. "Standing by the Stathmos: The Creation of Sexual Ideology in the *Odyssey.*" *Arethusa* 26, 19–50.

Woodford, S. 1986. *An Introduction to Greek Art.* Ithaca.

Woodhouse, W. J. 1930. *The Composition of Homer's Odyssey.* Oxford.

Woysch-Méautis, D. 1982. *La représentation des animaux et des êtres fabuleux sur les monuments funéraires grecs.* Lausanne.

Zancani Montuoro, P. 1959. "Odisseo a Cariddi." *Parola del passato* 14, 221–29.

Zeitlin, F. I. 1981. "Travesties of Gender and Genre in Aristophanes' *Thesmophoriazousae.*" In Foley, 1981, 169–217.

Zeitlin, F. I. 1984. "The Dynamics of Misogyny: Myth and Mythmaking in the *Oresteia.*" In *Women in the Ancient World: The Arethusa Papers*, ed. J. Peradotto and J. P. Sullivan, 159–94. Albany.

Zeitlin, F. I. 1985. "The Power of Aphrodite: Eros and the Boundaries of the Self in the *Hippolytus.*" In *Directions in Euripidean Criticism*, ed. P. Burian, 52–111. Durham.

Index